SOE Hero

Bob Maloubier and the French Resistance

ROBERT MALOUBIER

The History Press

To Serge

Thank you to François Kersaudy
for his valuable advice

First published as *Agent de Churchill* in French, 2011
This English-language edition first published 2019

The History Press
The Mill, Brimscombe Port
Stroud, Gloucestershire, GL5 2QG
www.thehistorypress.co.uk

British Library Cataloguing in Publication Data.
A catalogue record for this book is available from the British Library.

ISBN 978 0 7509 6607 8

Typesetting and origination by The History Press
Printed and bound in Great Britain by TJ International Ltd

Contents

Preface

by Jean-Louis Crémieux-Brilbac

This book contrasts sharply with all the memoirs of Resistance members that have been published to date, due to the colourful personality of Bob Maloubier, the exploits and adventures of war it recounts, and a style of writing that carries the reader along at breakneck speed. Another unusual point is that the author's role in the war was played within a covert organisation reviled by de Gaulle and almost unknown in France: the SOE, Britain's Special Operations Executive.

In the summer of 1940 Churchill created the SOE on the edges of the Intelligence Service with the mission 'to set Europe ablaze'. For obscure reasons, the official account of its activities was forbidden from being translated into French for fifty years after the war – this account could not be published until 2008![1] And, due to either chance or hostile reception, none of the accounts published in England by its agents have so far been translated into French.

However, the SOE was a key driver of resistance to German occupation. From the start of the war until liberation it was the SOE that supplied the secret services of France Libre, training its agents, ensuring its parachute drops, supplying it with radio sets, directing its radio links and providing arms to the Résistance. What is more – and it is well that de Gaulle did not

1 Michael Foot, *Des Anglais Dans la Résistance. Le Service Secret Britannique d'Action (SOE) en France, 1940–44* (Tallandier, 2008; 'Texto' collection, 2011).

admit this as he held that all French nationals reaching British soil must be available to Free France – Section F of SOE, under the authority of Colonel Buckmaster, created in France its own underground networks. These were often supervised by French men and women who had reached London with a determination to 'bash the Boche' and who, like Bob, were totally unaware of the tensions between the masters of the game.

The British circuits numbered more than fifty in June 1944 and had means at their disposal that were unavailable to the Free French networks. Direct action, without any political involvement, was their law: their mission was to increase sabotage, each network working in a strictly defined area, and then to organise or support the Maquis therein, thanks to whom three or four of these networks were able to make a major contribution to the liberation of their area.

The young Bob Maloubier was parachuted into France during the night of 15–16 August 1943 so that he could lend his talents in sabotage and act as an instructor in sabotage to the SOE network known as 'Salesman', which was active in Upper Normandy between Rouen and Le Havre under the authority of the journalist Philippe Liewer, alias Staunton. He arrived at a crucial time. The Allied landing on the Continent was planned for the following year, but the English believed that the arrest of General Delestraint, then that of Jean Moulin and the secret staff in the southern zone, which had occurred in June, had reduced the military potential of the Résistance by some 80 per cent. The militarisation of the Résistance was becoming urgent and the harassing of the enemy's machine of war imperative.

The reader will be carried through the mad course of events which made an adventurous 18-year-old high-school student, outraged by the armistice of 1940, into a tough guy, die-hard fighter and lifelong adventurer. For (it is not the subject of the book, but such was his personality) after the war, Bob Maloubier would go on to be parachuted into Laos on behalf of Force 136, SOE 'branch' for the Far East, and there he would be wounded for a third time. Later he would be the founder of the Service de Documentation Extérieure et de Contre-Espionnage (SDECE) combat unit of divers, a forester in Gabon, an oilman in Nigeria and in the Persian Gulf, the list goes on ...

Month after month, therefore, in a France that had seen more than two-thirds of its territory occupied and was locked in by the Vichy authorities, the high school boy did his utmost to get away and become a war pilot in the Free French ranks, each time meeting disappointment, failure and even time in prison. Finally deciding there was no better way to leave France than to join the Armistice Army, in November 1942 he found himself on guard at Bizerte aerodrome when the Germans landed in Tunisia. He escaped with great speed to Algeria, where Admiral Darlan had been forced, a few days earlier, to switch to the Allied side. It is there, lacking any contact with Free France, that he was enrolled in the British secret service as it promised him the most action.

With six months' training at SOE's secret schools, three weeks after being parachuted into France he was involved in the most spectacular operation accomplished by the Salesman circuit – the destruction of a small warship being repaired in the Ateliers et Chantiers Navals de Normandie (Naval Shipyard of Normandy), for which he supplied the explosives. The following month, in the space of three weeks, he had two more feats under his belt: paralysing the factory of Française des Métaux in Deville, which was producing parts for fighter aircraft landing gear, and putting the power station transformer in Dieppedalle, which supplied the whole Rouen region, out of action for six months. The breathtaking ups and downs of such exploits are astonishing to read. But life expectancy was short for saboteurs. Arrested and seriously wounded by the Germans in December, he escapes. You don't become a daredevil without having an exceptional dose of quickness of mind, and audacity in the face of danger and the indomitable energy to survive it.

Bob survives, he is cared for by the SOE and recuperates. He is parachuted into France for a second time on the day after D-Day in June 1944 as a reinforcement for the Limousin Maquis and is involved in the actions of the 'préfet des Maquis', George Guingouin. As a result, he is able to record the activities of this unorthodox communist Maquisard chief and to evoke the atrocious reprisals inflicted by the Germans in Tulle and Oradour. Such meetings with extraordinary characters, and his timely presence behind the scenes at historic events, make his tale much more than a mere Résistance autobiography. In Algiers in November 1942, he became fast friends with a number of the young patriots who contributed to the delivery of the town, without any fighting, to the invading American forces; he met an old childhood friend there in the person of Fernand Bonnier de La Chapelle, who was to shoot Admiral Darlan, and he made contact with some of those involved in the murder plot. Parachuted into Normandy, it is with the co-operation of Claude Malraux, André Malraux's half-brother, who was soon arrested and deported, that he carries out the sabotage in Dieppedalle. He takes advantage of the illegal landings organised by the most spectacular double agent of the war, Déricourt, at whose trial he would later testify. In the course of the tragic episode in the Limousin in 1944, among his colleagues was the heroic Violette Szabó, one of some thirty female agents sent to France by Section F, SOE, 'one of the best shots and most ardent spirits in SOE,' according to historian Michael Foot, and who, less fortunate than Bob, was shot in the neck before being burnt in the Struthof crematorium. Finally he could not resist the temptation to follow the rise and fall of Robert Maxwell, one-time agent of the Mossad Intelligence Service, and, until the end of the 1980s, a British press mogul.

A French survivor of SOE, of which he remains one of the defining characters, Bob Maloubier unfolds the saga of the Résistance like a great adventure where courage is commonplace, where the actors jostle and facts are circumvented. Is the way he tells his tale, at a galloping pace stuffed with dialogue, surprising? It's how he tells stories: he writes as he speaks and as he acts. Is the dialogue reconstructed? Yes, of course. How better to show that the Résistance was at each stage an affair of pals without whom nothing could have been achieved – pals who laid down their lives? Let yourself be carried away then in his galloping adventures; his tale is more thrilling than a gangster heist film and, what is more, it is all true ...

1

Achtung Feldgendarmes!

Rouen, 20 December 1943

'What the hell is Pierrot doing? Half an hour late, that's not like him!'

Georges Philippon pulls his head out of the dismantled engine on the bench. 'You're right, Bob, not like him! Don't worry, he'll be here!'

Running his hands along a bundle of tow rope, he smiles at me reassuringly. Georges is a typical Norman – a typical *Cauchois*, in fact: stocky, broad, short-legged but powerful, level-headed. Beneath his crown of red hair, cropped short and greying in patches, his face is smattered with freckles. If he ever speaks, it's only after careful consideration. He's my deputy and solid as a rock. I appreciated his composure when we carried out attacks together.

Punctuality: the golden rule instilled by the Special Training Schools or STSs, the British espionage schools; they made me into the secret agent that I am, operating behind the Atlantic Wall that Rommel is consolidating during this winter of 1943. I taught this same rule to my little company; Pierrot observed it to the letter until this evening. This boy is a pearl, as calm as Georges but chubbier and younger – 25 perhaps – but just as indispensible since, as an independent carrier licensed by the Occupation authorities, he owns a Citroën P45 lorry powered by gas and the magic words allowing him to move around freely: a German *Ausweis*, and a French *SP*. For six months now, he's been transporting weapons dropped from the sky over the Rouen countryside, taking them to my arsenal, a garage hidden away at the end of Rue des Abbattoirs in Sotteville, a Rouen suburb on the left bank of the river.

On this icy evening in December, in a field near Elbeuf, it's my job to take delivery of the last parachute drop of the year.

Frowning, George mutters, 'Stay put, *mon ami*. I'll go find out what's happening.'

He slips on his jacket, a *Canadienne*, jumps on his bike and disappears into thick darkness. As Normandy is within close range of the Allied bombers, the blackout is strictly observed here; a badly camouflaged lamp would attract the *Feldgendarmes* like flies to a corpse. If you're careless, you risk ending the night in solitary. And, should an attack take place, the *Kommandantur* might take it upon itself to go and round up some hostages. The minutes tick by. Half an hour, an hour passes. Anxiety begins to gnaw at me: has 'something' happened to Pierrot? Another hour rolls by; this is torture. I imagine the worst: Pierrot's been arrested, the Gestapo set a trap for Georges … Get away, before it's too late!

A discreet cough makes me jump. I had forgotten about him, the humble town hall secretary I was supposed to be entertaining with the great game of the night-time parachute drop. Charles Staunton, the head of the circuit and 'my' boss had come up with the idea: 'This chap's getting us identity and ration cards that are one hundred per cent real. He steals them from the stocks. He's a gold mine! In his way, he's risking the same dangers as we are! He complains, quite rightly, that he's nothing but a tiny cog in a war machine he knows nothing about. I thought seeing weapons dropping out of the sky would boost his morale! First chance you get, take him along!'

He's tense. I reassure him. My tone was convincing.

Suddenly a door creaks; I jump. Pushing his bike, Georges comes in, growling, 'Excuse me! Pierrot wasn't at home. It's his birthday, he's out drinking, going from one bar to another with his friends. He was wasted when I caught up with him! He said to me: "We're having one last one and then we'll be there. Don't worry, I won't let Bob down!" You bet. It's us who are going to have to let them down now.'

Impossible. It's too late to contact London by wireless and cancel the plane. A 30-ton bomber, alone, without protection, and its five crew, are going to get a dose of the Atlantic Wall with its anti-aircraft batteries, as they sneak between the Luftwaffe fighter bases … for sod all! Better if it brings us the latest transmitter, which would bloody well improve communications. We have to go! Georges will drive Pierrot's truck.

Georges objects. The *gazo*'s off. Needs a good hour to get it going.

Fortunately, there's the *Blue Bird*, a turquoise 125cc moped. It's kept for emergencies as petrol is so rare and George can only collect a few drops. 'And the 200 kilos of containers that'll be dropped thick and fast, you going to carry them in your little arms as far as Rouen, my dear chap?'

'Come on, Georges, what d'you think the ox carts are for? The farmer who's waiting for us will help; we'll plonk them in the barn, and that twit Pierrot will come and get them when he's sobered up.'

New objection: the curfew begins in half an hour.

'Bah, we'll have more than enough time to get out of town. We'll be okay in the country. The Jerries won't do a decent search there; you know that as well as I do.'

'Excuse me ... where am I in all this?' queries the town hall secretary. 'Your bike won't carry three!'

The wan ray of light from the headlamp of the *Blue Bird* in the blue of the civil defence shakes on the bumpy cobbles along the Elbeuf road, criss-crossed by frozen tramway rails that I take great care to avoid. Should one of the wheels of my moped get stuck in a rail, it would certainly be the end of the adventure. The glacial wind pierces the layers of newspaper, jumpers, cardigans and the sheepskin I am wearing like armour. Tears ice up in the corner of my eyes. On the other hand, the pen-pusher is stuck to me like a limpet so my back is hot. The orders of the 'boss' are law, so I have given him priority. Sotteville's streets are deserted; on this cold winter night the crowds of wage slaves who fill them when the factories close are now snug behind their shutters. They are gathering their dead wood, bits of coal, butter, eggs on the sly from various farms, and leftovers on the black market to make sure that this fourth Christmas under the Occupation, so heavy behind the 'wall', turns into a feast day.

Charles has given me permission to celebrate the festivities in Paris in the warmth, with oysters and foie gras. I picture the trembling lights of the chandeliers in Monseigneur, a luxury night club; those lights dancing in the blue eyes of Maguy moulded into a satin sheath; and gypsies cooing over blonde moss on her neck. She is one of those rare French women who does not wear synthetic fibres and is not perched on wooden wedge heels. For her, real wool, real satin, real leather. Privileged among the privileged ... she is a model chez Heim, the couturier on avenue Matignon. A real blonde, her hair as long as her legs or neck, and whose 19 years have never yet known a bra. A curtain of light eyelashes filters her grey gaze while a Mona Lisa smile often plays enigmatically between two dimples ...

On the other hand, Ann, the sweetheart waiting for me in London, has a frank gaze, green like the Channel in autumn; a diadem of curly flaxen hair under her Royal Navy cap; and soft round curves that the machine-made uniform, a stiff collar, tie and thick black grandmother stockings cannot hide. She does not pirouette on a podium; she polishes a submarine of 800 tonnes based in Weymouth.

Having passed the last dwellings of the town, I ride over a level crossing leading into the open countryside. The enormous red moon that had risen above the horizon has turned white and paints the meadows and trees silver. I'm smiling contentedly; here I am safe, a quarter of an hour before curfew! Suddenly I hear a roar behind me. At this hour, on a country road, it can only be one of those doctors authorised under the Occupation, along with the top civil servants (and, of course, the collaborator), to live the high life. I keep to the verge to give him room to pass. A large car passes, then suddenly cuts in and stops sharply in front of me. I almost crash into the number plate marked with a black WH* on a white background, the 'Double Vache' of the Wehrmacht! I hardly have time to recover, as a 'kolossal' *Feldgendarme* gets out of the car. I identify him from the steel plaque he wears on a chain, the inherited *Rink* of Teutonic knights.

'Zir,' he calls out to me, a nasty smile on his lips. 'Red laight, *nicht gut*!'

I repress a sigh of relief. That's all it is? I promise to change the incriminating bulb, if need be the entire electric circuit! However, his face does not brighten.

'And your *Kamerad, Weg?* Gone? Why?'

I turn round. My passenger has vanished into thin air without my realizing! I remain helpless a few seconds then I reply: 'Not a comrade! Don't know him, met up on the road. Hitch-hiker!'

A second German appears, lanky, wearing specs, a military cap plonked upright on his head, and he calls out to me in atrocious French: 'Do you often stop at night to pick up strangers who have so much to hide that they flee at the sight of us? That you will explain to the *Kommandantur*. Get in!'

He pointedly places his hand on his pistol. The fat 'Göring' holding me tightly does the same thing. Side by side, one quite round, the other puny: spitting image of Laurel and Hardy! One of their fellow travellers occupying the back seat of the Mercedes gets out to let me in and then pushes up close against me. I am sandwiched in. Gone, my beautiful optimism! They're blocking the doors; out of the corner of my eye, I watch the hostile profile under the 'coal bucket' steel helmet, visor falling over the nose. Fear crawls through me. God knows it was repeated often enough during the safety course at the end of our training: 'Never get locked up! You're licked between four walls, toast! Get out of there even if you only have one in a hundred chances of survival. Better death than torture.' All very well in the classroom! What would old Colonel Spooner do in my place, he who had drummed these instructions into us; 100 per cent effective … on paper. These Krauts aren't giving me the smallest chance! I know only too well that eventually under the Gestapo's quick-fire, trap-laden questioning, I would give myself away. I've experienced it 'in class' during the simulated but realistic arrests and interrogations. Instructors disguised as SS pulling us out of bed at dawn and breaking down our best alibis.

I yell automatically: 'And what about my bike?'

'We are taking charge of it,' replies 'Laurel' smugly. 'Roly-poly' has already straddled the *Blue Bird* and goes furiously at the kickstart without eliciting a sputter from the engine. Taunted by his companions sprawled in the warmth of the Mercedes, he explodes: '*Fransözische Mechanik, Sheisse*!' ['French mechanics, pile of shit!']

He doesn't know that, out of habit, I closed the fuel valve, which is located out of sight under the tank. And I'm certainly not going to tell him!

'Go help him,' *Laurel* orders me.

My heart leaps in my chest. The chance of my life!

The fat *Feldgendarme*, choking with aggression, moves out of the way for me. This old moped, struggling on the anaemic wartime petrol, has no secrets from me. Pretending to do up my laces, I unblock the gas tap with my fingertip then hit the kickstart with repeated blows. I deliberately make the engine stutter several times … When at last it starts, as it backfires I shout over the noise, 'If I stop, it won't start up again! You go on and I'll follow you.'

Everything is clear in my head: at the first crossroads, controlled skid, somersault, and I vanish into the woods! My dream is short-lived: behind me the fat man climbs astride the *Blue Bird*, which sags under his weight and the entire frame groans. He places the icy barrel of his Luger deliberately against my neck, growling: '*Weg*, get a move on!

Hah! In the slipstream of the car, everything is still to play for!

Alas, the Mercedes doesn't move off in front, but behind me. The beam of its headlights licks at my vehicle and slight pressure from the pistol brings me back to heel if I accelerate too much. On the right as well as on the left, the flat fields are completely naked, no cover … Already, a town is emerging; houses rise up too quickly! I come out into a square. At the end, an imposing building topped by the sinister Nazi flag. Soon there is less than 100m between us. Neither the car, nor the Luger, gives me an inch. My hope of staying alive is limited to a few seconds, as I'm absolutely decided on chancing everything on a throw of the dice: fly off my bike's saddle while braking aggressively … And if the car doesn't run over me, if a bullet doesn't blow my brains out, if the *Feldgendarmes* sent after me don't catch me … I'll survive.

What an 'if' and how I regret having thrown into the first toilet bowl I came across – out of pride, because at 20 you believe you are king of the world – my cyanide capsule, the 'insurance against torture' you're supplied with before the great leap into the unknown. Major Morel, head of operations, personally delivered it to me last June at Orchard Court, the elegant mansion in the chic heart of London that serves as the base of the French Section of SOE, a distinct service carrying out acts of sabotage, guerilla warfare and hits of every kind. Gerald Morel – Gerry – had handed me a blue pill box and a capsule of colourless glass, advising me with a thin smile, 'Don't get them confused, Bob! The blue pills, Benzedrine, will keep you awake for hours, the other, the potassium cyanide, will put you to sleep forever. In thirty seconds, you will go out with a bang, if one may say so, while putting the fear of God into the Nazis with your convulsions, eyes popping out of your head and sticking your tongue out at them! Should you be arrested, keep it in your mouth and if you are afraid of giving in to the torture, crack it! By the way, don't do a dress rehearsal when it's freezing and your teeth are chattering!'

His wry humour didn't offend me. I was prepared for it: I was familiar with 'understatement', the self-effacing deadpan the British employ even in the most dramatic circumstances, thanks to my mother, who had launched her career as a private tutor in England during the belle époque. The training officers certainly didn't lack this trait, just like Churchill, who, in July 1940, created out of thin air the SOE, which he proclaimed his 'Secret Army', his 'Fourth Arm'. Churchill even requested that the three bald pates who formed SOE 'Set Europe ablaze!' – no joke!

That night it's not Europe that's in flames but my head: fear, doubt, the ifs and the buts jostling to overcome me. I am fighting back the panic. I don't even have an opportune minute to get me out of it; thirty seconds at most … An idea comes to me suddenly … While the Mercedes begins a turn to pull up in front of the building, I go straight on without slowing down.

'*Rechts*!' grumbles my charge, prodding the muzzle of his gun into my neck.

Pretending that I am grappling with the handlebars, that I am struggling to regain control of my motorbike, I cry out: 'I can't turn, I'm going too fast! *Bremsen*, the brakes … *nicht gut*!'

My guard seems to believe me.

When we finally come to a standstill, the Mercedes has stopped under the swastika … a good 30m from us! Its engine shuts down, its lights go out. A rectangle of light projected by a door that opens reflects on the hood. Three silhouettes sweep into the opening. The *Blue Bird* groans in relief when old chubby dismounts, ordering me to follow him.

Everything comes back to me.

Mediocre schoolboy, maybe, but I was an exemplary student-spy, memorising the rules taught at the STSs as if they were gospel. For example, 'Never telegraph your moves. Put the enemy to sleep by appearing docile, terrified, stupid.' I apply the lesson to the letter: 'asleep' due to my perfect docility, and, like me, numb with cold, the big fellow lets his weapon hang down and cranes his neck towards the half-open door. Carried on a light breeze comes the smell of coffee! Hardly do I have the time to glimpse the Wehrmacht slogan '*Gott mit uns*' ['God with us'] engraved on the buckle of his belt around his belly, than he turns his back to me!

Now or never!

I pull myself together, I gather my forces, I tense my muscles and I hoist the 50kg of the *Blue Bird* from the ground up to shoulder height; then I hurl it with a wild howl into the German's back. He goes down with a squeal like a slaughtered pig. I make a dash for a street that leads off from the corner of the square. As soon as I reckon I've got 50m away, I feel as if a weight has been lifted from me: Major Sykes, director of SOE's shooting programme, demonstrated to us that at night and from that distance a shooter cannot hit a moving target.

I redouble my speed as the expected fusillade bursts behind me. Suddenly, a helmeted soldier, weapon at his feet, stands in front of me! Swerving, I avoid him and a chain extended treacherously between some shells concreted into the ground. Fortunately, he isn't the enemy but a stone *poilu*, part of the Great War monument that stands in the middle of the square. I almost smile at this, until a searing lash whips into my loins like lightning, cutting me in two, throwing me forward. The bullet struck me at waist height and has surely pierced a lung, the liver and the intestine. I stumble, recover somehow, and keep running. A mouthful of tasteless liquid rises to my throat, my lungs are hoarse, my mouth wide open, I'm gasping. Yet, without ever slowing down, I reach the end of the esplanade. The Jerries are in hot pursuit.

To my right, a street; I throw myself down it. Unfortunately, it's a cul de sac. At the end, a wall, completely black. It's the end. Just as I'm expecting to be nailed to it by a hail of bullets, a pale semicircle opens up before me – a tunnel. The moment I reach it, the Mausers thunder, the Schmeissers crackle; the slamming of bullets, the whistling ricochets ring out under the tunnel's roof, almost deafening me, but luck is on my side. I come out on to a dirt road vanishing off into the countryside. The racket is followed by a surreal silence. Have they run out of bullets, these buggers? No boots stamping behind me. A reprieve … About time! I'm finished, overcome. A fever throbs in my temples; a sharp pain runs from waist to shoulder. I stop to catch my breath. At that moment, ferocious barking brings me back to reality. They are going to hunt me with their military dogs. I get moving again, all the while coughing, wheezing … and still I flee.

A kilometre further on, my path gives way to the Seine. Exhausted, I consider giving myself up to it; miniature icebergs drift in front of a ghostly island low in the water. My frail survival instinct holds me back. Then I notice some huts, half-hidden by a fence. Refuge! I climb over, coughing my guts up. Behind it, a narrow canal. The cries of the dogs get ever louder, the men urging them on. There's no question of hiding. My scent, I have to drown it. I let myself slide into the icy water. I'm not giving up. Finally I grab the opposite bank, clutching at the muddy ground, and there I collapse. A meadow is laid out before me, flat and covered with frost. I crawl as far as the middle of the field where, counterintuitively, I dig myself in – a bet that has often paid off … that is, in training. I noted that the instructors acting the part of the enemy never imagined for one moment that it is possible to hide in plain sight. They were content to beat the undergrowth without even glancing at the open spaces!

My clothes stiffen, their folds digging into my groin and armpits. At times I lose consciousness. The hounds seems to be crossing the canal. Behind me, under rows of searchlights, locomotives pant and whistle, wagons bang into each other, loud speakers bellow in German. It's at Saint-Pierre-du-Rouvray, where the many lines of the large sorting station in Sotteville begin, that I will meet my end …

Suddenly air raid sirens begin to wail. The spotlights are extinguished instantly and with them the yapping of loud speakers, the puffing and chuffing of train locomotives, ramming and crashing … and the growls of the dogs. Everything is quiet except the roar of the four engines of my Halifax, come to sow panic. I have warm thoughts for its captain; he's going to go back empty-handed but he certainly didn't come for nothing!

The Halifax having disappeared into the distance, the searchlights light up one after the other, the sorting resumes, the loudspeakers belch, the wagons bang against each other, but the barking of the dogs is fading. The trains are whistling enough to awaken the dead … me. My limbs are already growing numb. The water in my sodden clothes is freezing and making me a coffin of ice.

A black veil descends. Farewell Ann … Farewell Maguy.

Death at 20 … because of a cock-up.

2

Churchill's for Life!

A whistle shriller than the others pierces the nothingness where I'm wiped out. But I recognise it: the little *Les Halles* train; every morning it rattles over the tram lines that run beneath the windows of our building, on Avenue du Roule in Neuilly. Delivering the Colombes and Argenteuil market gardeners' vegetables into the heart of Paris at dawn, it wakes up the bourgeoisie of the fashionable districts with a start, not to mention me – and my pain. My legs are burning, burning. I call my mother, who's dozing nearby: 'Maman, it hurts!'

She rushes over, tears in her eyes. What can she do? I remember the 'He's lost!' murmured by our old family doctor when he beheld my scalded legs, invaded by blisters. A basin of steaming washing placed on the tiles at the foot of the cooker. I was running – at just over 3 years old, I only moved at a trot – I stumbled. He wrapped them in sofra-tulle, these perfectly cooked legs. He immobilised them. Leave it in God's hands ...

I remain rooted at the bottom of my little crib, stiff as a mummy. At night, bad dreams. In the morning, the sounds of Paris: shouting from the glazier, the goatherd on his panpipes, the knife-grinder, the vendor of 'pimpernels for the little birds!' Jacques, my brother, plays the ragtime tunes our father brought from New York on the gramophone, over and over until they are worn out.

My ribald grandmother, Papa's mother, claims to have had Napoleon III giving her the eye at Bois; that during the siege of Paris, in 1871, she had a natter with Verlaine, smashed on absinthe; that afterwards she went to the Moulin Rouge; that she heard Big Bertha fire. She had been young, beautiful, with a pretty, thin voice, frivolous and a big-time gambler with it. Not surprising that, one day, my grandfather went out to buy some cigarettes and disappeared forever. That was in 1887, thirty-six years before my birth. So as not to be left out, my maternal grandmother, a native of Franche-Comté, let us know that she, too, saw the Emperor. He was crossing the frozen Doubs region by sleigh ... He patted her on the cheek.

Maman herself tells me how, as a young teacher, she taught French to rich kids in Germany and England, before being appointed as a teacher at the Adelphi College in New York: 'It was inconceivable in 1900 that a young 18-year-old girl should leave her family. Just think, under Félix Faure, chaps who went from Montbéliard to Besançon "emigrated". I had to fight hard, you know. More than your academic father! He was entitled to be a teacher, of course! When he arrived at the Adelphi, he had already taught in Italy, in Spain, in Prague, in Austro-Hungarian Bohemia where he fought with a sabre. We were both confirmed bachelors ... In 1914, exempted from military service, this Don Quichotte raced to enlist. Four years of war on the Somme ...'

Jacques was born in 1920, in a New York that Papa no longer recognised as 'his': the human-sized city of the 'Gay Nineties' had transformed into a metropolis out of all proportion, with gigantism, business and dollars beyond measure. He had an aversion to Coca-Cola, chewing gum, hamburgers, so, with his newborn in a Moses basket and his wife on his arm, he boarded the *Île de France* and turned his back on America.

I was born in Neuilly, where Maman chose to make her nest 'so that the little ones benefit from the good air of the Bois de Boulogne'. The good air ... I don't feel the benefit in the depths of my bed of pain. Yet I survive day after day, week after week.

'Miraculous!' exclaims our doctor when one morning he dares to unwrap two drumsticks – my legs – parchment skin, depigmented, the colour of ham fat, but clear of necrosis and infection. It only remains to force into movement tendons and joints that seem to have seized up forever. After months of martyrdom, victory.

Papa brought a love for sport from the United States. For Jacques and me, swimming, ice hockey, athletics. We shine more on the sports field than in the classroom. I aim for neither *polytechnique* nor a doctorate; I want to be a pilot, a fighter pilot. All I have to do is join up, war will do the rest. War ... from the thirties you could feel it. Press attaché, polyglot, Papa reads between the lines of the dispatches. One day, overcome, he tells us: 'My children, I have repeated to you that I was in the last war to spare you the next one. I was wrong. Hitler won't leave you in peace!'

The apostles of 'peace at any price', the soft democracies of England and France, cede to the Führer the Rhineland, Austria and Czechoslovakia. Chamberlain, the 'clergyman with rabbit teeth', wing collar and umbrella, and Daladier, the so-called bull of the Vaucluse, lead their resigned herd to the slaughter. Papa is still angry but he's preaching in the wilderness. '*Tout va très bien, Madame la Marquise*!' ['Everything is just great, Madame la Marquise!'] sings Ray Ventura.

On 14 July 1939, wild celebrations for Marianne, the 150th anniversary of the Revolution, a grand feast. All Paris is in the street, they storm over the Velodrome d'Hiver. Marlene Dietrich sings *Mon Légionnaire*.

My heart swells with pride to see the parade of our latest and most modern fighters and bombers, Moranes, Blochs and Potezs, flying over the Champs Elysées. Back in Neuilly, I declare, 'We have the best air force in the world … Papa, I want to join up!'

My father looks at me with a mournful stare: 'It's out of the question, you're only 17 years old… and anyway, those planes you were admiring are the only ones the military can muster. A façade. Behind that, there's only worn-out old birds. Statistics just don't lie. And I've been keeping my eye on them for over twenty years! Happily, the RAF hasn't fallen so low. But I don't believe they've got it in them to confront the Luftwaffe. If I were a believer, I would pray. It's the only thing for it because the war's coming for us.'

Without warning, on 1 September the Wehrmacht enters Poland; in one night the Luftwaffe brings down almost the entire Polish air force. 'We will be in Berlin in three weeks!' clamours the French press. But France does not move, its weapons stay on the ground.

The 'phoney war' sets in: 'patrols' along the Rhine, air reconnaissance on both sides. As soon as an enemy craft flies over the Maginot Line, sirens blare all over France, and it's down to the cellar for good measure the first few weeks. Afterwards, there's no need, we stay warm in our beds. The Civil Defence, pensioners in berets, armband, sometimes in blue uniform, blow their whistles and shout themselves hoarse when a ray of light escapes between badly drawn curtains. Maman, a dyed-in-the-wool patriot, and I are doing a first-aid course. I already see myself, at 16, resuscitating a pin-up that I have pulled from the rubble. A sweet dream!

May 1940, the Panzers sweep through the Ardennes, deemed 'impenetrable' by our various Colonel Blimps, through the open window that is

Flanders. As Belgium had declared itself neutral, it was considered unnecessary to continue the Maginot Line as far as the Channel – in spite of the fact that in 1914 the Kaiser showed no respect for Belgian neutrality!

'He's on guard ... Subscribe!' declares a poster inviting the French to get rich by investing in Treasury bonds. The masterpiece consists of a slim squaddy in a long greatcoat, puttees and a helmet, with the tricolour as the background.

'Puttees and barbed wire, don't remind me! I've already done my bit!' grumbled Papa. 'As for the 20kg bag, against the Panzers ...'

These Panzers continue all the way to the sea. Nevertheless, more than 300,000 Englishmen and a few hundred thousand Frenchmen bid them a rude farewell at Dunkirk. Elsewhere Gamelin's regiments are surrounded, disarmed, captured. No more news about Jacques, my brother, but we're confident: mobilised in the artillery, off to war following a Percheron horse pulling a 105mm gun, he will never get to the front!

Shortly before the charge of enemy tanks, I win the *L'Auto* cross-country, a gathering of the best cross-country competitors in France organised by the paper. Contravening the amateur code, I receive as a prize a superb cyclo-tourism bike with balloon tyres, derailleur gear, bags and every type of gadget. I have no idea how timely it will prove to be.

'Swot up on your maths if you want to become a pilot,' Papa tells me.

Easier said than done! Short of teachers who've been mobilised or required elsewhere, my *lycée*, Janson de Sailly, only opens its doors in the morning, and only to pupils with their gas masks. You only have to forget it to be left out in the cold.

Temptation: nearby, in the Bois de Boulogne, is the green nest of the Racing Club of France. Dreamy mermaids anointed with suncream basking on the edge of a turquoise lake. In the evening, surprise parties. The parents turn a blind eye. How could one refuse the kids a party when they may fall at the front tomorrow? I'm certainly planning on being there – at the front. My role model is a close relative of my mother's, Émile Bonotaux, a commander. He covered himself with glory at a very young age in the Great War. When he comes to dine, bristling with medals, I imagine myself in a blue uniform, pilot badge on my breast ...

At Neuilly's dances, there's a holy truce between the liberals of the Pasteur Lycée and the bible-thumpers of the Sainte-Croix Institute. It wasn't so a few years ago when I made friends with a 'papist': Fernand Bonnier de la

Chapelle, a handsome, clever boy, straight as a die. He admitted to me that the 'de la Chapelle' was just the transcription of his mother's surname 'della Capella' – a Dupont-Durand Italian style – added to his father's. We didn't argue over girls; both of us just dreamed of 'bashing the Boche'. He carved fleurs-de-lys into the noble stone of Haussmann's grand buildings, believed in God, in a king blessed by Him and in Joan of Arc.

On 5 June, Papa comes home early from the office, aghast: 'Tomorrow my firm withdraws to the south-west. Two seats have been reserved for me in a car ... no more.'

Maman refuses to leave me behind. My intellectual of a father shows how Cornelian he is: the 'little one' has a duty, priority: in three days he has to sit the *baccalaureat*, so he can get into Flying School. Then I, too, put Maman in her place: 'You weren't crying when you had to leave your mother's skirts at 17; you, a girl! So ...'

My father cuts in, 'The roads are chock-a-block, reaching Saintes by car will take days. But Bobby can cycle 200km in one go. He'll get there before we do!'

The morning of the exam, I arrive at the *lycée*. On the door there's a note: 'Due to recent events, the *baccalaureat* exams are deferred to a later date.'

Wartime communiqués, meanwhile, are assuring the public that the enemy is being contained by strategic withdrawals in a clever 'elastic defence'. Hogwash! The Panzers are surrounding Paris. It's time to get out of here!

The following day, at dawn, in the frighteningly empty streets, overflowing bins spew their rubbish to the wind. An impenetrable fog stinking of sulphur and burnt rubber catches in the throat, stings the eyes, and the sun has an eerie halo; the fuel and tyres depots of the army must be on fire. The ghost of an obelisk in Place de la Concorde appears to be bathed in moonlight, as if in a Magritte painting. At the Porte d'Orléans is a potpourri of sedans, old bangers, buses, lorries, taxis and dumper trucks from the *glacières de Paris* and a hearse. Even little donkeys from the *jardins du Luxembourg*, harnessed to their toy carriages, are fleeing from the city! As the men are at war, women and kids who've never held a steering wheel before play at dodgems, make the gears squeal and insult one another worse than fishwives.

In Chartres, great peace. The cathedral spires lauded by Peguy spring up from the harvest fields into a serene sky, but a humming makes me prick up my ears; a swarm of Stuka fighter bombers, shrieking sirens, hits the road, one after the other. Geysers of earth, iron, bodies explode. Mattresses tied with string to the roof of vehicles prove to be hopeless shields; they tumble like confetti. Pursued by the screams of the wounded, I launch myself across the fields, the cut wheat cracking under the wheels of my prestigious and providential bicycle.

Saumur is set against a backdrop of flames. More burning depots? It's rumoured that the cadets from the cavalry school are ready to mount a gallant last stand. The bridges across the Loire are stormed. Fortunately, there is a railway bridge away from the main roads that spans the river.

Beyond the Loire, the great retreat thins out.

At Saintes, my parents having taken refuge with an uncle, cover me in kisses. They thought they might never see me again, the news is that bad.

Papa announces: 'It's a debacle. Barely even a curtain of troops between us and the Germans. Even so, Reynaud could have turned it around. Churchill proposed that France and England form a single nation. But Pétain, who now has full powers, Laval and Admiral Darlan, laughed in his face. But Churchill, he's a somebody, believe me! I knew him on the Somme in 1915. As a minister he'd been sidelined, so he joined up rather than lounge around in parliament. I've seen him standing on the parapet of a trench haranguing his battalion with a French helmet on his head, gift from a general. Bullets whistling around him, men falling, drunk from the smell of powder. And what a visionary! Sixty-five years old, he will absolutely be able to turn the tide. He could raise the dead, this super-man!'

On 17 June, Pétain quavers: 'Peace in honour ...' Tears in her eyes, Maman murmurs: 'This honour, where's he finding it? At the same height as his ...?'

She bit her lip. My mother, a saintly woman who spoke like a duchess!

The next day my father, who continually listened to the walnut wireless set, seems almost cheerful: 'Some tank officer called de Gaulle, who to my mind is ahead of the game, is calling on the French to continue the fight. He has followed Churchill to London. Ah, if I was twenty years younger!'

'I'm forty years younger, Papa!'

My father stares at me seriously: 'I have thought about it. I even managed to convince your mother that not only the Jews, but the young like you have everything to fear from these paranoiacs, Hitler and Stalin. They've formed an unholy alliance to butcher Poland.'

I can't believe my ears as he continues: 'You want to be a pilot? Ah well, go on! I'll give you half of what I have, twelve hundred francs, there, take it! And then letters of recommendation for my old friends in London.'

I am jubilant: 'Churchill and de Gaulle can count on one more pilot' – and what a pilot!

3

Zell Dreiundneunzig (Cell 93)

At 17, you go off to war full of naive enthusiasm; at the end of the road, victory, glory. To get to England, all I need to do is jump on board one of those ships docked in the Atlantic harbours. It'll be child's play … I'm not wrong!

Saintes is out of the way of the great migration that is swallowing me up at the entry into Bordeaux. Opulent, bourgeois Bordeaux is now nothing more than a Romany camp. A canvas village, canteens, a shantytown on the imperial Esplanade des Quinconces, under the majestic facades of Chartrons. The last waves of the exodus have washed up there along with the government, and public services. Its 700,000 inhabitants have been overwhelmed by 2 million refugees. Worse: bombardments, the first series since the Fronde, have spawned ruins, desolation and death.

The British consulate is besieged by a crowd so dense that you couldn't slide a visiting card through it, much less a boy and his bike. I fight my way back towards the docks. There are heavyweights defending boat bridges against the hordes brandishing thick wads of banknotes. In quiet corners sailors are selling spaces on board at a high price. Better to wait. Cunning as I am, I'll find a way to force the hatch in the night. The implacable sun makes the Garonne a brownish broth of culture exhaling the fatty stench of low tide, silt, fuel, and rotten plants. With a dry throat, I seek shade in a quiet lane. Slumped over their kit or on the floor of the seedy café's terrace, stray soldiers ruminate bitterly.

'Weygand said he'd regroup his forces in the Pyrenees, do you think it's true?'

'My arse! He's got no balls, the old f*****! I'm putting my civvies on and going straight home to my missus. They won't have a clue.'

'If you get caught, it's a court martial.'

'Caught, who by? There's no army any more! It's the Jerries we gotta dodge now ... You need to listen more, nitwit!'

From the depths of the bar, the nasal voice of the wireless: 'Bordeaux ... declared an open town ... the troops of the Reich must be allowed to enter without resistance.'

Sounds to me like there'll be some fighting. Best head south.

The route to Spain, first a line drawn with a ruling pen through the pine forest of Les Landes, rising and falling around the inlets of blue water ridged with low houses, a church, a pelota, in front of which dance white figures in berets and wide red belts. Here I bump into a racing friend, Roger Nordmann.

'Where're you off to?'

'Like you, *mon ami*, I'm off to England.'

We end up in the picture postcard port of Saint-Jean-de-Luz. It is overrun with holidaymakers flocking around the front of the fish market, which has been occupied by disciplined soldiers who salute their officers. In the distance, endless streams of boats depart with a full load of men on to the quay and return empty. We cut through the 'paid leave brigade' in vests and shorts, kids with peeling shoulders, trailing prawn nets and rubber ducks. A young soldier comes over: 'Are you looking for someone?'

'No, we were just wondering ... The eagle on your collar, what is it?'

'The Polish eagle, see! We fought as long as we could, we withdrew in good order. Now we're heading for England.'

Nordmann, older than me by three years and a future engineer, can be convincing. We're offered *borscht*, uniform (albeit without an eagle), and a bed for the night on the marble slabs of the fish market. The bed is hard. Even so, I'm floating on a cloud.

In the pale dawn light, lines of Poles are trudging their way to the docks. Roger and me with them. After an eternity we reach the landing stage. I'm bursting with pride, 'Father, if you could see your son! I've already got one foot on the ladder.'

Roger, who's in front of me, hurtles down ten steps and jumps into a launch about to leave. As I jump, the embarkation officer who, leaning over the docks, turns his back to me, drops his arm in front of me like a chopper.

Loaded to the gills, the boat moves off with Roger on board who, standing on a bench, waves at me shouting. 'See you soon, Bob!'

The officer then turns around. He looks me up and down and growls in Polish. As I remain silent, he says to me drily in French, 'Ah, you're French! Well then, get in the queue over there! My men first. If there's still room, we'll take you.'

Head lowered, I head to the back of the queue, so long it's frightening. As I reach the end, a car careens over and screeches to a halt. The driver shouts, 'The Jerries are coming!'

All at once, ranks break and scatter, the pier empties of people, the launches flee, the ships in the harbour, engines bellowing, lift anchor.

'See you soon, Bob? No, farewell, Roger ...'

Soon, no one else is on the cobbles except me – and two boys lying in front of a Traction Citroën. When one of them says to the other, 'Let's be off to Irún!' I intervene: 'Do you *still* believe in Father Christmas as well? Franco's in league with Hitler; he's got no love for the French. He'll slam the door in our face.'

The older of the two moans, 'What're we going to do? Pierre's been at the wheel for sixteen hours straight from Paris. He's shattered and I can't drive.'

I offer to take over. En route, we introduce ourselves. The 'old one', in his 30s, is Czech, a fashion designer who had taken refuge in Paris and taken the name of Boucher. The other, my age, Pierre Bourillet, is the son of a senior official. He's driving his dad's car. We drive as far as Marseille without stopping. Cargo ships are still sailing for England from the port of Joliette. At least, that's what the sailors 'in the know' tell us in the bistrots. They promise us passage for a small 'down payment'. They take our deposits and then take off forever. I've still got a lot to learn!

Boucher remembers that a friend of his, a fabulously wealthy collector of American art, lives in a château in Cassis, 20km away. He'll surely have a tip on how we can reach London.

In an antique robe and a nymphet on his arm, the aesthete welcomes us in a cinematic setting, white ruins spread out along the flank of the cliff highlighted cleverly by spotlights. Stars often frequent the place: those washed up there by the exodus are Denise Grey; Albert Préjean, seductive rogue who looks just like his friend Gabin; Carphin, the accomplice of Raimu in Pagnol; and Robert Lynen, a flamboyant shark of my age who was made famous by the film *Poil de Carotte* [Carrot Head] and who now only dreams, like Fernand Bonnier and me, of 'bashing the Jerries'. The others' only ambition is to win pastis tournaments at pétanque in front of the Bar de la Marine. Carphin gets me on the team: I 'shoot' the ball well.

'See, Bob,' he repeats to me, 'forget about the English. When the studios of the Victorine reopen, I'll take you with me.'

Not a chance. Lynen, my new friend, is in cahoots with a big Irish rogue who claims he's a dynamite specialist for Sinn Fein and boasts he'll clear our way to England.

Cassis, picturesque port, sleeps at the foot of Cap Canaille, a 400m cliffhead beloved of suicides. Cassis and its delights: on warm nights, sardines grilled on the bare rock under the green flashes of the lighthouse. Intoxicated on the local white wine, the failed starlets staying with the American become emotional, both in soul and in body. Superstar Lynen attracts them like a magnet; I pick up the crumbs.

I realise quickly that the American's route and the tips from the Irish fellow are dead ends. On the 'Côte', bathing in sunshine, olive oil and pastis, means de Gaulle doesn't cut it, especially since at Mers El Kébir – the Vichy rags drumming it every which way – the English killed 1,500 of our sailors. Best that we, his diehards, keep a low profile.

In Marseille, I come across two childhood friends, Jean and Pierre Ducroquet, sons of a well-known surgeon, who, taken to the hills in the Midi, are continuing their medical studies. Jean opens up his arms in greeting: 'Ah, you couldn't have come at a better time. Would you believe it, I'd stashed my weapons in my father's apartment in Paris.'

Fisherman and hunter, Jean is absolutely infatuated with weapons; he's studying medicine during the spare time that the workshops of his gunsmith and joiner allow him.

'And you know my dad's big mouth,' he goes on. 'A set-to with the Jerries, a search and it'll be the firing squad! Gotta get rid of them and you're going to help me.'

The Demarcation Line runs between Marseille and Paris. Without an *Ausweis* and an identity card for the Occupied Zone it's not possible to get through. We have no fear. We buy two blank cards from a bookshop, write our address in Neuilly in a fine violet ink, authenticate them with an official seal – Marianne's profile, from a 5 franc coin we borrowed, inked and hot-pressed – and mark them 'For the Préfet'.

The Café de la Gare, in Buxy, a village about 15km away from Chalon-sur-Saône, the first town in the Occupied Zone, is a playground for smugglers. For 50 francs, a good man takes us to a line of barbed wire running from the corner of a forest and covered in signs '*Achtung Minen*.'

'Don't panic, it's pure codswallop. No mines. On the other hand, don't stray from the woods and covered paths, otherwise the Krauts'll spot your footprints in the fresh snow and with your bourgeois look you'll end up in the Villa in rue d'Autun, the prison down there.'

It's 24 December 1940, the cold is biting and a thick carpet of snow stretches out to infinity. We follow the advice of the passer-by and reach Chalon station by jumping from one copse to another. Heart in mouth at the sight of the first *Feldgrau* on duty. I've only seen *Feldgrau* in photos. He's no advert for them, this one: shaved head under his green cap, he looks me right in the eyes. As he bends over my identity card, my heart is pounding. He studies it carefully for a long time then motions towards the train.

At Lyon station, Jerries abound. Sentries with machine guns, the *Schmeisser*, on a chain; soldiers on leave walking along aimlessly. Some strange Christmas trees have grown on the square, poles studded with white-yellow-red road signs bordered in black. On the square the occasional green car and some vélos-taxis, strange carriages towed behind a bike in tandem. At the entrance to the metro, Jean and I stop dead before a poster, or rather an announcement with black edging, a freshly posted *Bekanntmachung* – 'notice' – dated the day before, the Military Tribunal of Greater Paris has condemned to death for violence the engineer Jacques Bonsergent ... who was shot this morning.

The métro is packed. Those occupied and those occupying, bayonet at their side, sit next to one another, indifferent – already.

When I ring the doorbell of our house in Neuilly, rue Borghèse, my mother almost faints. New Year's Eve will be a slim celebration with a warmish stove that, in the biting cold, Papa feeds with pretend coal, small pellets of newspaper crushed in water then dried.When I boast that jumping the Line was a doddle, he's ironical: 'You seem to be unaware that on the 13th of this month, Pétain sacked Laval, sent him into house arrest. Suddenly, furious, Hitler sent his henchmen to collect him in Vichy – in the Free Zone. Then, he sealed the Demarcation Line. No admittance even to those with *Ausweisen* and all the damned lot. And you chose that moment to 'jump', as you put it, while all the border guards were on the alert. With that recklessness, I pray that your hangman's luck stays attached to your body!

Poor Father. I stop myself from telling him that I didn't cross the Line just to celebrate New Year with my family but to carry across weapons. And from the first days of the Occupation the French have been required to turn in weapons, all the weapons, even the most ancient peashooters – on pain of death.

Is it a truce for Christmas? The Germans are smiling – but that's because Hitler has taken it into his head to mollify France by returning the ashes of Napoleon II, whose role my friend Lynen played on screen. On 15 December, at Les Invalides, Darlan, all starched and stiff, received them in the name of the Maréchal. Sacha Guitry played the diva; the entire press sounded a fanfare. But then, the next day in great charcoal lettering on the walls of Paris was written, 'He steals our coal. He sends back the ashes!'

Long swastika banners mar the Chambre des Députés, Sénat, ministries and grand hotels, all requisitioned. Their pavements, *verboten*, are guarded by helmeted sentries. Queues stretch out from shops' doorways.

On the way back, at Chalon, determined to spare ourselves a 15km walk in the snow, we try our luck with the owner of the first café along the Saône river, which forms the line, cutting the town in two. Jean whispers to him above the counter: 'Do you know any smugglers, by any chance?'

With a smile, the manager points out a client in a boiler suit: 'Say, Marcel, can you take these young people?'

'We'll go at night. Gives me time to finish my drink.'

He guides us towards a gateway on the gate of a lock. Suddenly, a gigantic *Feldgrau* surges from the shadows. I jump. Marcel seizes me by the arm,

'Calm down, lad! I work over here, I live over there, so I cross every day. This Kraut, keeping him in drink over the last six months, so he's learnt to keep his eyes closed.'

'Look how bloody big he is!'

Marcel bursts out laughing, 'No, no. He's wearing polar boots with wooden soles a good 10cm thick.'

The giant gives me a nice smile and a tap on the back as he passes. I relax. How could he imagine that Jean is transporting a big automatic pistol, a Browning, and me, with a Spanish Star with a long barrel tied around my stomach banging against my inner thighs. Marcel accepts just a jug of red in payment. A small price to pay since trafficking in arms is worth a dozen bullets in the chest.

Fortune smiles on the innocent. But does this rule hold firm?

Marseille is freezing. The Pyrenees are buried under a thick carpet of snow. Fleeing to Spain will have to wait until springtime.

While waiting for the thaw, I venture as far as Clermont-Ferrand. The general staff of our armies have taken refuge in the town and its environs. And with them, Emile Bonotaux, my 'cousin' the officer, to whom I confide, 'I'm looking to join up with de Gaulle. Can you help me?'

He looks around anxiously, 'Are you mad? You don't mention that name around here!'

'But Maman assured me that you wouldn't give up the fight.'

'She's right. But I'll take up the fight within the law. Don't you do anything stupid!'

His 'within the law' puzzled me; did he mean with Pétain, Laval, Darlan and the others? I didn't know then about the Résistance movements some of the Vichy officers were planning.

In February 1941, a dramatic turn of events! Berlin authorises Vichy to form a small 'Armistice' army of a few hundred thousand men: non-Jews, non-communists, non-Freemasons ... and the Maréchal's flock; that goes without saying. That army will defend the country and its colonies against all aggression ... British to begin with. The new recruits will choose the location they are assigned to.

My friend Jean Kisling, the son of the fashionable painter, and I are off to enrol in the air force. Option: Tunisia. It is the perfect choice; as student pilots, we'll be heading for either Malta or Libya on our first solo drop, where the British are wiping the floor with the Italians!

I spend four months at soldier school under an iron fist on a starvation diet, in the glacial embrace of the Isère valley, then under the torrid sun of the Tunisian Zaghouan plateau I'm sent to Sidi Ahmed, a base near Bizerte, Jean to El Aouina, a bomber base at the gates of Tunis, but both of us as ground staff as the pilot schools have closed their doors *sine die*. Malta is only 500km away, but that's swimming, and the British area of Libya is more than 1,000km away on foot, along the beach.

One evening, pursued by Spitfires, two Italian Fiat fighters (very easy-to-handle biplanes) are taking refuge on our base. While I'm on guard, I commit my first sabotage; with the point of my bayonet, I trace a line of perforations under the lower part of aircraft; I invite my relief guard to continue. 'If these wings are cut to shreds in the air, it means covering them in canvas again, right?'

On 22 June 1941, the base reaches boiling point: Operation Barbarossa. Hitler has invaded the USSR. Joy in the camp, 'Just like Napoleon, he'll succumb in Beresina!' Meanwhile, the Panzers are dashing to Moscow.

I polish up the Dewoitine D.520; two years ago it was the latest fighter of Group 2/7. I'm an assistant mechanic. Faithful to the Maréchal, the group's pilots loop-the-loop in the serene sky. On the other hand, they cut their teeth on a LeO 25, known as the 'hen coop', a 1920s observation plane that gives up the ghost at 150mph. These were the aircraft in which the crazy non-commissioned officers were attempting to reach Malta. The squadron's ace brought down an English bomber who reached the coast. And rightly so, since Tunisia is neutral ... Meanwhile Axis aircraft land there and cargo ships loaded with weaponry destined for the Libyan front use it as a stopover.

It's thanks to our aerobatic pilots that the Dewoitines end up in the scrap yard. They joke around, flying low to sever a volleyball net using the ventral antenna, and fail spectacularly. They make mistakes, like when a captain twice confuses the lever for the landing gear control with the lever for the flaps. And best of all, when the best of the pilots throws down the gauntlet – the traditional simulated combat challenge – to the new commander on his arrival: diving spin, vertical climb, feints, bellies almost touching, breathtaking barrel rolls ... until the chief skids and crashes into the marsh that borders the airfield in an explosion of smoke, flames, metal and mud. His opponent makes a disastrous landing, his machine wrecked, but emerges unscathed. The squadron leader is buried with great pomp at the cathedral, with the bishop present. In the space of one morning the '2/7' has lost four aircraft and a commander. England, for her part, is short of planes and pilots ...

7 December: Pearl Harbor. America enters the fray. So now all that's missing is me.

There is reason to believe, I hear on the grapevine, that an Anglican pastor in Tunis might be running an escape route. I approach him cautiously; all the same, he greets me like the young, foolish 17-year-old that I am. 'Sorry, my boy, but I'm only tolerated if I remain strictly neutral. Otherwise the Italian–German armistice commission will obtain my expulsion, just think. However, I can tell you that Bizerte, being the key to the Mediterranean, is where the Allies will land one day and soon, within a year.'

Thanks, Padre! I can enjoy my annual leave, 'in the exclusively free zone', it says so in the regulations. But regulations don't apply to a hotshot Line-crosser!

I make a stopover at the College of Sports in Antibes, where my brother Jacques is in training. He welcomes me conspiratorially. He's actually a part of a Gaullist 'network' called *Les âmes du purgatoire* – the souls of purgatory! As he's an artist and poet, it was the name that attracted him. I'm worried about him. What the devil's he going to do in this hellhole? He's incapable of surviving undercover. He's an innocent abroad with no sixth sense, which is deeply rooted in me – jumping over frontiers, loaded with weapons.

In Buxy, the atmosphere is no longer great. No more willing soft-hearted smugglers to slash prices for a youngster: 'Getting slaughtered in Russia has made the Jerries nasty. At the littlest trifle, *nach* the Eastern Front. So, orders is orders!'

But I know the score … and the way. I get over the barbed-wire fences surrounding the false minefield, pick my way through the woods. The sky is leaden; the earth, the woods, the roads are covered in a blanket of white. It's bloody freezing; 18 degrees below zero. So what, I've plenty of time to catch the 13.10 Express from Chalon Station …

'*Zell Dreiundneunzig!* Cell ninety-three!' barks a prison guard with an angular face and little round glasses behind the entrance grille of the Villa de la rue d'Autun, the German prison in Chalon.

The courtyard, as vast as the nave of a cathedral, is surrounded by three floors of open-worked iron tunnels where the cells are located. A century ago, the Villa must have been a model prison. Since then, its windows have become loaded with so much muck that only the dimmest of light filters through them.

A classic *Feldgrau*, threadbare trouser seat hanging from his backside and jacket too short like a bolero, walks in front of me on to the staircase merrily tinkling a bunch of keys the size of one of my grandmother's damson tarts along the railings. This jingling, and hammering of boots, slamming of iron doors, bolted locks, cell windows, will be forever engraved on my memory. Our nave harbours itinerants of all kinds, collared, like me, on the Line, kids, old people, gendarmes, a priest and Jews relieved along the way of their possessions in banknotes and jewels. Only men. The women's quarters and 'domestic prisoners' are, it seems, 'elsewhere'.

The ninety-three is a dark hole where there's a waste bucket, a small pile of wood, a cast-iron skillet, two raised boards for sleeping and a thin chap, with eyes that are rare like a beautiful day, wrapped in a blanket.

'You've turned up too late for the soup. So, take this, lad!'

When I hesitate, he adds sharply, 'Stop the circus act! You'll do the same for me some time ... Where'd you get yourself caught?'

I described my encounter with the *Feldgendarmes* between two corners of the woods I claimed to have come for 'fresh supplies' at a farm. A country fellow who was passing said, 'That won't wash, my boy. These two've been doing the Line for the last six months. They recognise a homing pigeon with their eyes closed!'

'You're as bloody stupid as me,' chuckles my cellmate. Comforting for me.

'How much does a passage across the Line cost?'

'For you, I don't know. For me, a packet,' he groaned.

'Oh really, why?'

'In the clink, questions are unhealthy, little fella. If I need you, I'll call. Keep it shut! It's eight o'clock, time for some shut eye, if you can ...'

Hardly had he finished speaking than the light goes out. Pandemonium erupts.

'What is it?'

'Vermin, of course!'

Springing from the straw mattress and crevices in the bedstead, fleas and lice mount an assault. My first night, I don't close my eyes and scratch until I bleed. At dawn, my cellmate, Gaston, comforts me, 'Gotta deal with it. They were there before us!'

A remedy, fleeting only. A splash with a stream of water falling into the courtyard from a stalactite. At -18°C – invigorating. A bucket of water, no more, reheated on a stove heated by three twigs and some pats of peat will have to do for washing everything, including bathing oneself in the afternoon. Diet: ersatz coffee, two servings of swede broth and a hunk of bread a day. On Wednesday and Sunday, a dice of meat floats in the broth.

Gaston softens – he decides to become mentor to the pup that I am. I become fond of his ferret snout.

Each evening the favourite marching song of the Wehrmacht arises in the streets – *Heidi, Heido, Heida!*' We argue over the basement window.

'It's my turn!'

'No, it's mine!'

'Last time I lifted you up!'

I climb up on to his shoulders and push my face between the bars.

Gaston asks anxiously: 'Have they got them?'

'I'm not sure – can't see very well.'

'You f****** me around?'

'If you go on like that, I'm not saying another word …'

'And I'll throw you on to the stove!'

'Take it easy! They've got them.'

This bickering for the basement window is a ritual; from there we can catch a glimpse of the detachments marching past under our walls. If they display white sheets it means departure to the Russian front.

Gaston gloats, 'Let's hope their balls freeze and fall off them, the shits, and Popov play marbles with them!'

If Gaston hates them now, it's because he's got good reason to. A squaddie from 1940, he was caught before he'd fired a shot.

'The first time I went on the run, I wasn't prepared. They collared me in less than 100km. The last time, I paid my own crossing from Germany, from Silesia, the forbidden zone, the Occupied Zone, it was a breeze … And I got stung 100m from the Line, near Saint-Etienne, at my place! Bloody daft as a brush, I had kept my military identity plaque to show it in London when I got there. For I was sure I'd get there … like you. I'm going to get a hammering but I'll get over it.'

One morning, Wilfred, the most obdurate of the guards, yapped at the cell's window, 'Gaston Baret, *Dripunal!*'

When Gaston got back two hours later he barked, 'I'm done for!'

'They're going to …'

'Shoot me? No, you plum! I copped two months in solitary … Let that be a lesson to you. Keep it shut! Especially here where there's grasses – easy to recognise them, they stuff their faces on the sly and they're fatter than us. Look at the Alsatian in 56, for example. If you blab to him like you did to me – Paris to Marseille with a popgun – it won't be Germany where you finish up, but lying in a ditch, for sure.'

On 2 February 1942, a surprise! Gaston produces a birthday cake of real chocolate decorated with resin candles and raises a thimbleful of liquor, humming, 'To your 19th!'

When he leaves, he gives me an embrace just like a minister.

I am transferred to 56. In spite of the sweeteners with which the little Alsatian showers me, I play the idiot, just as Gaston recommended: 'You mustn't force it, you gotta stay natural.'

I will always keep the memory of Gaston's thin smile, his half-closed prying eye, his stubbly chin, his hair in untidy spikes.

When it came to my turn, the *Dripunal*, composed of a single officer, only condemns me to two months' detention and authorises me to write to my mother. She sends me a parcel with six eggs, thus depriving herself. I must render thanks to Gaston's lessons. I don't bat an eyelid when Wilfried breaks them one after the other 'in case they should contain a message', all the while watching for my reaction from the corner of his eye. That day, I swore to myself that he would pay dearly for my mother's eggs. And I kept my word – with mixed results. Alas, at times, forgetting Gaston's advice, I can't resist mimicking a guard or smoking on the steps. Then I'm sent down to solitary, a narrow vaulted cellar, pitch black and bare with nowhere to sit. We're piled up with ten standing and squatting first in the cold then in tropical humidity, and a hellish pestilence from the moment that the waste bucket overflows. Got to sleep standing up. At dawn, when Otto or Karl opens the door, a stinking cloud of shit and tobacco makes them recoil.

'*Sie rauchen*? ... *Verboten*!' they shout.

'*Nein*!' we reply in a single angelic voice.

At dawn, sometimes, we hear creaking bolts and muffled cries. 'They' are removing prisoners 'in secret' from the cells on the ground floor. Then shouts mingle and fuse, 'Courage, you'll be revenged! *Vive la France*! Long live de Gaulle!' accompanied by drumming, the Marseillaise. A farewell to hostages who are going to pay for an attack with their lives. The atmosphere is electric!

'You, *bakages*! *Weg*! Leave!' barks Wilfried on a chilly spring morning.

At Chalon station, a dashing French captain, shiny riding boots, is chatting with his opposite number in grey-green and monocle. In the background, a modest woman in a woollen coat: Maman. She flew to my rescue while my father remained tied to his work. Ten hours on a freezing train did not deter her. She threw herself into my arms, lamenting, 'My poor baby, you're so thin!'

My clothes having fallen into tatters, I float, ghostly and pale, in cast-offs – a dinner jacket, in fact – given to me by the nuns who visited, having permission to comfort prisoners.

'Don't forget to thank my cousin Emile!' she insists. 'If, at my request, he hadn't sent in the cavalry, the Germans would have kept you in the Occupied Zone! Without him, you would never have got back to Bizerte. You'd've been condemned for desertion to the enemy.' Her voice becomes a murmur. 'You, who've tried for the last two years to join up with de Gaulle!'

The train draws into the station. The dashing French officer bends over her wrist. Just think, a lady who has contacts at headquarters! The *Hauptmann* clicks his heels. She squeezes me tightly to her chest but, sarcastic, whispers in my ear, 'When will you ever leave your mother's skirts?'

4

4

Special Detachment

One fine day, weeks after my return to Bizerte, Colonel de Montrichard, commanding officer of the Sidi Ahmed base — a handsome, old-school sky fighter, greying, decorated, scarred and limping low — summons me to his office to scold me. 'Headquarters is concerned about you, the famous border jumper whom I gave two months' prison for insubordination! No doubt Emile had a lot of clout! What I am reprimanding you for is getting caught, but since I like chaps who run risks, even absurd ones, I'm transferring you to the guard – you will have a gun.'

In the course of the following months, I fuss over my Oerlikon 20mm gun, a paragon of Swiss precision. I practise handling it, and hit the bullseye on the very rare occasions of shooting practice.

The progress of the war is no secret for Henri Silol, my friend who operates the switchboard. He just listens in on conversations exchanged between the high command and the colonel!

On 8 November 1942, in the morning, his hysterical voice crackles over our battery's telephone. 'Bob! The Allies have landed in Algiers!'

'But, they're supposed to land here! My pastor promised me …'

'Do you want me to ask for a refund? Wait and see; Darlan, the admiral, is there as well. He came to visit his sick son, and he's found himself cornered. So he's made himself their heir apparent to the Maréchal, opened fire and killed thousands of men.'

'I hope they hang him, the bastard!'

'Obviously. Until then, if you want to come and follow all the action, be my guest.'

At the switchboard, Henri stuck a phone in my ear; the voice of the Governor General of Tunisia, Admiral Esteva, says with a nasal twang, 'Colonel, I transmit to you the orders of Admiral Darlan, the Maréchal's deputy; "As the Allies have attacked us, we must fight them alone or with assistance." If they advance, you must push them back!'

'Pardon me, Admiral,' exclaims our chief, sounding distressed. 'But if we do, we put ourselves on the side of the Germans!'

'Those are the orders!' cuts in Esteva imperiously. 'They are countersigned by the head of the government, Pierre Laval, in person.'

Montrichard isn't a man to submit to Laval, who has sold himself body and soul to Hitler; he hangs up abruptly.

In the afternoon, Tunisia's bombers flee to Biskra.

The next day, rumours circulate; waves of giant Blohm & Vosses drop thousands of *Feldgrau* over Aouina and they move calmly into Tunis without firing a shot. The base was deserted as they arrived. Jean Kisling is, therefore, already in the Allied camp. Lucky bugger!

Over the coming hours and days, the telephone calls become increasingly contradictory. 'General Juin speaking, commander of the North African forces. I'm calling from Algiers where I have the situation in hand. The Allies are moving towards you, Colonel. It's for you to welcome them and push back the enemy!'

'Did you actually say: "push back the enemy"?' replies the old fellow cheerfully. 'At your orders, General!'

Unfortunately, who takes over the line the next day? – Esteva, 'The instructions of General Juin are cancelled! Remain neutral, keep the army ready to act!'

11 November, usually celebrated in style every year, is replaced with a brief whistle.

Shortly after this, Esteva surfaces again: 'I've received a signal stating that a German squadron is off the coast at Bizerte, to which the Colonel replies: 'Should I hold them at bay, send reconnaissance patrols?'

'Certainly not!'

Next, Admiral Darlan appears in person. A political end. Don't they say he's done more navigating in the channels of power than on the oceans? He expresses himself calmly, heightened by a slight sing-song accent, 'You must stay neutral at all costs, Colonel. Welcome the Allies if they present themselves – the Germans, too.'

'As you command, Admiral,' mutters Montrichard, without much conviction.

A final call from Esteva brings it to an end. 'From now on it's General Noguès, Governor of Morocco, whom you are obliged to obey. The marshal has delegated all powers to him in North Africa, and has ordered him to defend against "any and all" invaders.'

'But not long ago Admiral Darlan ...'

'The Maréchal, who has just discharged Darlan, has ordered me in no uncertain terms to respect the conventions of the armistice. I command you to fire – on the Allies!'

'And on the forces of the Axis if they appear, yes?'

'Not at all! We're not *de jure* in a state of war with them, but we certainly are with the Allies who invaded us. Must I repeat it?'

Montrichard, a great lord whose gruff courtesy is legendary, mutters a '*de jure* – my arse!' before hanging up in a rage.

When during the night the governor tackles him again, Montrichard cuts him off hissing, 'Allow me! Our squadrons received the order to join up with the units in the south, 9,000 poorly armed men of General Barré who took the side of "our" allies. Do you, Admiral, wish to cede to the enemy a land that you are supposed to defend? I shall continue to respect the orders, along with a handful of creeps who aren't up to pushing back anyone or anything. But you won't have any gallant last stand!'

On his high horse, the admiral yapped, 'I command you to obey the Maréchal! You must resist to the last man ...'

Montrichard hung up on him.

'Handful of creeps ... and the last man, that's us!' exclaims Silol. 'They don't give a f*** about screwing us, these old schnucks ... and for nothing! The Jerries are f*****, that's bloody obvious. I'm not taking my last bow, no way! Time to get out, it's now or never.

In the morning, when I go on duty with my Oerlikon, black dots appear in the sky.

'Fortresses!' crows my supplier.

'With three engines? Junkers 52, you mean! Give me the shells!'

The battery NCO, haircut square as per the rules, interposes, 'Forbidden to fire! You, get down from the lookout and get lost.'

I reach the switchboard, Henri is on the look out, 'You've only seen the vanguard, who gave Admiral Derrien, commander of the navy, an ultimatum: "Capitulate! Otherwise you will be classed as an insurgent and shot!" He's already a collaborator, you can just see how he's going to come a cropper!'

By chance, I come across a truck that is in working order behind the engineering hangar. I approach it after nightfall and a sergeant leaps from the shadow, a pistol in his hand. 'What're you looking for?'

Pathetically, I report this failure to Henri, who replies in a good humour, 'Bah, 1,000 kilometres, on foot, no big deal! I'm joking, I spotted two bikes under the staircase of the CP and I intercepted the password for the checkpoints. En route, my boy!'

The sentry who, that evening, raises his bayonet against us until my friend whispers the famous 'word', points to the bivouac fires, 'The Krauts are there! Go through on this side and you'll bypass them.'

Without this well-trained squaddie, we would've fallen into their hands. We reach the tarmac Mateur road without incident. At the end is Algiers, a few hundred kilometres away. I notice in the moonlight that Silol sways his hips oddly, I shout to him, 'You're pedalling all wrong. Aren't you wobbly?'

'"Wobbly." Shit, the only wobbly on the base is the colonel. Did I filch his bike? Bah, he doesn't need it any more, since his legs are done!'

Poor Montrichard. An admiral stole his honour, the Nazis his freedom and a squaddie on the run his bicycle!

100 kilometers and ten punctures further on, sweating and frozen, we climb the steep meanderings of the route leading to the Algerian border. At our feet, we leave Tabarka, a cute little port, dozing under the tamarisks. At dawn when we finally reach a plateau we hear backfiring and throw ourselves in the ditch. Two motorcyclists in khaki pass right under our noses at full pelt.

'But they're coming from the west!' exclaims Henri. 'So they're ...'

'English, yes. I recognised their bikes, Nortons. With no protection, they've got some nerve! They're scouts; the bulk of their troops must be following behind.'

'I've been waiting for this moment for two years and – I didn't even shake their hands! Shit!'

We come across the mass of troops at the first township, La Calle. It turns out that it's only an advance guard of tracked vehicles full of astounded Tommies, who are catching the bouquets of flowers thrown their way and giving the V for victory.

The inhabitants are enthusiastic and the town decked out better than for 14 July.

There is light at the end of the tunnel. The route to Algiers – open. And it leads right to the recruitment office for the RAF, I bet.

Maman, I'm out from under your skirts!

A cool-headed corporal is out alongside me, his Sten gun barrel glued to his stomach, shooting magazine after magazine into the sky, showering me with a downpour of burning cases. The tack-tack of his machine gun is lost in the roar of the Junkers 88 bombers skimming the treetops at 500kph. The crackling of individual weapons, the staccato of machine guns, the thudding hammering of pom-poms mix with the exploding bombs. An unbelievable racket. A deluge of fire falls around us, severing branches of the fig trees in Bône's central square, as a result of which the 36th British Brigade chose to sacrifice its sacrosanct five o'clock tea. Henri and I had just been invited. Suddenly, a procession of bombers came down the avenue. We rolled up in a foetal position between the roots of a tree, under a shower of leaves and branches.

Finally, calm reasserts itself. The roadway is ruined, jammed with damaged and burning vehicles, bloody bodies; the wounded are groaning. A major, covered in white dust, going from one to another, cries out, 'Anyone around here speak French? I need local doctors to assist me!'

I raise my hand, as in the classroom. Henri and I hunt out the doctors and help transport the wounded and dead to the hospital. By the evening, we're muddy and exhausted.

To show us their gratitude, Wilson, the major, suggests we sign up to his brigade as scouts. 'An honour,' he affirms. I exercise all of my diplomacy to decline. Becoming fighter pilots is our dream, isn't it? Fair play, the officer gives us a letter of recommendation and a valid safe conduct with His Majesty's forces.

The next day at dawn, the goods train into which we had climbed draws to a halt on an outcrop overlooking Algiers, strafed, like Bône, by the Luftwaffe. Enchanting spectacle; multicoloured garlands rise graciously towards the stars; these are the strings of beads from tracer shells fired by all that the town and the bunch of ships moored in the harbour has in the way of batteries. The bombers scatter geysers, brownish on the land, immaculately white on the sea.

On the single intact rail, the train pulls into a ruined station whose shattered glass dangles miserably.

In battle dress, cap over one ear, Players hanging from a lip, off we go, striding down rue d'Isly, Algiers' smartest street. The major's 'open sesame' does a great job. At the remote depot of the British forces, at the Lycée Bugeaud that dominates Bab-el-Oued, a navy lieutenant welcomed us with open arms. He first of all tried to 'sell' us an engagement with the Merchant Navy, which is cruelly short of manpower; the U-boats of the Kriegsmarine send so many cargo boats to the bottom of the sea. It's not for us. Without resentment, the officer supplies us with a pile of regulation uniform, lace-up boots, tack, spares – everything except for the rifle – explaining, 'Us English are just tolerated in Algiers. The landing is an American affair. Also, don't count on finding a recruitment office. Instead, go see the Yankee side – and you are welcome to stay with us as long as you wish.'

At the prestigious Saint-George Hotel where the Allied headquarters are based – exclusively American, or almost – a *female* officer, uniform *à la* Chanel, Max Factor make-up, advises us with a film-star smile, 'Sorry, boys, in an advance operations theatre there are no recruitment offices. You need to revert to the French army. It is with us now.'

At the garrison's office we are introduced to a Gothic colonel wearing the *bleu horizon* of the Great War and sporting a handlebar moustache. I'm full of doubt. Too late. He chokes when I tell him naively that we wish to rally to de Gaulle.

'What, that renegade? he sputters. 'You owe allegiance to the Maréchal and to him alone. Guards,' he thunders, 'conduct these traitors to the barracks' prison at Pélissier!'

Fortunately, our 'guards' amount to one single infantryman, wearing a fez as worn out as its owner, who, while swearing by Allah, won't say no to a drop of sweet-flavoured *anisette*. The first has him describing to us his Marne of 1915. With the second he avows his admiration for 'di Golle'. After the third, we abandon him anchored to a counter, with his blunderbuss, bayonet on the barrel, wedged under his arm.

I grumble, 'How can we be such dummies! Especially after having intercepted the conversations of these old phonies left in place by Roosevelt!'

Wild rumours run rife in the streets of Algiers: Admiral Leahy, US ambassador in Vichy and confidant of President Roosevelt, would have convinced him that Charles de Gaulle has no following in France, that the only, real head of government is Pétain, father of the country! For Roosevelt, the general is an odious dictator in power. In standing alone against the invincible Wehrmacht aided by Stalin, England has bankrupted herself. Now dependent entirely on Roosevelt to bail him out with men, arms and gold, Churchill plays Roosevelt's flunkey; he and de Gaulle have a love–hate relationship. Winston persists in counting on Grand Charles, stubborn and irritating enough to make him swallow his cigar. Churchill recognises the government of *France Libre* – Free France – while Franklin swears by Vichy.

Be this as it may, Operation Torch being purely an American affair, Churchill subscribes to it. The majority of British troops en route to the Tunisian front are merely crossing through Algeria. Roosevelt left the governance of North Africa in the hands of Darlan and his clique.

In Algiers, the shop windows display portraits of Pétain and Darlan. Better to avoid the old mustachios under the emblem of the Vichy government of the Légion des Combattants and the Bureau du PPF,[1] a breeding ground for French Waffen SS! They're still well established. The emergency laws introduced by Vichy even before the Nazis demanded it are still in force. Public office and army positions, among others, are closed to Jews. Their identity cards bear the mention 'Indigenous Jew'. We keep our heads down just as much as the known Gaullists who are wanted by the Admiral's police.

We surf without making waves in this devil's pool that is Algiers. It attracts the flotsam and jetsam of society, deadbeats who have found their groove there and who deal in tips, often shit. The latest one, for example; 'At the corner of rue Rameau there's a Gaullist office at 7 rue Charras!'

We are in English uniform, so where's the risk? A sign on the door, Bureau des Carburants, doesn't tell us anything. A flight of stairs leads to a room furnished with a bookcase, a white wooden table. A young officer cadet, thin and blond, looks up at our approach, 'My name is Peauphilet. What can I do for you?'

Put off by the fossil Bureau de Garnison, I beat about the bush. The cadet smiles at me, 'If I had the power to get you to England, I would already be there! On the other hand, I can enrol you in a Gaullist course ... le SD.'

'SD? As in the *Sicherheitsdienst*, the Nazi security service? You're joking?'

He bursts into happy laughter, 'No, SD for Special Detachment! It's a, let's call it paramilitary, unit equipped by the English.'

1 Parti Populaire Française, French Fascist party active during the Second World War.

'And what does this SD do?'

'Perhaps one day, it'll do Darlan and his clique good and proper. If that sounds like your thing, come back tomorrow morning at 6 a.m. A lorry will take you.'

'Where?'

'You'll see when you get there.'

I look over at Silol, questioning. He nods, 'We'll be there.'

We almost didn't get there. Each evening as darkness falls, the Luftwaffe Ju 88s appear, flying low from the heights of Algiers on to the fleet of grey boats tucked into the port. This time, one of them aims short. There is a shrill whistle. I throw myself under my bed, shouting to Henri, 'It's for us!'

The sky falls in on our heads, the walls follow; we find ourselves back in the fresh air. Our room is nothing more than a patch of wall bristling with long glass shards buried there by the explosion. Outside, the courtyard has given way to a gigantic excavation. Everywhere, corpses. Twenty dead, a hundred wounded. We help to evacuate them, as in Bône.

At dawn, the place has been cleaned up; we make our way to rue Charras. From there, after having driven for about an hour, the lorry drops us off at the door of a vast estate at Cap Matifou. Behind a long wall, fields, barns, a manor, some outhouses. A little tubby man in battledress and jodhpurs, with tortoiseshell glasses on his nose and thinning hair, introduces himself, 'Captain Sabatier. I command this camp. Come to the mess and have a coffee.'

The mess is a barn where a group of young people are gathered dressed, like us, in battledress. As I enter, a voice is raised, 'Hey, Pasteur is returning to Sainte-Croix from what I can see!'

With a huge grin, Fernand Bonnier de la Chapelle holds out his hand. His look is as frank as ever; a boy scout, dimple in his chin, he really is my friend from Neuilly!

'How'd you get here, Fernand?'

'I took part in the protest at the Arc de Triomphe on 11 November 1940. As I was only 17 I only got a beating and eight days in the clink. My father, a journalist in Algiers, got me a pass. Hold on, let me introduce Pierre Raynaud. We were in the coup of 8 November last ...'

Raynaud looks old, more than 21 perhaps, because his hair is in a pudding bowl and there's not much on his temples, and he frowns and chews a pipe.

'You should come to dinner at the Chien Qui Fume to celebrate our meeting again,' suggests Fernand. 'My father's treat!'

Fernand drives Papa's venerable Citroën, *Rosalie*, to town at breakneck speed. Our meal is boozy. On the way back, he negotiates the curves like a virtuoso and tumbles into a ditch. We weren't too sloshed to get *Rosalie* back on the road. That evening, Silol, who isn't given to introspection, mutters, 'A Bureau des Carburants without petrol, an SD which isn't; Gaullists disguised as English hidden in a farm and who're having a wild time at the local bistrot; while Darlan's cops are hot on their heels – what is all this jiggery pokery about?'

In the morning, Sabatier asks us, 'Have you two been in the military? If so you'll be teaching drill to the rookies.'

These rookies are the *pieds noirs* – the French Algerians, mostly students – and Jews. They want to have a go at the Nazis, but the army closed the door in their face. How did they find their way to the SD – a mystery! Sabatier lifts a corner of the veil, 'Some of them gave a helping hand at the landings. Since then, they've been on the run. Matifou is their refuge.'

'And the Americans are in the dark about it?'

'For the moment, they're leaving us alone. I don't know for how long. The English have set up their official channels. The owner of this farm, Demangeat, has put it at our disposal, in whose name, I ask you? The day after the landing, "they" delivered 17 tonnes of English weapons to us, some uniforms, enough to equip a regiment. And our budget is enough for us to feed everyone.'

Another odd thing about this 'English' camp is that its canteen is managed by the survivors of the Brigades Internationales, desperados in the style of Hemingway – red scarves, berets and belts, moustaches and sideburns à la Pancho Villa. They concoct spicy stews and aren't stingy with the *vino tinto*!

Raynaud, Bonnier, Silol and me soon form a separate group, which two phlegmatic Normands join, Bures and Lucas,who is blond like wheat, small moustache, pipe sticking out of his face, more British than Colonel Bramble. They are dropouts from the officers' diploma course.

The night of 7 November, our friends, along with Pauphilet, had overrun Algiers – in the space of a morning. Raynaud tells us the story:

'We were among 100 or so conspirators who, that evening, showed up with some crafty tricks at Doctor Aboulker's, a Jewish surgeon, one of the leaders of the coup. There, the commanding officer of the garrison, Colonel Jousse, handed us armbands stamped VP for Volontaires de la Place, a phony militia, charged with, you know, assisting the troops in the event of "unforeseen circumstances"!

'Two hours later, without firing a shot, all strategic points in the town were under control. Under Pauphilet in his cadet uniform, we relieved the guards on duty at the villa of the general in chief, Juin – softly, softly! It only remained for us to wait for the Americans to land. Everything was going swimmingly when Bob Murphy, the United States Consul, turned up with Colonel Chrétien, the boss of the Deuxième Bureau.'

'He was also part of the plot, was he?'

'I believe so ... Murphy had Juin woken up. He comes down in his pink striped pyjamas and Murphy says to him, "The Americans are about to land. Hold back your troops!" Son of a gendarme, wedded to the discipline, Juin cries out. "But, I don't have the power to make decisions! I have to refer any to my superior, Admiral Darlan!" And this idiot of a Murphy lets him do it! Put on guard, Darlan puts the garrison of 25,000 on alert. The Americans are welcomed with cannon shells. The hundred or so VPs that we were with had no weight to fling around, of course. Many managed to get away but two were killed. All his own doing, Murphy just avoided his men being pushed back into the sea!'

The next day, a British major, all 6ft and 100kg of him comes into the camp as easy as you like. In a Faubourg Saint-Germain French he introduces himself, 'I'm Jacques Vaillant de Guelis, charged with teaching you the basics of shooting and unarmed combat, the art of killing silently, young people!' A superior officer – just think – attached to a handful of squaddies to teach them kick-boxing when a corporal could pretty well do the job. What's up with that? Better still, he's treating us like friends, listens to our adventures, laughs at them, tells us a bit about his:

'In 1941, I was in the Free Zone. Imagine, Roosevelt, who detests de Gaulle, had it in his head to surround himself with "representative" French politicians who would give Washington and London the upper hand with the General. I had a mission to get Daladier, the trade unionist Jouhard and Edouard Herriot on board. They weren't exactly keen on the idea after ... you know ... Mers-el-Kebir. The "pink" politicians didn't care for de Gaulle at all. And let's not even mention Herriot!'

I burst into laughter, 'Herriot didn't want to get wet! My father often repeated to me Clemenceau's words, "Herriot is a flag. He turns whichever way the wind is blowing".'

The good giant bursts out laughing, 'Good God, that's a good one. I'll have to repeat that one to Churchill. He worships the "Tiger" and adores witticisms.'

'So then you're a spy?' Silol asks.

'A spy? My God, no. With us, spies in the strictest sense are those who listen at doors, belong to the Secret Intelligence Service or MI6; me, I'm just an SOE agent, lend a hand, sabotages, executions, behind the back of the enemy. The Intelligence Service is answerable to Foreign Affairs, SOE directly to Churchill.'

'Executions? Is that common?'

'No, rather rare. An operation "homo" order, for homicide, must come from the top, right at the top.'

Hands in his pockets, de Guelis calls me over. 'You, Bob. Attack me!'

'If you don't defend yourself, I can't, Sir!'

'Come on, it's an order!'

I had played around with boxing before the war under the eye of a former world champion, Routis. I threw myself forward. A foot catches my leg, my hand is taken in a vice and, making a circle in the air, I land on my back and a knee crushes my chest while my elbow is jammed at a funny angle on a thigh and the side of his palm hits my throat like a blade. To finish with, two forked fingers aimed at my eyes halt only when they are close enough to brush the lashes. The major gets up, dusts off his trousers and taps his pipe on his heel, 'That's what unarmed combat or silent killing is all about, Bob. You've still got a lot to learn!'

'It's all very well, this unarmed combat,' cuts in Henri, who isn't encumbered by bowing and scraping. 'But we actually want to fight in the sky not on the ground. Couldn't you find us a little place in the RAF, by chance?'

'Sorry! Aviation isn't in my remit. But if SOE tempts you ...'

'Do the secret agent stuff? What an idea!' mutters Henri. 'To be sent straight back to France when I've had such a hard time getting out, never!'

One morning, Sabatier says to me, 'It seems you shoot well? I'll have you as a bodyguard.'

'Are you under threat then in this camp?'

'Of course not! But in town, it's better to be on your guard'!

That comes as no surprise – Algiers is a madhouse! The Vichyist government, I am shortly to learn, has been infiltrated by Gaullists, monarchists, upstarts and opportunists who are watching Darlan for the slightest wrong move that will allow them to eliminate him and take his place.

Hassled by Churchill, and under pressure from de Gaulle and from public opinion – England, France and even America itself are outraged by his reliance on a known collaborator – Roosevelt backs down: 'I've made a provisional deal with Darlan, which will be revised as soon as we see victory in Tunisia.'

This declaration has been redacted from the newspapers by Darlan's *cabinet noir* of 400 censors. It's a lost cause; the BBC and Radio Brazzaville are having a field day. Graffiti appears on the walls: 'The admiral – out to sea or in a watery grave!' *Combat*, a Gaullist underground paper, carries the headline, 'There's water everywhere and he's going to sink!'

I struggle to follow events as they unfold; I've got too much to do. Sabatier's organising one meeting after the other at a frenetic pace. We jump from Doctor Aboulker, Gaullist; to Marc Jacquet, a cabinet director who until then I thought a Pétainist; to Henri d'Astier de la Vigerie, director of police and one of the promoters of the Volontaires de la Place formed from all sorts. I thought him Gaullist, he would turn out to be a monarchist! He's one of the '*Cinq*', supposedly neutral, powerful men imposed on Darlan by Eisenhower – recommended by Murphy – to thwart his Pétainiste ardour. Free from such constraints, the admiral would soon have had all opposition put behind bars.

I come across Lieutenant Cordier who, during the night of 7 November, occupied the telephone switchboard. In civvies, if you can call it that, he is a priest, confessor to Henri d'Astier and my friend Fernand.

On 27 November, a warning shot at Darlan – the French fleet, 'his' fleet, is scuttled in Toulon just before the Germans, who invaded the free zone, reach the port. Naively, Roosevelt hoped right up to the last minute that the fleet would join up with the US Navy. Now the mighty admiral is just the incompetent captain of his own destiny. He would have been demoted by Pétain anyway, for black market trading! It's said that at his home in France the marshal's police uncovered hundreds of kilos of sugar, coffee, oil and ham – goods so rare that the ordinary people never even see them.

One day in mid-December, while I'm escorting Sabatier, we are trailed by the very caricature of a spy – felt hat with brim pulled down low, dark sunglasses despite the pouring rain, and a long, putty-coloured trench coat. It's a silhouette that isn't unknown to me. Where've I seen it? I've got it – in the headlines. It's the figure of Henri d'Orléans, the immutable claimant to the throne of France offering his services to the marshal just a while ago. Laval has responded by offering him the Ministry of Supplies. It's like offering him a rotten egg; 'Supplies' is the hated target of 40 million starving people dreaming of skinning the minister alive. His Highness declined, not amused, and then flew off to Rome where he hailed Mussolini and threw himself at the feet of Pious XII.

So what is he up to here in Algiers, this pillar of the monarchy who is banned from French Republic territory? I learn that Abbot Cordier, Marc Jacquet and Mario Faivre, a young sympathiser to his cause, went to fetch him at the Moroccan border – country under mandate, therefore 'foreign' in law – where he was residing, and smuggled him into Algeria under the pseudonym of Robin Hood, probably. D'Orléans took rooms at Henri d'Astier's and immediately offered his services to the '*Cinq*', then to Darlan. None of them, it seems, brought up the fact that His Highness's position was highly illegal. But they all let him make a fool of himself. Convinced that God and man had opened up a royal way for him, the pretender, between saying masses at his portable altar, drafted a *Proclamation au Peuple de France* to be disseminated when he becomes 'Prince President', and several versions of the composition of his future ministerial cabinet. On one occasion, de Gaulle and Giraud were included in it, one and then the other head of government and heir apparent. As for Darlan, His Highness imagines him as ambassador to Washington! At first Churchill, whose sense of humour is legendary, is amused by these antics, but then he and Roosevelt put an end to the sport.

By contrast, Giraud's star rose to the firmament. Giraud, a general in the old tradition, tall at 1m 92cm, sports leggings and a Gauloise moustache. In the eyes of Roosevelt, the perfect understudy in the event that Darlan ... one never knows, does one? Jacques de Guelis' SOE, the Intelligence Service and the Bureau Central de Renseignements et d'Action (BCRA) all combined their efforts to extricate Giraud from the German fortress where he had been rotting since 1940. As soon as he was liberated he ran off to pledge allegiance to the Maréchal. An emissary from FDR then persuaded him to come to Algiers by dangling a carrot – the command of the Allied Armies in North Africa. The submarine *Seraph* of the Royal Navy, having become a clandestine ferry, that transported secret agents to and from the French shores, took him on board at Ramatuelle near Saint-Tropez and delivered him to Gibraltar and into the hands of Eisenhower – whom FDR had made general-in-chief of all the forces of North Africa. Ike offered him, as a small consolation, the command of the French forces. Giraud ensured they begged him before consenting to be flown to Algiers. Alas, his plane was diverted to Boufarik, a secondary and deserted aerodrome. The triumphal committee he had been expecting was absent. He wound up getting caught in the middle of a full-blown shouting match – one of many – between Darlan and Clark, Eisenhower's second, who, infuriated by the duplicity of the admiral, offered his place to Giraud. Noguès vetoed that. Darlan has one more star than Giraud.

Clark has, it appears, admitted defeat. Giraud will only agree to being the 'most obedient servant' of the admiral. And Darlan proclaims on posters: 'In the name of the Maréchal I assume authority in North Africa. The officers keep their command. The administrative and political arm remains in place. No change can be effected without a new order from me. Long live the Maréchal!'

Shocked by the sickening turn of events, Churchill did not hesitate to double-cross Roosevelt – this Special Detachment constituted of reprobates who wouldn't hesitate to take a shot at the admiral.

The Matifou farm overflowing with volunteers, the SD has annexed the small Ain Taya station, which is just a stone's throw away; it is disused now, as is the small local line that served it before the war. There I became involved with three GIs occupying a bourgeois seaside villa. They are operating a marine gun targeted out to sea – without much zeal, as the closest Germans are spread from Tunisia to Sicily, 1,000km from Algiers! Entente cordiale, I trade fresh vegetables and plonk for tinned foods, cigarettes, Louis-Philippe beds with soft eiderdowns. And I keep the ovens going to general satisfaction.

Christmas Eve. I'm frying *boudin blanc* and *pommes reinettes* when, through thick static and in an indefinable language, a radio spits out the fragmented message, 'Admiral Darlan assassinated – murderer apprehended…'

I drop my pan and, with Silol at my heels, I run to the station. Pierre Raynaud is there, his customary pipe in his mouth.

'You heard the news, Pierre? Hey, isn't Fernand with you?'

He remains silent, before dropping a bombshell, 'No. He killed Darlan.'

'How do you know that?'

'I was in on it. I set it up with the others, including Sabatier, Henri d'Astier and his son, Cordier, Mario Faivre. Took lots. Fernand pulled the short match. Operation succeeded, except he was taken. It isn't serious, he's covered. Yesterday, after his Confession with Cordier, he admitted to me, "I don't fear anything. I've got a passport in the name of Morand, a visa for Spanish Morocco. From there, I'll join up with Leclerc's army." He was full of energy again. He's covered. D'Astier is director of police and his right arm, Commissaire Achiary is Gaullist through and through. The English are taking care of the escape route, it's their speciality. As for Giraud, he'll be so happy to inherit power, he'll turn a blind eye!'

The first news bulletin on the mormimg of the 26th stuns us all: 'Urgently recalled from the Tunisian front, General Giraud assembled a military tribunal to try the murderer ... who was shot this morning.' Apparently Roosevelt gave the trial his blessing, declaring, 'It's first degree murder!' and thus a premeditated homicide, without attenuating circumstances!

What aberration pushed Giraud to have the head of a boy scout of 20 years of age for the price of that of a traitor? Didn't Darlan wish for victory of the Reich, give the Nazis the Syrian and Libyan bases and on 8 November sacrifice thousands of men, for nothing? Worse, Giraud sanctioned a miscarriage of justice; as a minor, belonging to no recognised combatant unit, Fernand should never have been subjected to a military tribunal.

At dawn on 26 December, two black cars came to a halt in a dry moat of the Hussein Dey Fort. In one, a pine coffin, in the other, Fernand. As the firing squad raised their weapons, he cried out, 'I gave a traitor his justice.'

He was put into the coffin. Nobody shed a tear. A kid with bright eyes, 20 years and 57 days old, he believed in France, in the King, in the Good God.

He had confided to Pierre, 'You know, Henri IV said, "Paris is worth a Mass." So, France is worth my life, for sure.'

In the afternoon of this damned day, I walk up and down the earth platform in front of our little station in a melancholy mood. A blue coach sweeps in, preceded by a black Citroën motorcar. Descending from one, a troop of mobile guards who fan out; from the other, two plain-clothes policemen emerge and address me: 'I would like to speak to men named Sabatier, Raynaud, Pauphilet. Are they here?'

Yesterday, all our friends disappeared. Henri and I alone remained. And for good reason – we have no pied-à-terre in the town. As cool and calm as can be, I reply, 'Don't move, I'll go and get them.'

I go into the station, collect Silol on the way and, via a service entrance we leg it to the villa of the *Américains*, then from there at a trot to that of Major de Guelis. That evening, he has guests: the chattering officers, glasses in hand, behold two breathless squaddies arriving at the front door. The major pushes us into the kitchen, listens to us and concludes, 'Ah well, my boys, if you want to escape Giraud's police, you have no other choice than …'

'Than to join your SOE?' cuts in Silol.'Okay, Sir, we have no other choice!

The admiral's grandiose funeral is held in Algiers' cathedral. The catafalque blessed by the high clergy is entirely covered in wreaths and sheaves of flowers. Eisenhower and his people salute behind the rows of their 'allies': Giraud, Chatel, Noguès, Bergeret and the others, bronze and silver oak leaves in the wind. They are unaware that in private, Ike and Clark have nicknamed these old capricious whores the 'YBSOB' for 'Yellow Bellied Sons of Bitches'.Churchill will later say of them, 'They hate one another more than they hate the Germans. Rather more than liberating France, what really interests them is power!'

However, the President does not see things from the same angle and Winston is simply his most obedient servant, alas!

Immediately after the funeral, on the basis of a measure that stinks of Nazism, the new high commissioner, Giraud, goes hunting. Carts loaded with suspected Gaullists depart for the Tunisian front; there they will almost certainly be shot in the back, or deported directly to the Sahara with the prospect of being forgotten there forever, not to mention those who are thrown into prison without trial. Doctor Aboulker, for example, is pulled from his bed without being permitted to fit his artificial leg – the original remained in a trench in Champagne.

Hopping to your prison cell – a first for a Great War invalid, don't you think?

5

The Crazy Bomb Disposal Expert of Gibraltar

Minuscule walnut shell in a blue universe, the *Tarana* sails on.

'What, we're setting sail in this leaky tub?' Silol had joked when he saw it, overwhelmed by the mass of large buildings and liberty ships jamming the port of Algiers at daybreak.

De Guelis was almost angry: 'This is a corvette of 200 tons in the service of SOE! In the jargon of the profession, a "felucca" – a name doubtless inspired by the feluccas on the Nile, which crossed from one river bank to the other. Disguised as trawlers, it and its sisters land and evacuate dozens of agents on the coasts of Provence and Languedoc! And believe me, it's hardly a walk in the park! If I hadn't acquired it, you'd go to Gibraltar on a cargo ship, nowhere near as comfortable. Besides which, if one day you have the Gestapo on your tail, you'll be thrilled when this leaky tub turns up to save your bacon!'

I can well believe that; while the navy sails dry, aboard the *Tarana* beer, Spanish wine and Scotch flow freely.

While Algiers-la-Blanche fades away on the horizon, two men spring from a hatchway like jack-in-the-boxes. One of them, dry, lithe, blonde with clear eyes, says to us, 'Good day young people! I'm François Vallée, Breton, cavalier, and this here is my friend, Henri Gaillot. We've just left a penal colony in the Sahara. Pétain had sent us on holiday there.'

Gaillot, massive, short neck, hair and beard both thick and grey, takes it up, 'I'm a Walloon, and so very old, nearly 50, that they call me Grand-Père. And, of course, we call one another '*tu*' not '*vous*'! In Liège, we don't use '*vous*'.

The two men, officers who refused defeat, had become friends in Tunis where the debacle had left them. Here they had joined a resistance network who had put together a radio transmitter and by some miracle had managed to make contact with the Intelligence Service station in Malta. One of them, Mounier, an *avocat* [barrister], then sailed to Malta on his cutter and acquired modern transmitters that could send signals reporting the passage of Italian convoys, which English bombers could then pick off. He and his men looted the ships that had sunk in the shallows and the mass of documents they recovered reached such a volume that the radio admitted defeat. There was a submarine that made deliveries to Malta; one night, it took Breuillac, the head of the network, and entrusted him on his return with submarine bombs called 'limpets'. If you believed these Englishmen, sticking them to a boat was child's play ...

'Yeah, right!' scoffed Gaillot. 'Those damned limpets were so heavy that the first one fell out of my grasp. The magnets on the second one, which I'd fitted with a bladder, wouldn't stick because of the barnacles covering the hull. On the third attempt we scratched the sheet metal for so long that our fingers lost all feeling. At the end of winter the water is freezing cold, even in Tunisia, and we were in swimming trunks! Over time we have seeded several Italian cargo ships and we think they sank ... there's no proof, since the delays in setting the bombs off were calculated in such a way that they sank out at sea and, as you can imagine, the Italians did not broadcast their losses. But then we sank an ore miner whose cargo left a dark trail to the docks and Italian divers discovered what had been going on. The guard was reinforced, and so it seemed wiser to wait for better days. Sadly, a fine tanker arrived – so fine that Vallée couldn't resist. If I had been there, I would have made him listen to reason. But he got in the water and was intercepted and knocked senseless with an oar. I joined him in prison a little later. Direction south ... the clink. When, on 8 November, the Germans got a foothold in Tunisia, we thought we were f*****! Out of the goodness of his heart, or because he caught a glimpse of the future, a guard let us get away.'

Not long after we reached the HQ of the Intelligence Corps in Gibraltar, a lovely Hispanic dwelling perched at the top of a lane climbing the Rock, de Guelis joined us. 'You're not having much luck: Churchill, Roosevelt, de Gaulle and Giraud, meeting up again next month in Casablanca, have monopolised most of the planes! I've grabbed two seats for Vallée and Grand-Père. They're expecting them in London. You others will go by sea. And as the boats are currently under attack you'll have time to explore the Rock! You know it's like a Gruyère cheese – riddled with holes and a subterranean town. Nearly 100,000 mole-men live in the warmth down there but without a single woman. So, suicide is very fashionable!'

'But the brothels aren't made for dogs!' exclaimed Raynaud.

The associations of mad spinsters had them banned, so the poor blokes continue to die, but with their souls intact, thank goodness!'

If there's one person who will refuse to die, it's Lionel Crabb, head bomb disposal expert and Gibraltar's star. They call him 'Buster', alluding to Buster Crabbe, a super American swimming champion, Buster and Toad. He has disarmed dozens of bombs the Italian frogmen work so hard to plant on hundreds of boats stopping off in Gib.

These French frogmen who outstripped the first Italian ones, who have just recently sunk their first English ships at Alexandria, were invited here by him. 'You're a good swimmer. Come with us!' Vallée said to me.

This place the Toad has nicknamed the Bastion is only a rickety sheet-metal shelter on a corner of a quay, greasy, covered with ropes, pipes and boxes of tools.

The Commander, as his own people call him, although he's only a ship's lieutenant, is a small, badly shaved, carrot-top with a sunken chest and a nose like a snorkel. His left eye blinks unwearyingly and unendingly, irritated by the smoke of the butt that never leaves his lips. Just like his French counterparts, he has no diving suit, scuba or flippers. His diving mask is a gas mask in a football skin. Holding out his hands – damaged fingernails, chapped, blistered and cracked – he scoffs, 'Mustn't complain. Soon we'll be getting gloves. And the Admiralty, having already raised the diving subsidy to near five of your francs, has given us a double ration of booze!'

At 20 he had already sailed the seas of China and done 100 jobs. Once the war had started he had hurried to enlist. The navy rejected him as 'too sickly' and put him in the 'auxiliary', a wheezy trawler claiming to hunt submarines. From there he was expected to standby along the coasts. Standby for what? Submarines, invasion fleets? He was vigilant in keeping watch for long periods in every pub posted strategically between Folkestone and Dover. By happy coincidence, they lacked bomb disposal experts. Two months later, the bomb disposal school lets loose this madman who would defuse the most sensitive mines with chisel blows. Quite rightly, Gibraltar loudly claimed the bomb disposal experts as theirs. Received as the Messiah, the future Buster discovers then that he must exercise his talents underwater. However, he can't swim. He learns on – or rather under – the job.

'Come and have a tot of rum to warm yourself up!' he suggests. 'Ah, if we had some flippers we could darn well patrol our 50 hectares of docks and our hundred ships' hulls more quickly! Well, we've already got Davis aqualungs – rubber sack with a pipe at one end, there! Thirty minutes of autonomy – if you breathe half the time.'

'It's new?' asked Vallée.

'And how! Conceived under Queen Victoria, patented around 1910! A little tot for the road, Gentlemen?' He fills with rotgut our enamelled quarter-litre mugs, more than good enough to lay out a Cossack!

In the evening, between clear turtle soup and over-boiled leg of lamb with mint sauce, de Guelis adds a touch to Crabb's character. 'He invented protection nets, grenade launcher pipes, sub aquatic floodlights. He fished up dead *nuotatori* in his nets and then buried them at sea with full military honours, bugle, laid out in their flag, covered with flowers and blessed by a Spanish Catholic cure, entirely at his own expense. As a result, the Italians named him 'Gentleman Crabb'. And do you know by what criterion he judges his candidates as frogmen? The length of their nose! He claims that's the sign of a good future diver. So, Bob, you should be in the running, shouldn't you?'

He doesn't know how prophetic he is. Ten years later, I will be contributing to forming a corps of French fighting frogmen, and, more astonishingly, equipped with a Davis: regulation grant from our French Admiralty! As for Crabb, I will cross his path again before he bows out at the end of many tours.

All through the night, every three minutes, a great bell rings the alarm – the Toad's invention. The undersea grenades explode with the regularity of a metronome at the entrance to the habour.

The day of their departure, I accompany Vallée and Grand-Père to the aerodrome, a concrete strip thrown across the isthmus marking the frontier and bordering a shanty town of crates pierced with windows, bristling with stovepipes – the packaging of apparatus delivered in the form of spare parts to be assembled on site, from which the mechanics make their home. Around, strewn any old how, are 1,000 aircraft, ready and waiting for their pilots.

The final touch: the Spanish highway, which crosses the middle of the runway, is closed by a gate that opens for just a fraction of a minute, between two landings, to let through a riot of Spanish workers who gallop like zebras to avoid being chopped up by the propellers of the next monstrous flying machine! Gibraltar Airport is without contest the most deadly in the world: winds swirling at the foot of the 400m-high Rock, while aircraft follow one another hell for leather down a runway divided by a level crossing that serves crazy pedestrians, which ends by plunging into the sea.

Two weeks are dedicated to feeding the impudent monkeys squatting on the Rock, pulling passers-by by the sleeve and chattering all the time. It's a long time. These Barbary apes have every right: legend has it that if they were to disappear, so would the English soon after.

Finally, the *Laetitia*, a liner converted into a troop carrier, is ready for us. All things considered, a good week spent crossing in a zigzag movement to deceive the German submarines that abound in the Atlantic. And, in February, the Atlantic is tempestuous.

Immediately after having crossed the Pillars of Hercules, we dance on mountains of water that intersect and then break; over them, the *Laetitia* dances a jig. The third night, the klaxons blare, sirens howl, loudspeakers bark, 'Standby to abandon ship!' Pierre, Henri and I fall from our bunks, put on our Mae Wests and muster in the gangways with the line of soldiers, who stagger blindly ahead, hands stuck to the walls to keep their balance. Outside, the storm is raging. Unleashed, the wide beams of the searchlights slide over the crests of monstrous waves, which the destroyers pierce like needles, throwing up gigantic fans of foam. Boom, boom, sounds the great bell of Gibraltar. Underwater grenades explode without pause. Geysers burst forth. The DCA enters the fray. I call out to an officer, who has his nose pointed towards the sky as if he could pierce the cavalcade of low clouds. 'What are you firing at?'

'One of those bloody bastards of a Focke-Wulf Condor that's been reported.'

The Condor, the eye of the Kriegsmarine, is a long range four-engine monoplane that directs U-Boat packs towards Allied convoys.

Suddenly, one of our escorts – a small aircraft carrier – appears. It pitches in such a way that at times it seems to be a hair's breath away from vertical. Above, two antique reconnaissance biplanes turn. They are hesitant to land on this see-saw. Finally one risks it. It lets itself come in at the very second the deck becomes horizontal, runs on for a few metres. A team rushes out, pins it to the deck and drags it off the runway. Encouraged, the second follows – just at the moment that the bridge rises. It crashes, nosedives and slides inexorably towards the void. I hold my breath. Suddenly, just before the old bird tips nose-first overboard, a small grey silhouette, the pilot, jumps free!

'Good show!' applauds the officer. Tonight, Dönitz (commander of the German submarine fleet) might as well have spared himself the trouble.

'But I didn't see anything! You're sure we were attacked by a submarine?'

'Certainly, but when you're not part of it, you can't see anything in this stir,' he replies, his hand gesturing at the foaming swell. 'Nevertheless, the Atlantic is swarming with U-boats, more than 300 today! Up to now they have sunk more of our tonnage than American shipbuilders can produce!'

Silol whispers to me, 'We did the right thing refusing to enlist in the Merchant Navy, huh?'

Bah, if I had inherited my mother's gift for dodging U-boats, I'd have nothing to fear. She defied one in 1915 from the bridge of the *Touraine*, on a transatlantic voyage she knew well. That year, having it in her head to surprise my father on the front in Picardie, she had embarked in New York without a word to him. 'We were the only three women on that boat and treated like princesses,' she often recounted to me. 'One night, the moon was dancing madly from one porthole to another, making me dizzy. You know me, I went to have a chat with the captain. I surprised him at his post on the bridge: "Why are you veering like that, Captain? It's driving me crazy! And … well, I'm finding it rather cold for the season. Aren't you sailing too far to the north?"

"Madame!" erupted the pasha. "I've got a submarine up my backside and I'm manoeuvring to avoid it. Get off my bridge, for God's sake!"'

At that moment a phosphorescent trace brushed the stem; another, the stern. The *Touraine* took a steep turn and Maman slid down the poop deck ladder on her bottom.

On the quay of Greenock Port, in the Scottish drizzle and damp fog, a perfect specimen of a British officer appears; trench coat, straight helmet, pale butter-coloured gloves, stick covered in pig skin and sparkling boots.

'*Je me présente*: Captain Bisset, your conducting officer – your nanny, if you like – responsible for getting you as far as London.'

Unbelievable! This fashion plate speaks perfect French with the distinctive accent of Paris's Belleville district. He enlightens us, 'That took you by surprise, didn't it? I can't help it. My father was posted in Paris. I went to primary school there. They call me Toto. And I call everyone Toto! *En route mes Totos!*'

At daybreak, a car picks us up from the *Scotsman*, the Glasgow–London express, on arrival and drives through the fashionable areas of London, comes into Portman Square behind Selfridges, goes through a gateway and deposits us before an elegant private house.

'Terminus. Orchard Court!' announces Toto. '*La cour du Verger*. And you'll notice – not a single apple!'

No danger of that, it's all smooth asphalt, as if it had been ironed, this courtyard!

A comic-looking major-domo appears on the steps, tall, well over 40, shining hair on a smooth forehead, lips pursed giving an outline of a pinched smile. He articulates in a refined French, '*Bienvenue au Verger! Je suis Park, le factotum*. Colonel Buckmaster is waiting for you, follow me!' And he leads us to an impersonal office on the top floor.

There, as I prepare to face the steely gaze of the head of the troops whom Churchill had ordered to set Europe ablaze, it is the round and kindly eyes of a lanky, somewhat awkward pastor that meet mine. A few small red and white frizzy curls beat a retreat up his large, intellectual forehead. A warm smile shows his piano-key teeth. He welcomes us with a '*Merci à vous de nous rejoindre*!'

'It's an honour!' replies Raynaud on our behalf.

The colonel's accent owes nothing to the Belleville; rather to Oxford. You could cut it with a knife. Yet, Bisset confirmed, he lived for a long time in Lyons and in Paris! The gift of languages must not be his cup of tea, that's all. The exchange of banalities comes to a stop and Major Nicholas Bodington, Buck's overwhelmed deputy, has by some miracle found us a timeslot.

Nick, to his friends, is a different beast. At first sight, his slightly heavy features may be deceptive until you notice his eyes, incisive, very mobile behind his small round glasses, and his cynical moue. He sizes me up it seems like a horse dealer would a cow; me, and my life expectancy. Human warmth is absent. He's a spy, a real one. He was press correspondent during the Spanish war and honourable correspondent for the Intelligence Service – you couldn't be one without being the other. After that he was an attaché at the Embassy of Great Britain in Faubourg Saint-Honoré in Paris, where his father was the *éminence grise*; among other things he covered the official voyage of King George VI to Paris. Infiltrated into France on the *Tarana* in 1942, he set up several SOE circuits. Thanks to his prestige he became the linchpin of the French Section.

Afterwards Park takes us to see the man in charge of Operations, Gerald Morel, called Gerry, an insurance broker who lived in France for a long time. In the course of his first and only mission, he was betrayed and delivered to the Vichy police. An emergency operation was performed for peritonitis. He then managed to escape from the hospital, where he was under guard, on the arm of a nurse, his stomach stuffed with dressings. He crossed the Pyrenees, crossed Spain and reached Gibraltar, and finally London.

Next we meet Bourne Paterson, called BP, the administrator, the dossier man. He is an affable Scotsman who jumps with equal ease between Spanish, Portuguese and French.

Park kept the secretary-general for last; her office exudes the fragrance of Oriental tobacco. While rolling a long cigarette holder between her fingers like Marlene Dietrich, she looks at us with her sapphire–blue inquisitor's eyes. She is a beautiful woman, expertly made up, with full lips and a defined jawbone, whose auburn hair is rolled into a twist. Her smooth, smart, Mayfair accent drawls so that her last syllable seems to go on forever. Pillar of the section's brain trust, she has her say on everything. She is manager and confidante of agents, a little like a mother, while the colonel does try to be father-like. She can make or unmake any of them, since Buck trusts only her judgement, they say. They call her 'the Madonna', which says its all. Her name is Vera Atkins. While the male staff of the section make no mystery of their origins – Eton, Oxford, Cambridge, liberal career, temporary officers – Vera's are impenetrable, a closely guarded secret. A high-flying aristocrat, desirous of remaining anonymous, no doubt. Her accent pleads in favour of this hypothesis.

God did she know how to deceive her world, the Madonna! Only Nick Bodington surpassed her. It is only in the last act, at the grand dénouement of

SOE, that it proved to be that agents who passed for white were blacker than soot, that others one believed 'single' were 'double', that some 'doubles' had been had by the 'triples' and that Vera wasn't everything that one believed!

When she dismisses us with a warm smile, Silol whispers in my ear, 'I got the impression she was stripping my thoughts bare!'

'And your thoughts, vis-à-vis her – were they pure?'

'Humm, that depends.'

We are then welcomed by a jack of all trades of the French Section, rather leaning towards air operations since he is an RAF squadron leader, André Simon. Son of an eminent importer of Bordeaux, he is French but, a product of English colleges, massacres our language to the point that in 1941, on his first and only mission in France – in the free zone, fortunately – his accent betrayed him. The Vichy police threw him in prison. Luckily, an officer recognised him as an interpreter who had been under his orders. A Lysander repatriated him. His booming laugh rivalled that of Jacques de Guelis who, glass in hand, doesn't hold a candle to him. André soaked up whisky, port, champagne and Bordeaux (of course) with equal gusto. At hardly 40 years of age, his nose bloomed like a bunch of lilacs. But what humour, what joie de vivre!

Orchard Court is a madhouse, in the hands of 'bloody amateurs', idiots who got lucky because they supposedly know French culture; put in uniform, ranked haphazardly and working under verbal orders. No plaques at the doors, service notes as rare as sunny days. They nicknamed the house 'pass house'. From morning to evening, there is one meeting after another between debriefing officers and agents returning from or about to leave on mission. All the rooms are monopolised, including the black marble bathroom with a bidet – a rarity in England. As Orchard Court is full to overflowing, I am sent to '64', No. 64 Baker Street, just two steps from the Orchard. SOE headquarters has a mix of all sections and is supposed to be top secret. A jest from the old hands, 'If you get lost in London, with your foreign accent ask the first taxi to take you to the house. They will drive you straight to the HQ of BCRA, 10 Duke Street, to the Orchard or to '64'.'

London has been invaded by a million soldiers – British, American, Free French, Belgian and Polish, and later refugees from European countries under the Nazi boot. Officers proliferate, and the military salute has been abolished so that those without rank don't live with their hand riveted to their military cap. The first day, Bisset drives us to a Patriotic School, a large building, grand but with soot-blackened walls, in Wandsworth, a South London suburb.

'Queen Victoria founded it,' he explains to us, 'to accommodate orphans from the Crimean War. Today, it's a filtering centre. Every foreigner who sets foot in England passes through there. For you, being sponsored, it's just a formality. But don't be complacent. Stumble over a trap question and you will stay for months being grilled, and if you get in a muddle, you'll finish with a rope around your neck!

Once the 'formality' is concluded, in less than an hour, Toto plays the part of tourist guide – Westminster; Whitehall; Big Ben; St Paul's Cathedral, intact, upright like a finger of God in the middle of a field of ruins. The city has been razed by the Luftwaffe. Buckingham Palace is surrounded by barbed wire and clad with ramparts of bags of sand, as too are monuments and administrative buildings. At each corner of the street, a container of water, and around that, bricks or quarry stones piled up properly – the remains of a building having received a direct hit. The water containers are for the firemen. Stuck on a still-standing pillar, a small poster: 'By the grace of Herr Hitler, our shop, which was beginning to date, has been transferred to 10 Jermyn Street. Our kind clientele is invited to visit our new completely renovated premises.'

'Don't do anything stupid,' Bisset told us. No danger of that! Our pay hardly covers the price of a portion of fish and chips, traditionally coated fish and chips wrapped in yesterday's newspaper. Mobilised or doing men's work, and dying as often as they are under the bombs, the English women no longer have anything in common with Thackeray's butter-wouldn't-melts. They put the men in their place or show their preferences. Alas, without a penny, we remain window shopping.

Toto finally brings us to Chicheley, a charming village with thatched whitewashed cottages *à la* Walt Disney. In a cottage, we're taught unarmed combat and shooting, accompanied by obstacle courses. We let off steam there.

One evening, muscles in knots, ears still ringing from gunshots, I take myself off to a village dance. In a hangar, three old beaux in dinner jackets are murdering an out-of-tune piano, an accordion and a violin. A battalion of female soldiers, nurses and a few girls in organdie dresses and lamé pumps are arguing over a handful of military males. My sunburned colour attracts their attention. Several of them invite me to dance; I shy away from that. Dancing, for an English girl, is a sacred art, and a sacred sport that demands years of practice – arabesques in the slow waltz, the huit in the paso, pirouettes in the tango. Don't even mention the jitterbug or the acrobatic swing imported by the GIs.

A young nurse sits beside me, 'You're not dancing? So, let's chat …'

She is fresh, svelte, chestnut hair and large clear eyes. I've come from elsewhere and I know how to listen. Her father, her brothers are at war, her great middle-class mother has enrolled in the Civil Defence. As for her, she interrupted her studies so she could serve. She will remain a nurse while the fighting continues; afterwards she will be a doctor, her vocation. She looks at her watch and cries, 'My God, it's late. Walk me home, would you?'

The night is inky dark. So she takes me by the hand to guide me along the forest pathway. Dead leaves crack under our feet. Suddenly she stops and says, point blank, 'Give me your raincoat!' She spreads it out on the ground, covers it with her ample nurse's cloak. Holding my arm, she lies down, raises her legs to the sky. Her skirt flies away, uncovering a white triangle which, in its turn … a whisper follows, 'Darling, prove to me what they say about Frenchmen isn't exaggerated!'

I didn't think to ask her name. I never saw her again. My only memory of her is the discreet and expensive lavender scent, *à la* Lady Chatterley, mixed with that of composting humus.

One of my saintly mother's musings comes to mind: 'Alas, to a foreigner, Frenchwomen have a reputation as having light morals, especially in England, where a lady's conduct is irreproachable!'

What debauchery has flowed under the bridges of London, my poor Maman, since you crossed them in an elegant Victoria carriage?

'At the selection school, Special Training School No. 5, in Wanborough, a ruthless screening will take place,' proclaimed Bisset. 'You pass or you don't, my Totos! Only the best of the best will be admitted to be trained.'

Wanborough Manor, an Edwardian manor house on the Hog's Back, a few kilometres from Guildford, looks over a large park harbouring a shooting range and a demolitions quarry. Here we find a dozen trainee agents, among them three young women. A striking brunette with a pretty, matt complexioned face and with hair the colour of polished chestnuts calls out to me, 'Are you French?'

'Yes. You too, I guess.'

'No, Spanish by my mother, English by my father, who does business in Europe. They brought us up partly in France, my brother and me, that is. Born Eliane Brown-Bartroli, I'm Plewman by marriage. Here,' she adds, pointing to a redhead with green eyes standing at her side, 'this is Diana Rowden, a pure British product who grew up on the Promenade des Anglais!'

Diane hit back, 'Whatever! I didn't grow up in Nice, but in Cannes, where my parents anchored their yacht. I did my studies there.'

The third young woman is a pink sweetie with foamy blonde hair, immense eyes behind tortoiseshell glasses, her eyes so faded they seem not to be inhabited.

'She's our chaperone,' guffawed Eliane. 'Her name's Prudence – seriously! As if we needed a chaperone!'

Among the men, Eric Cauchi, a brown-haired, brown-skinned colossus, prefers to speak 'pied noir' than to massacre his maternal language, 'However, I'm British, Maltese in fact. As I followed my father from port to port around the Mediterranean, I learnt Greek, Italian, French and just three words of English.'

While he's just let us know that dynamite explodes at the least shock, at the least spark, the instructor juggles, cigarette in his beak, with a lump of explosive and lets it escape! By instinct, I roll into a ball. Not a sound! The officer guffaws: 'Fortunately, this isn't dynamite but high-explosive plastic composed of a fraction of accelerant in an inert excipient – therefore stable, ladies and gentlemen! It's an ideal weapon. In a ball, flames of hell will leave it as cold as marble, but put a match to the detonator with mercury fulminate, super sensitive, it'll detonate at 8,000m a second and will slice through steel and concrete!'

Our turn to knead, to set the wick in the detonator and the detonator in the charge. What happy drunkenness exploding the first rolls! Sensing that in order to get through this 'ruthless' course we might be better working together, Eric, the girls and us three 'Africans' – as we had come to be known – helped each other out. When Diana wrestles to reassemble a Sten gun in the dark, I whisper, 'Don't forget to lock the breech!' This is our greatest fear – if the breech of a Sten, a pressed-steel machine gun produced by the millions in three parts, is left to fall free, it bounces like a ball. If the cartridge is engaged, the entire round explodes in every direction!

Map reading, orientation marches, demolition lessons and shooting lessons become increasingly demanding. I ace the shooting test, completing the forest and 'haunted house' course without a single fault. At Wanborough, it's not ghosts and skeletons that jump out at you, like at the funfair, but cardboard cutouts of SS men. They slide from tree to tree along a cable, jump up from behind a bush, a door, at the top of a staircase, even in the toilets. You need to beat your shadow to the draw, otherwise bad points rain down on you! In the Morse code class we try to outdo one another in speed and skill until Eliane breathes to us, 'I learnt that SOE is short of wireless operators. So stop making sparks, otherwise ...'

Wireless operators, or 'pianists', are prima ballerinas, umbilical cords and pariahs of a circuit or network – all at the same time. They are cherished because through them orders, instructions and calls for help are transmitted. They are so precious that they are kept away from parachute drops and sabotage. They live a cloistered life until – all too often – the Gestapo's 'big ears', their radio direction-finding equipment, track their signals and thus locate them.

'In their line of work, losses are 25 per cent higher than the average!' Eliane tells us with a well-aimed blow. 'Take heed!'

Overnight, our fingers knot themselves up, jamming on Q, da-da-di-da, that we had previously been churning majestically to the rhythm of the Wedding March, on the V, di-di-di-da, like Beethoven's Fifth, the H translated by a salvo of four sharp percussions! Mike, our signals instructor, will no doubt never get over this unprecedented epidemic: six wireless operators slipping through his fingers!

The final days, the exam days, are feverish, even without Morse code on the menu! We appear before long tables loaded with a flea market of explosives, grenades, weapons from all over, Mausers, Parabellums, Lugers, Hersthals, Brownings, Colts, Smith and Wessons, Spanish Llamas, Stens, Brens and even the redoubtable *Sturmgewehrts* of the German parachutists, which, timed and blindfolded, we must dismantle and reassemble without leaving out a single piece. This is child's play for our friends. Having grown up on a ship, Diana understands mechanics and has a good sense of direction. Eliane has nimble fingers; daughter of a businessman, she is a master of rhetoric. When she doesn't know an answer she drowns the instructors in empty verbiage.

The exercise at the end of the course starts in a faraway forest. We have to find our bearings without light, without a compass, without maps and without being caught by our professors, who play the enemy spotters. Final objective, take the office of Major Watt, commanding officer of the school. Having slipped between their fingers, I reach the façade of the manor. I hoist myself up along a vine to a window; its shutter opens easily! Stealthily, I slip inside.

'My God, who is it?' groans an afflicted voice.

A bedside table lamp lights up a rumpled bed. In the bed, Prudence, the chaperone, barely dressed, flaxen hair spread out, stares at me with her large, myopic eyes. A pink breast peeps out of her mauve satin negligée. I whisper, 'Don't be afraid, Pru! It's only me, Bob, we're doing a break-in exercise. I got the wrong room ...'

She murmurs, 'Ah, that's right! I was to go with the girls but I've got the 'flu!'

The sheet unveils the other breast. I fall on my knees; my mouth places itself on Prudence's half-open lips, which come to life. Suddenly, against her pearly skin, I have a vision of Article IX of the school's rules: 'The Ladies Quarters are strictly forbidden to males.' As delicately as possible I unfold the arms locked around my neck, and regretfully wrest myself from this enchanted valley perfumed by Yardley. I slip into the corridor; ten paces further on, I slide into Watt's office.

Prudence or not Prudence? Have I foiled a set-up or have I disappointed an ingénue who wanted to test, yes, her too, if what they say about the French ... I never did find out. On the other hand, I am judged 'suitable to continue my training'.

On Saturday, we are afforded free quarters in Guildford on the express condition that we keep away from the Red Lion, a pub in the centre of town. In the evening, Henri comes back fidgeting with news, 'I've met a ravishing woman. We drank a beer at the Red Lion.'

I jump, 'Are you mad? It's out of bounds, forbidden, get it!'

'You don't really believe that SOE has spies disguised as beer pumps, do you?' he replies laughing.

The next day, stubbornly he meets his lovely creature. When Pierre and I get back from the cinema, a note pinned on our friend's pillow attracts our attention: 'Good evening friends. I've been called to London. I won't be there for long, for sure. See you soon.'

See you soon? We will never see him again! Somewhere in the extreme north of Scotland is hidden a fortress called the Cooler or Purgatory, so they say. There, SOE sequesters agents who fail in total secrecy. Cut off from the world, without a calendar, without a watch, turning into zombies deprived of all notion of time, they would mix up dates and events. When one day the door opens, they will be nothing more than harmless neurotics, free to tell whatever enters their heads ... how, for example, SOE used to disguise spies as beer pumps.

In London, I occupy the guest room in Eliane's apartment at Queens Gate in upmarket Kensington. Eric shares with the lady of the house. They fell for one another, these two, between the throws of a grenade! We form an unbreakable trio. Playing the big sister – she's 24 years old – she calls me *hermano* [brother] and indulgently smiles like an angel at my night-time conquests whom at times she surprises as they are getting out of bed, asking, 'What do you have in the morning, tea or coffee?' As if nothing were more natural than finding a half-naked stranger under her roof. She even awards them marks.

Vallée, Gaillot and Pierre Raynaud, too visit us. Diana gives little tea parties in Chelsea, the Saint-Germain-des-Prés of London, in her mews house, a stable that has been turned into a bijou flat looking out into a lane, the height of chic! Eliane bills us in cocktails. Her favourite restaurant is Casa Pépé, Soho's fashionable Spanish eatery. There, Pépé, a chubby Latin hunk, brilliantined hair, pale blue suit and pink shirt, crushes her to his chest, covers her palms with kisses.

No one can make Eliane yield, not even Vera whom, at the end of the month, I face, head lowered, due to a cruel lack of funds.

'Vera, a small advance of ten pounds, please.'

She gives me a glacial, piercing look:

'By God, Bob, you know I'm forbidden to give an advance to anyone! Ah, you Frenchies!'

'Look, Vera, if I survive only three weeks on mission, you'll be more than reimbursed!'

She gives a heartbreaking sigh, holds out a little square of soft blue flimsy paper the colour of her eyes to me, 'Fine. Sign here.'

The parachute school or 'parachute factory' in Manchester delivers parachutes like a vending machine delivers sandwiches. They are sent rushing down the length of the ramps, at the foot of which we queue. Before we jump, ground training: apparatus, tucked rolls, jumps from a dummy bomber or a tower, visit to folding rooms and inevitable joking from the duty sergeant who wisecracks, 'See, each of these folders inserts a card with his or her name into each bag! So, if your 'chute doesn't open, you will know who to address your complaint to.'

A swarm of Whitleys, way out of date bombers, drops thousands of men each day to the four winds. Before jumping, you bawl out, 'I want to find a sergeant who forgot to hook me up! 'Cause I ain't gonna jump no more!'

The green meadows of England as seen through the circular hatch renders the twenty faces, framed by the visor and ear protectors of the foam helmet, deathly pale. We propel ourselves, each of us following the last as if our life depended on him, through the gaping void, which swallows us whole. At Ringway it's not so much count your chickens as it is count your birdmen – the sky teeming with them. Instructors bawl through their megaphones, 'Number Thirteen! Keep your legs tight together just before landing! Impeccable position. Shit. Ambulance for Thirteen!'

Stunned on impact, poor Thirteen is dragged listlessly behind his 'chute, which inflates like a great sail in the breeze. Mercilessly, one guy, a cockney, yells at him as he passes, 'Throw the anchor, old chap! There's a quay at the end!'

Eliane and Diana have their own aircraft, which drops them out of sight. As no woman is supposed to fight – say the war conventions – what would they be doing with a parachute? Unless they were being specially trained, which is nobody's business. Incidentally, neither they nor anyone else will get the blue winged badge, either. In order to deceive the enemy, aren't we supposed to pretend we are pen-pushers? And of course, pen-pushers don't jump out of planes, do they?

6

Adios Hermano!

The Security School, or Group B, occupies a huge area on the estate of Lord Montagu of Beaulieu – pronounced 'Bewley' – south of Southampton. An endless string of pasture lands, of hedges and thickets where cows, half-wild horses and herds of deer wander.

A major welcomes us in an Edwardian manor. 'Welcome. This is Boarmans Chalet, or STS 36, and is traditionally reserved for members of the French Section. Why "Beau Lieu"? Because the French Cistercian monks who built a gigantic abbey here translated it into their language from its Latin name "Bellus Locus" – meaning "beautiful place". In other words, this site was enchanting. They prospered here until the Pope excommunicated our good king Henry VIII. Straight off, he grabbed the monastery, its treasures and 3,000 hectares of land, which were ultimately sold for a pittance to a Montagu, an illegitimate relative of the Stewarts. But enough history. Today, the estate has a dozen or so cottages like this one, housing Belgians, Czechs, Yugoslavs, Norwegians, Danish and so on. And you.'

On the programme: composition of the armed forces and Nazi subsections, which include the RSHA, the Reich central office of security, and its offshoot, the *Sicherheitsdienst* or SD – of which Section IV is the Gestapo. Not forgetting the *Abwehr*, the military secret service directed by a literary hero, Admiral Canaris. His photo is pinned to the wall – white hair, his face sharp-featured and lit by a metallic glance, which, they say, pierces his interlocutors.

As for Heydrich, the mystical head of the SD – sadistic with a face like a knife blade – three agents from the SOE's Czech Section bumped him off last year.

Himmler is the supreme head of the SS – executioners dressed in black uniforms with a skull and crossbones, hence their nickname *Totenkopf* [death's head].

The boss of the anti-terrorist section of the Gestapo in Paris, our public enemy No. 1, is *Sturmbannführer* (equivalent to major) Karl Boemelburg. In his early youth, before 1914, Boemelburg studied in France – and then visited several times in his long-time role of spy. Passing himself off as an expert criminologist, he even collaborated in the protection of George VI at the time of his visit to Paris in 1938! Really, like Bodington? He even had access to French police documents! When in June 1940 he took over the premises of the Sûreté, rue des Saussaies, he felt at home. His services requisitioned the majority of fine buildings at the end of Avenue Foch, on the Port Dauphine side, of which No. 84 was dedicated to interrogations of captured SOE agents. He is backed up by *Haupsturmführer* (SS captain) Hans Keiffer, who is a straight-as-a-die ex-cop from Karlsruhe; and Götz, a Herr Professor made *Obersturmführer* (lieutenant) expert in *Funkspiel*, getting captured radio operators to work for him. He juggles with codes. As for Karl himself, an Epicurean, devoted to sensual pleasures and luxury, especially good food, he has a thing for French cuisine and the little women of Paris ...

Our face-painting lessons, led by a young officer named Captain Follis with the physique of a film star – christened Follis Bergères by Eliane – unleash much raucous laughter. Making ourselves up with whatever comes to hand – white shoe cream to grey the hair, ashes to accentuate wrinkles, chewing gum and cotton wool for the jowls – we are aged thirty years and become hunchbacked, lame, at death's door.

We swot up on the codes and we concoct invisible inks from egg whites, lemon juice and urine. To interfere with the mail without leaving a trace, there's nothing better than rolling a knitting needle very delicately under the flap of the envelope.

Afterwards, Captain Green, called Killer Green, arrives on the scene. 'Killer' because he teaches criminal activities which, contrary to what one might imagine, does not mean bloody executions but scientific poisoning with cyanide, arsenic, aconitine, botulism toxin and others, administered by means of drinks, food, the glue on envelopes and stamps, coffee or tea. As if the Germans would drink tea! Green also picks locks. It appears he's a virtuoso cat burglar that the SOE had released from prison in order to teach us his art. He cracks the combinations of safes by ear, takes fingerprints with chewing gum and modelling clay, chisels to the millimetre counterfeit keys in Plexiglas. He cracks safety locks using a hairpin.

I apply myself – to no avail. It's a real blow when Killer tells me, 'It takes ten years to become a decent burglar, my dear Bob.'

Shadowing lessons follow. Instructors and pupils take it in turn to shadow or to be shadow. The chosen area: Southampton, where we jump on moving buses, run though buildings with two exits and lose ourselves in department stores. Diana and Eliane are sharp customers and draw their pursuers into the rows of panties; there, under the eyes of shocked ladies, they turn to jelly.

We are now familiar with the town and its port thanks to this little game. The bombs haven't spared them. As in London, the stretches of water surrounded by a low wall fill the voids left by destroyed buildings and businesses. At times, the sign is all that is left of a pub, shored up by a pile of ruins. One of these, The Swan, makes me smile – *La Mort du Cygne, à l'anglaise.*

One night, we break into a cottage stuffed with booby traps of talc hidden behind doors, in drawers and even under the seat in the loo. We return from the expedition white as snow.

Outside of the classroom an old sergeant-major evokes the good old times, 'Under Victoria, Baden Powell, you know, the inventor of the Boy Scouts movement, a real workhorse and straight as an arrow, and yet he knew how to pull the wool over their eyes! He ran around the world disguised as a Sunday painter who sketched all the fortifications, all the cannons that he came across – without getting caught! A star of the Intelligence Service! Among his friends were Dansey-the-Sock and – Churchill. The Sock because he liquidated the Boer sentries with a sock full of wet sand. They say Winston really valued him. These two belonged to a unit that left their uniforms in the lobby to attack the Boers at the back. No surprise that they founded SOE. Today, Dansey is No. 2 at MI6. In fact, he is the real boss. He's got Menzies, the titular head, eating out of his hands.'

A brilliant brain of the Firm – as the Intelligence Service was dubbed – was the inspiration behind this school. His father, Saint-John Philby, gentleman explorer, was the first to cross the immense Arabian desert and, having become a staunch supporter of Ibn Saud, negotiated extractions with the American oil magnates. His son, Kim, graduate of Cambridge, entered into the IS and laid the foundations of our Group B and the STS 17, the higher school to train saboteurs. After that, he climbed the ladder of the Firm until taking the head of a very sensitive section, that for the USSR. We know what follows – with four of his comrades from Cambridge, he sells the secrets of the IS and its agents over a period of at least thirty years, before escaping to Moscow where, as a colonel of the Red Army and Hero of the Soviet Union, he is buried with all honours. He never needed to worry, as no gentleman of the establishment could conceive that a fellow of Cambridge, a fraternity brother, would get a kick out of betrayal!

'*Heraus* ! Get up!' Three well-imitated Gestapists – black uniform as per the *Totenkopf* and mouth in keeping – erupt into my room and drag me into an empty room, under an arc lamp. Between dream and reality, I attempt to gather my wits. Questions rain down. My torturers taking turns, churning out the same questions, hurl abuse at me, force me to give myself away. I get out of it as best I can. This true-to-life rehearsal of an arrest by the Gestapo utterly wore me out. Nevertheless, the course director judges me 'suitable to continue his training'.

Tomorrow, I will face the final test of the session, the '96 hours scheme': a simulated full-scale mission.

The coking plants, blast furnaces and steelworks of Sheffield taint the sky for 20km in every direction, and the neck of my shirt in less than an hour. My aim: to unearth a ton of information on the central post office and transmit it discreetly. Bisset didn't hide from me how tricky the expedition would be.

'Each evening you will telephone us the name of your hotel.'

I hit back, 'I'll be followed then as soon as I put my nose outside and you will pick me up in bed!'

'That's up to you to get out of the shit, then. You haven't spent four weeks in Beaulieu for nothing! Good luck!'

Luck smiled on me – Sheffield, no long-distance direct calls. Playing La Fontaine's fox, I laud the twitterings of the telephone operator. She tells me she is single; in town, no more young men; they've left for the war; life isn't much fun there. Her plumage isn't, alas, equal to her song. All she had going for her is golden hair, styled any old how, eyes as green as her tweed suit hidden behind her glasses. A few large glasses of Claret put her on top form. In an hour she tells me more about the post office than my questionnaire requires. I make it up to her afterwards by lavishing on her all the fervour

I'm capable of at the age of 20. End of mission: transmit the information collected to a slightly paunchy 50-year-old at the Hotel Terminus the next day. Impossible to miss him as he's reading the Times.

On the dot for the meeting, I scan the bar. A voice calls me, 'Lieutenant Mortier?'

It is that of a fiery-haired vamp, with too much make-up. Seated on a high stood she offers me an unobstructed view of her generous thighs sheathed in smoke-coloured stockings. In Sheffield, I am Roger Martin, the identity card that Orchard Court delivered to me certifies this. This vamp is therefore a Mata Hari made by SOE to try to trap me. So I continue on my way without blinking. La Dalida pursues me and whispers the password in my ear that a paunchy 50-year-old should have produced for me. I reply with a sweet smile, 'You're mistaken, Madame, you've got the wrong person!'

She insists, but I remain Martin. She persists. I decide to let myself be tagged: 'Even if I'm not who you think I am, I am blessed by this misunderstanding – may I offer you a drink?

During lunch, I only talk about her – all the time – nothing but her. During the walk that follows, under an apple tree, I put my arms around Doris. She doesn't push me away. I start to strangle her – as taught by de Guelis – which I interrupt at the second where her eyes are sliding upwards. When she comes to, I murmur to her, 'See, Doris, there's no one around. Hidden under this hedge your corpse wouldn't be discovered for days. I'd be long gone by then! Be so kind as to mention in your report to Buckmaster that you were assassinated by an unknown person who fled at three minutes past five. Okay?'

How could she hold me to account? We became so close. She confides to me that she is the sister of the commanding officer of one of these STSs that I go to. It seems the French Section is something of a family affair.

When, the next day, I cross the hall of the hotel to get a taxi, two men dressed in civilian clothes walking up and down the pavement bar my passage. I jostle them. Tempted by the promise of a large tip, my chauffeur jumps in and scatters them. Effort wasted, three of their colleagues spot me at the station. As I'm taken, cuffs on my wrists, the crowd gathers around: 'This fine-looking young man you've taken, is he a criminal? At a time when so many others are giving their life for the country! Shocking!'

At the police station I'm grilled until the morning as rigorously as by the 'Gestapists' not so long ago. These cops are applying to the letter the orders from Orchard Court. In any case – thanks to Doris? – my sense of security is recognised. I am judged 'suitable to fulfil a mission in the field'. For real!

'Mortier, do you know Poitiers?'

'Not at all, Sir.'

'Perfect, perfect,' repeats Buckmaster, who has summoned me. 'Thus you will not be recognised. I have something down there for you. A straightforward matter – to orchestrate the sabotage of the major canal locks – if you're volunteering?'

'Of course, Sir.'

Point of arrival – the abandoned hippodrome in Poitiers, situated 9km from the town near a hamlet called La Torchaise. A blind parachute jump.

Aïe! Being dropped blind and alone means I can't count on anyone to unhook me from a tree if necessary, help me if I get a sprain, bury my parachute, erase my tracks, help me to carry my suitcase that weighs a ton, put me on the right road. And that's without even envisaging the worst: that 'this bloody navigator' gets his degrees muddled up and drops me out into the blue 100km from the prearranged point!

My operational order doesn't much concern itself with details:

> 18 May 1943. Operation Porter. Your codename: Paco.
> Identity papers in the name of Robert Mollier. Cover person and history: to be constructed. After parachuting you rendezvous at your safe house: Monsieur Gâteau. Auctioneer. 19 bis rue Boncenne. Poitiers. Password: 'My friend Pierre told me that you could introduce me to his cousin.'
>
> You will reconnoitre the drop zone that we suggest here and receive demolition equipment at the beginning of the June moon. You will define the itinerary between the DZ and objective. You will reconnoitre the objective in such a way as to take a team there and be in a position to fill in the joint questionnaire.
>
> Your contact on your escape route: Señora Dona Jacoba Robredo. Calle Bravo Murillo 107. Secunda Izquiera. Madrid.
>
> Your signature for recognition for all mail: Anastase. In Spain, you will be able to require the assistance of the British authorities under the name of Lieutenant Robert Malley – Number 13191.
>
> You will learn these instructions by heart stamped under the Secrets' Act and will not divulge them to anyone, even family and friends.

'Porter', 'Paco', these are good classifications for the SOE pen-pushers but I won't be using them. Instead, in France I will run as Mollier, and if by misfortune I have to jump over the Pyrenees, after having got rid of my papers I'll become Robert Malley, British officer, escaped. I will demand that my Spanish jailors communicate my name and my number to the closest British consul. They'll have me released, hopefully, while they're at it.

Next morning I recite this text from memory the right way up and backwards. In all modesty, I announce to Pierre, Eric and the girls that I am first on standby. At the supper Diana gives for the occasion, Vallée and Grand-Père reveal to us that they are also on their marks. But I am sure I can overtake them.

The month of May 1943 is abloom with lilies of the valley; the sun is shining. Heinkels and Dorniers respond to the appeal of springtime and subject us to a mini-blitz – a modest downpour of bombs, irreplaceable buildings disembowelled, a few hundred deaths. The RAF and the anti-aircraft (ack-ack) batteries spread across the whole city are now extremely heavily manned.

At 8 a.m. the dormitories for disaster victims fitted out in the Tube stations wake up. Between the curtains concealing bunkbeds, school boys in blazers and gentlemen of the city emerge: business as usual!

The summons of the Colonel does not surprise me: I'm ready to go … and the first to leave, as I anticipated …

'Hum, hum! My dear Bob,' Buck says to me, 'Plans are scuppered. Mission cancelled at the last minute.'

Diane and her freckles as well as François Vallée leave us on 16 June. Pierre the next day.

Eliane, Eric and I remain at large, melancholic.

'Bob, do you know Rouen?'

'No, Sir.'

'Perfect! You'll therefore go and replace the saboteur of the Salesman Circuit, in the Seine-Maritime. He's had some bother. Clément, his boss, is waiting for you.'

Clément is the pseudonym of Captian Charles Mark Geoffrey Staunton, a seasoned agent who, in 1941, already belonged to a circuit of the Côte d'Azur. Arrested by the Vichy police, he was interned in the Mauzac camp, in the Dordogne. He escaped in the company of a dozen or so SOE and Gaullist BCRA agents, by taking out a guard! Through the Pyrenees, Spain and Portugal, they got back to London. Fabulous! This escape is discussed as a case study in Beaulieu. Last March, Staunton went back to France. In Rouen, he created a network that is cited as an example.

Once over there, I'll be Robert Mollier, orphan, single with no children, born in a suburb of Le Havre whose town hall has been reduced to ashes. Ingenious, don't you think? My letter box: Micheline-Modes, rue des Carmes, Rouen. The password: 'Have you any shirts size 46?'. If the boss, our 'correspondent', is absent, the seller will think I'm mad – I have a neck as skinny as a swan's. When I'm chased by the Gestapo, I'll no longer take refuge with my 'aunt' Dona Robredo in Madrid but with an 'uncle' Lionel Martin, Rambla Santa Monica in Barcelona. It's closer!

Final briefing formality: Morel handed me the traditional sweet box, 'Blue pills: Benzedrine ... colourless capsule: cyanide! Don't get that wrong, eh?'

Eliane, Eric and I enrolled for the July moon 'tour'. Ah, this bloody moon, SOE and its agents are at its mercy! Its rays delineate the meanderings of rivers, paint meadows white; they contrast with the forests that remain ebony black. These are the only points of reference available to 161 and 138, the clandestine squadrons of SOE, who, with radios off, navigate by dead-reckoning above the ground that the blackout makes even blacker. And in the cockpit of the four-engine 30-ton Halifax, another four men act as lookouts! On the other hand, there is just one man at the controls of the little pick-up monoplane, the Lysander, or Lizzie as it is known affectionately! His only breadcrumb trail is the map that tends to slide on his knees, lit by the pale glimmer from the instrument panel. It is he who must overcome the storms to 300km and land like an acrobat on a pocket handkerchief – and a badly paved one at that! These squadrons are so reliant on the rays from the queen of the night that they are dubbed the Moonlight Squadrons.

Eliane and Eric cherished the dream of an adventure together; the '64' squashed it in the embryo stage, 'Two agents who are emotionally involved will never be parachuted together. If one of them is taken, the other will try in every way to save that person, even as far as betrayal ...'

Good sense prevailed. It was enough to see Eliane fold herself against Eric, insinuating her head bit by little bit between his chin and shoulder groaning with pleasure, her eyelids beating like a butterfly's wings, to be convinced that it was the right decision.

Ann was in my heart, but it was nothing like the passion that submerged these two. She lands at Portsmouth without warning, gets rid of her beret, her jacket, her collar, her tie, shakes out her curls, then melts in my arms. For the first time, that evening she wears the lace undies I bought her. She is still amazed; if a gentleman dares to enter a ladies underwear shop alone then in her eyes that is an act of heroism.

She has two adorable dimples at the corner of her lips, two others in the small of her back.

I have one last jaunt to Chorleywood, an STS 'à la carte' everyone can take part in whatever activity takes their fancy – shoot, demolitions, motocross. The wireless operators practise scales on their radio sets. I get chatting to Peter Newman, an Englishman coming back from a mission. In fact, his real first name, Isidore, brings him out in a rash. 'I adopted Pierre or Pépé in France,' he tells me.

I take my fill of plastic explosive and Bazooka shooting. The Bazooka is a brand new American rocket launcher: light, no recoil, pierces tanks like Gruyere. I'm not so brilliant with the 'three-inch' mortar – at more than 75mm, it's a proper cannon.

At first light of the July moon, a huge Humber takes us – Eliane, Eric and me – to Hasell's Hall, an STS departure building about 100km north of London and ten minutes from Tempsford, the base for the Halifaxes in the Moonlight Squadron. The hall is a brick mansion dressed with a peristyle of colonnades. In the entrance hall we find the main attraction: a large felt noticeboard on which, ceremoniously at teatime, the head of Operations pins a sheet of paper – the list of those departing that night.

The second day, my name is on it.

I have the privilege of inviting my friends to a private room.The old Bordeaux and Drambuie – Scotch whisky – flow freely. At coffee, Eric crushes me to his chest, tears in his eyes, Eliane embraces me tenderly, 'Goodbye *hermano*. See you soon on the Champs Elysées!'

A quarter of an hour later, after having manoeuvred on the track between enormous shadows that are bombers in the parking area, my car drops me in front of a hanger dubbed Gibraltar – you need to go there to know why! Batteries of dazzling lamps light long tables; its walls covered in shelving crawling with a jumble of parachutes, sacks, and clothes, tins of conserves and weapons of every description. A sergeant conducts a full strip-search, looking for forgotten tickets, small change, laundry marks or labels 'Made in England'. However, my suits and shirts have been tailored 'in the Parisian style' by a little Central European artisan in Vera's pay. The man checks my identity papers, my ration books, my work certificate ... and the capsule of cyanide in its case. They cram my suitcase with tins of conserves, bars of chocolate and cigarettes made from the butts of cigars in blue paper packing with no label. Unheard of in France! When I make a gesture of refusal, an officer intervenes, 'In a country where everything is scarce they are invaluable as a currency to trade!'

Currency? A single ticket for Buchenwald, more like! I climb into a flying suit with twenty pockets loaded with shovel, pickaxe, first aid kit, maps, compass, dagger and an antique Mauser with an oak butt, vintage 1914, disposable – just like me. I'm hoisted into the Halifax, whose engines are already roaring. It shudders, the brakes squeal and then it rolls. We're off! Next stop, Rouen! Suddenly it makes an about turn, stops, the engines die. A navigator jumps out of the cockpit, 'I'm your captain ... Weather overcast. Not going over.'

'But – what, the weather people didn't warn you?'

'The weather people in Occupied France? Think about it: the Huns won't communicate the weather to us and their U-boats sink our sea stations! So we get it at the last minute and it's often just guesswork!'

In the lobby of Hasell's Hall, a statuesque tall girl in a white shirt and black trousers is waiting for me, 'Would you like supper?'

'What? After midnight? Is that usual here?'

'Often the case with chaps like you who've made a u-turn – I'm the duty cook.'

'You, a cook?'

'I belong to the FANYs, you know, elite corps that provide HQ and those services where they stamp the documents "burn before reading" with secretaries, chauffeurs and ... cooks. By the way, I'm an officer, like you. My name is Mary.'

'Breakfast – another time, Mary.'

In the evening Eric invited us for his farewell dinner. Eliane and he let their hair down with fine words and Saint-Emilion, but in Eliane's eyes you could read infinite sadness. I retired discreetly.

Eric returns at daybreak. Two evenings later, another melancholy dinner. Eliane is off. The next day we have breakfast together.

While the moon is shining to burst, I am 'on' again. 'My' Halifax takes off. The pilot invites me into the cockpit. In a riot of stars, a great part of the heavenly body of the night rises; the Channel is silvery.

'We are flying at 6,000ft,' says the captain. 'We're about to fly over the coast of France.'

'2,000m? Not too low, is it? If we're hunted, what will you do? You don't even have a tail machine gun, I notice?'

'Not just in the tail. We haven't got any at all! We are totally unarmed, which allows us to carry extra containers. If a Focke-Wulf sees us, I can promise you a damned chancy dance.'

'Has that happened to you before?'

'No. However, this is only my sixth mission. Apparently, the routes we are told to follow, well away from the hunter bases of Beaumont-le-Roger, Evreux and Saint-André-de-l'Eure, are viable. So many squadrons fly over France that the Jerries don't now where to start. Since their radars aren't as good as ours, single planes still manage to nip in and out all over the place. We'll get through "under the radar" again this time, no problem.'

As it happens, it's not Focke-Wulfs but a summer storm that chases us. And we dance! The Halifax pitches, bucks and somersaults, jumps 100m in the air to fall back 200. The sheet metal seems to tear, the parcels knock one another about, their straps creaking, the rain drumming. I brace myself against a corner post so I don't fly away. My parachute is long gone in the wind. After an hour of this circus, the dispatcher comes in, zigzagging like a drunk:. 'Vis. nil, but the cabby wants to have a little more fun trying to position the craft over your DZ.'

So as not to look death in the face, I swallow a great mouthful of Scotch from my first-aid flask. It knocks me out. I leave this tunnel of death.

A blaze of purple beams falling from a bubble of Plexiglas wakes me. We're flying without a jolt. Beside me the dispatcher is snoring. I go up front. Everyone is sleeping, pilot, co-pilot, navigator, radio operator, mouth open, head back. Under automatic pilot, the controls shudder. Like the mare of a country vet heading for the stable, the Halifax trots itself off towards Tempsford.

When the moon sets, they send us back to London. Eric bursts out laughing. 'Seven false starts for us three and how many litres of Bordeaux knocked back! "Crazy like the moon" – now, I know what that means!'

After two weeks of sweet nothing in Queens Gate, Eliane puts the key under the door. Return to Hasell's Hall.

On 11 August 1943, my Hali and I push off to Rouen. The indicators are green, time to check out the surrounding area. We have followed the meanderings of the Seine, I have put on my parachute, and the air is racing through the uncovered hole; we turn in a circle, then twice, then a third time. The dispatcher shouts to me, 'We are spot on for your DZ. No beacons. We go back.'

The conclusion of a 'bag of transmissions': storm, crash landing, interference and jamming or cut on the sly fearing being spotted, resulting in truncated messages or no message at all, which is the daily norm for wireless ops. As such, the DZ dates are uncertain. For one successful operation, three are aborted.

Eliane, Eric and I are the last clients of the manor, which at moonrise held a good dozen agents. We're becoming part of the furniture.

On 13 August, all three of us are 'on'. On the Tempsford tarmac three Halis are waiting for us. Lost in a jumpsuit that could have contained two of her, Eliane gets up on the tip of her toes to kiss me before being swallowed up by the bomber – engines howling. She forces a wan smile; Eric has already departed in the first one. Mouth on my neck, she murmurs, 'Believe in my feminine intuition, *hermano*, this time it's the big departure! I'll never forget you. See you soon on the Champs Elysées!'

In my car, I sniffle; I wipe my nose so that my chauffeur, a pretty FANY, doesn't notice the small trembling tear on my cheek. I believed I had a heart of stone. But Eliane is my sister, after all …

'You need a pick me up!' Mary says to me as she sees me reappear at dawn. 'I recommend the chef's special – soft-boiled eggs with a porto flip cocktail. And I'll join you; this empty manor bores me rigid. Although we don't show it, we get attached to you all as you pass through. At each moon, we have to have stout hearts!'

Only one remains. It's me!

I wander about like a lost soul in the park, in the empty rooms. At the bar, an old major on the staff who's drowning his sorrows in a Guinness offers me a glass, 'We're going to land in Dunkirk soon and the old crust that I am won't be there!'

And what about me? The only comforting news, which reaches me only now, is that de Gaulle has taken Guadeloupe – and the gold of the Bank of France that Pétain had put 'securely' in the Antilles!

The next day at teatime, a name appears on the board, mine, of course. Mary appears, 'This evening you won't be dining alone – if you want me there?'

I really want that – in all innocence and honour – this tall girl with hair cut like Joan of Arc's.

At Drambuie hour, she tells me, 'My birthday strikes at midnight. It will bring you happiness, I feel it!'

7

Death of a Swan

15 August 1943. Midnight.

The wind rushing through the jump hole hits me in the face. Might Mary really have made this happen?

'Go – and *merde*!' yells the dispatcher thumping me and shoving me out. Carefully articulated, this *merde*! Only French word he knows – and only recently learnt. I have just explained to him that *merde*, meaning 'shit', wishes someone luck. My canopy opens in a rustling of silk like a lover's silk nightie falling at her feet. I enjoy the silence of the night for thirty seconds at most, as secret agents are chucked out close to the daisies so as not to attract attention. Rows of apple trees rush towards me. I roll between two of them. A shadow approaches me:

'I'm Clément!'

I note his round forehead and big, pale, penetrating eyes.

'Roll up your parachute and let's get out of the DZ!' he continues.

'And the parcels?'

'The reception team will take care of that. Come on!'

'No. 4 is full of provisions. As you're short of everything ...'

Clément, in London known as Captain Staunton, gives a small smile. He leads me to a farm, opens the door into a big room and a long table covered in charcuterie, chains of sausages, Breton-style *andouilles* by the metre, terrines, loaves large as tyres and a large slab of butter. Stout women are slamming pans on a red stove big enough for an army. Each of them gives me three brisk kisses on my cheeks in the Normandy way.

'You'll have a little snack, especially as you've got nothin' to eat in England!'

My supper of Yorkshire pudding is still weighing on my stomach. Clément whispers to me, 'No question of refusing. You'll vex them!'

Bowlfuls of cider and glasses of Calvados finish me off. I throw my guts up at the bottom of the garden. At dawn, the *gazogène*'s fan wakes me up. Without reflecting further, I throw my cyanide capsule down the loo. Torture, I'll manage to beat it!

The containers that the Halifax has dropped are already loaded on to a *gazogène* lorry and hidden under some logs. My boss, Pierrot the chauffeur, and I tuck ourselves into the cabin. Pierrot, a placid boy, drives carefully amid occasional vehicles, German for the most part. At the entrance to Louviers, I notice my first *Feldgrau*. In Elbeuf and Oissel, they're more numerous. However much I try to steer clear, it seems they are staring at me suspiciously. Suddenly a soldier plonked at the crossroads in front of us brandishes a red sign. A checkpoint! Instinctively, I seize the door handle. Clément grabs my arm, 'Calm down! It's only a *Feldgendarme*. He's signalling to us to let the tanks pass – there – on the right!'

Pierrot puts his head on the steering wheel and suddenly falls asleep! Clément smiles, 'He's solid, you see! You can always count on him.'

Panzers come into view, wedged on trailers mounted on so many wheels they resemble millipedes. The turrets reach the level of the roofs and their caterpillar tracks go past at my eye level: 'a causeway of articulated plates, which, by distributing the weight over a large surface, allows an automobile engine to drive along over muddy soil', as per the words of my grandfather who, teacher of the technical college in Montbéliard, had invented this 'caterpillar' at the end of the last century, in cooperation with his most brilliant pupil, Kégresse. The French generals, still fighting yesterday's war, had sent them packing. The Tsar's generals, on the other hand, had invited them to present their baby in Moscow! Alas, grandmother railed against her Pierre, who invented the '*promenoir*' for agricultural purposes, going and selling it to the 'Tartar' warriors. Kégresse made a fortune – not Grandpa, who had neglected to put his name on the patent. Seeing the Panzers, it's clear that his baby has thrived!

Once the last truck has passed, we set off again. After several kilometres of jolts along Sotteville's cobbles, the P45 branches off into the narrow rue des Abattoirs and enters a warehouse. A stocky 40-year-old in a boiler suit, Georges Philippon, closes the door behind the vehicle. My boss points out a luxury bicycle to me with balloon tyres, derailleur gears and bag racks, 'Here's your carriage, Bob! The Fritz only gives out *Ausweisen* and petrol tokens to doctors and a few high-ranking people. Pierrot is an exception, as he's a working lorry driver and his lorry runs on coal! If there's an emergency, we use the *Blue Bird*, the put-put you can see over there. Open to all weathers, the bike isn't ideal to face the pisspot that is France – you'll realise that quickly enough. You'll get used to it. Come, it's time to meet your landlord.'

Maurice Gelé is my landlord, round and jovial, who lords it behind the counter of the Bar de la Marine, on the quai de la Bourse. Clément says to him, 'Here's your nephew. Get him fixed up with lodgings and send him back to me.'

Then he takes me to one side, 'Leave your suitcase with him and come find me at 12 rue Jeanne d'Arc, the main street that comes down from the station to the Seine. I'm on the second floor; there's only one door: "Denis Desvaux, Couture." I'll introduce you to the rest of the team. And not a word to your "uncle". It's none of his business, right!'

Maurice has a charming stone house on the Bihorel hill, which is painfully steep. Waiting for me are his wife, a plump blonde; a kid, his son; and a real nephew, who was hiding out with them having resisted enlistment in the Service du Travail Obligatoire – compulsory work service – in Germany. I'm offered some 70 per cent calvados, but I don't take the bait. In Normandy I'll not only have the Germans to worry about but also cirrhosis of the liver!

Rouen is teeming with Germans. A green tide flows toward the lower part of town, rue Jeanne d'Arc, which is bordered by respectable grand apartments. The Pucelle Tower, the town hall, a gothic jewel, and many buildings are flaunting more Swastikas than the Paris Majestic.

I reach 12 rue Jeanne d'Arc, second floor and stand stock-still. Reedy voices of a choir escape from the door indicated, massacring a musette tune: '*On n'a pas tous les jours vingt ans*!' ['You're not 20 every day!'] I hesitate to ring but orders are orders.

An imposing woman, immaculately made up, chin high, wearing guipure lace and with her hair dressed à la Saint-Honoré, opens the door and cries out as she administers the triple kiss of Normandy, 'You've come at just the right time! We're celebrating the birthday of one of my apprentices. Then *mezzo voce*: 'They're not au fait with "our" activities.' She lets me know all this is a screen to 'our' activities. 'So, you're a friend just passing through – innocent as a newborn babe, right?'

In the Louis XV salon, about a dozen girls, hair curled, dolled up, a glass of champagne in the hand, press up around a Pleyel baby grand piano chattering. 'Pierre, please, play *Fascination* for me!' 'No, *Rêve d'amour*!' 'Play me: *La Valse brune*!'

As I approach, the pianist turns his head and calls out to me. 'Here you are, at last? I've been waiting for you for goodness knows how long!'

It's Peter Newman.

The party comes to an end, the apprentices fly off, and he gives an embarrassed laugh. 'In my youth, I studied the piano and applied arts. You see, it has its uses as I create some dress patterns for Denise, my "cousin". My cover is therefore perfect. Of course, in spare moments I tinkle for Clément on a Mark III.' The Mark III is the most advanced clandestine suitcase radio and considered light – 4 kilos without a battery.

A boy of my age comes forward. He is slim, with an angular face, feverish grey eyes and a lock of hair falling over his forehead. He reminds me of someone – but who? Peter introduces him, 'This is Claude.'

'Claude is my second-in-command,' cuts in the boss. 'So, with you, the team is complete. Get used to the verdigris by sauntering around for a week in town. But avoid the cafés, the cinemas at opening times. They go there to chase out the idle! Don't forget, Morel has it hidden from you of course, but your false papers made in London aren't worth a damn: paper too thin, colour too faded. On the other hand, you've got the luck of the devil – a young woman of our circuit has a brother and repatriated from a Stalag. But he got sick and died on the way back and his death hasn't been declared! On sight of his repatriation certificate, the mairie of Le Havre will give you his iron-clad papers! Resident of Le Havre's "forbidden" coastal zone, you'll be able to go up and down the Atlantic Wall without a personal *Ausweis* and as you're repatriated for health reasons, you'll be exempt from compulsory work in Germany! Tomorrow I'm leaving for a week. On my return, I hope to find you swimming in *Feldgrau* streams like a fish in the sea.'

The next morning, my 'uncle' Maurice calls me, 'Friends of mine, the Beaus, members of our circuit, are sheltering an English pilot who's been waiting for weeks for a people smuggler to take him on. As he doesn't speak French, poor bloke, and the Beaus not a word of English, he's remained banged up in one room, so he's getting depressed. Do you want to go and chat to him in his language?'

The Beaus live in rue aux Ours. A little lively woman introduces me into a bedroom with closed shutters. The pilot, John, a small blond man with the pale colour of a recluse but ballooning out – his hosts are feeding him up, that's certain – brightens when I greet him in English. He tells me in a rush how his Lancaster was knocked out of the sky, how his parachute saved him and how the country folk hid him. To hear him rolling his 'r's I'm pretty sure he's Scottish. He replies, 'Not at all! I'm from Southampton!'

He's homesick, this good John, which I fully understand. Now, Southampton, I've just come from there! I'm going to talk to him about his town; his melancholy will disappear! In fact, I just keep talking: I can easily evoke the districts, fashionable shops. No response. The cradle of his childhood, he only speaks about it grudgingly. The monuments, the avenues, the squares, he describes them as – a tourist guide. What's missing? The ruins left by the bombing, the sandbags, the barbed wire, the black out – the war of course! An unpleasant waves passes over me. Then I have an idea: 'You know the Swan for sure, a pub near the port?'

'And how! Two months ago I was sweet-talking a barmaid!'

'Ah well, since then it's closed. A sex case!'

'Not possible! I hope to find it open when I get back!'

I feel sick to the stomach. If he is unaware that the Swan has been reduced to dust more than a year ago, it means he hasn't put a foot in England since, this John, or this Johann – a false pilot but a real German!

I remain impassive; I don't cut short my visit. But finally, using all the anti-tracking methods I learned at Beaulieu, I run to rue Jeanne d'Arc to put Peter in the picture. He pulls a grimace, 'If your John's a stool pigeon, the Beaus have been under surveillance for a long time. You, I hope you haven't been followed. That said, are you certain you're not being paranoid? You can see Gestapo everywhere during the first days of a mission, I've had that experience, you know.'

Claude, the veteran, is even more sceptical than Peter. My mind at rest, I go off into town. Here I am in the Vieux Marché, where Saint Joan of Arc burned. Opposite the butcher, the Auberge de la Couronne, which claims to be the most ancient inn in France, is reserved for the Wehrmacht. At the doors of shops, on the terrace of bistrots, postcard stands to commemorate the saint are on show. On other cards, Churchill is caricatured as a Bishop Cauchon, cigar in his lips, relishing her torture. What an injustice! In his *History of the English-Speaking Peoples*, God knows that he heaps praise on 'his' Joan of Arc, of whom he is an unconditional fan: 'Angel of deliverance, the most patriotic of women, virgin, maiden forever radiant, glorious, the most superb hero of France, etc ...'

On the cathedral square, protected with sandbags, an admirable Gothic residence with a sign '*Soldatenheim*', reserved for the Wehrmacht. In rue Saint-Romain, a medieval alley, a rather dilapidated placard '*Rechts gehen*', invites you to keep to the right. Dating from the first days of the Occupation, it is now out of fashion. Gallic disorder still reigns supreme, occupants and occupiers cross one another pot luck on the pavements.

As evening arrives, I return to the Bihorel house. I ring several times at the door. No response. I jump over the gate, and let myself into the salon through a half-open window. Suddenly, followed by her son and nephew, my hostess emerges from the chimney, 'Ah, you're free, are you! My husband has just been arrested! When I learned it, we hid!'

Ruffled and black with soot, she turns round, 'I don't know what to do – you'll have to leave tomorrow, I think!'

The Gestapo, I was taught, hunt at night. That it hadn't thrown its nets over the house already was miraculous. I have to get out of here right now, but where can I go?

'Relatives of mine live two streets from here,' my 'cousin' says to me. 'Luc can take you.'

It's after the curfew. Loaded with suitcases, pushing our bikes, Luc and I keep close to the walls until we reach the house. Behind the closed shutters, a woman whispers, 'Who is it?'

'Me, Luc! – Maurice has some problems.'

'What problems?'

'The Jerries ...'

Behind her, a man mutters, 'You, kid, don't mix us up in that! Get out of here, or else ...'

The shutter slams. Luc says to me, 'We're screwed. Several patrols pass by here each night. But thinking about it – our old housekeeper lives quite near. She's a patriot for sure! She'll hide us.'

By stealth, we reach a modest house at the end of a small garden. A nice woman in an apron opens the door, 'What, the Boches are after you? Come on in quickly, youngsters!'

No question of having a coffee and a 'little something' before diving under the flowery duvet. In the morning, after having destroyed the packaging, I give as a gift to the good woman some cigarettes and some of the 'made in England' chocolate. She takes out of mothballs the overalls, beret and the musette of her 'defunct' husband. Thanks to Follis Bergères, I paint lines on my face and crow's feet with cigarette ash, which ages me ten years.

Peter, his features hollowed out by anxiety, hardly recognises me, 'Is it you? Thank God! You haven't been followed, at least ...?'

'No. I took precautions. Well, you already know my landlord has been arrested!'

'Your landlord, arrested? First I've heard of it! I thought it was just the Beaus up until now ... Lord, Maurice as well? We really are in the damn shit!'

It doesn't matter if Maurice talks. The Gestapo'll have a hard job recognising me from the description given by the phoney pilot. My boats are burnt all over France! Peter is appalled.

'Now you're going to have Alie at your heels.'

'Ali, who's he? An Algerian?'

'No, Alie with an "e" is Breton and head of an anti-terrorist brigade that the Gestapo have given all powers to. He can arrest, torture, have any one shot. Do you have a safe house around here?'

'No, in Paris – perhaps.'

'So, let's go. Forget the Express, it's sure to be watched. Claude has a letter box in Paris. You'll leave your address there.'

'A letter box? What's the name?'

'Malraux.'

'André, the writer?'

'Claude is his brother ... Get a move on!'

There are no Krauts nosing around on the platforms at the little station. After twenty stops, my crawler train arrives at Saint-Lazare station in a torrent of cinders and smoke. A Franco-German team from 'Economic Control' rummages through the luggage in search of products on the black market. Fortunately, I've been relieved of the cigarettes and chocolate from Baker Street!

On the church square, arms dangling, I ask myself where am I going to sleep tonight? To be avoided: hotels – informers – hand over clients' fiches to the police. The only people in the world I can trust are my friends the Ducroquets. Alas, their phone doesn't answer. I have only one recourse – mine. I dial the Neuilly number.

'Who is it?' replies my brother, Jacques, at the first ring.

'It's Robi.' We are the only two who use this diminutive. 'I'm passing through.'

He represses an 'Oh!' of surprise and goes on, 'I've been very sick lately, but I'm no longer contagious. Let's meet up then as usual.' This 'sick, contagious' tells me nothing useful. Putting me on my guard?

Over the last three years in Paris very little has changed. There are just as many swastikas and directional placards. On the other hand, there are ever more 'patriotic' posters: 'Worker, go to Germany. You will be working for Europe!' or 'Join the LVF' (French Voluntary Legion). And placards in the windows of empty shops – 'Jewish enterprise'!

'As usual' – a rendezvous point, near the large bronze Ballon de Ternes of the Porte des Ternes, between the big Luna Park of Porte Maillot and the Institution Sainte-Croix, from where Fernand ran off to engrave his fleurs-de-lys.

Jacques represses a heave when a worker in a boiler suit stands up in front of him and yells at him, 'You contagion, what's the sense in that?'

'Ah, it's you? I've just spent four months in the Cherche Midi prison. I was a liaison officer for the Ames du Purgatoire. The Gestapo infiltrated us ...'

'And you were freed after four little months in the clink – that's all? Incredible!'

'Note that every day an SS man assured me that he would shoot me the next day. But it seems the ravishing sister of one of our guys caught the eye of some Gestapo big shot, a major, and she would have done whatever she had to do.'

'If, as I suspect, your major is called Karl Boemelburg, we're just across from his place now. He lives in this private house that you see there, opposite, on the corner of the rue de Rouvray and boulevard Victor Hugo. Don't let's hang around here!'

'Maman also pleaded for me ...'

In her most polished German, my mother harassed these gentlemen of the Gestapo day after day and the authorities at the prison until they gave her back her son.

'She'd hardly got over that shock, then she got another one! Just think, a fortnight ago, just after my return, late in the evening, the door bell rang at home. Trembling all over, Maman chokes out: "It's the Gestapo again!" At the door, guess who – Jean, our cousin from Saintes! A year ago this twit let himself get taken to Germany by the STO! He found no better way to escape than by climbing on to a wagon of potatoes, jumping off at Gare de l'Est and turning up here without warning. You're going to be the last straw!'

At rue Borghèse, I'm hugged, choked, bathed in tears. That evening, wishing Jacques good night, I burst out laughing.

'Have you lost the plot?' he asked.

'No, you might say I'm finally getting it: three years ago, right from here, I left for the war – I bought myself exodus, a failed departure from Saint Jean-de-Luz, months in prison in Chalon, a Bizerte-Algiers rally, Darlan's execution, cruise from Algiers to London, then this raid Tempsford-Rouen-Neuilly. All this to get to the departure hut and – no doubt about it – get back to London via the Pyrenees! And when I get there, in London, the war will be over! That's enough to make you die laughing, isn't it?'

One fine morning Captain Staunton shows up. I follow him, tail between my legs.

8

The Atlantic Wall

Bang! Bang! I draw my Colt at the speed of light, as I imitate the detonations. In the lecture room put aside for my use – that is, Philippon's garage – none of my pupils laugh. Under the Occupation, we manage without shots being fired ... anyway that would be superfluous. My men are woodcock hunters who shoot by automatic reflex. They would kill all the Jerries in the world, with real bullets, without a batting an eye!

A vigorous dressing down by Charles saved me from the Pyrenees–London rally, 'You committed an unpardonable security lapse. The Salesman circuit prospers because it is kept reasonably separate. I rebelled when Buck ordered me to serve as a relay in an escape line for MI9! But the order came from the top; there are so many pilots to be evacuated that the *passeurs* are overwhelmed. You almost screwed up my network! However, thanks to your luck of the devil, you didn't get taken in the Gestapo's search. The Beaus were completely unaware of you and didn't give up Maurice, who just barely managed to get through!'

'But he *was* arrested!'

'For black market activities and released against a hefty fine. I've severed all ties with him. You'll stay with your "cousin", Boucher, painter and decorator; rue Molière, behind Saint-Maclou. Now, enough joking about, you've got combat groups to train and factories to blow up!'

First stage – take 'my' shock team in hand in rue des Abattoirs – Philippon and Jean, his nephew of 17 who lives in his shadow, the brothers Broni and Félix Piontek, teachers of mechanics, and Hugues Paccaud, master carpenter with the Chantiers de l'Atlantique. Solid men, placid, artisans with the golden touch for dismantling a machine gun, booby-trapping a grenade or setting a detonator, that all goes without saying. We form a family of which Charles is the patriarch and I'm the minor master because I practise the art of weaponry.

I've become hardened, I no longer see a Gestapo bloodhound in the first territorial I come across. I approach the identity control checks without blinking. I pedal through the countryside, the bags of my bike loaded with my tools of the trade – Sten gun, Mills grenades, hunks of plastic covered by my Colt and two gammon steaks stuffed with a good pound of explosive and 100 nails. I go from farm to farm, where small groups of volunteers wait for the 'Englishman' as if for a messiah who's going to teach them how to stuff the Jerries. In the forest in Lyon, at Saint-Martin, in a bend of the Seine or the Risle, I unpack my essentials on a big farm table. The lesson ends with a ham omelette, bowlfuls of cider and a slug or two of Calvados, then I sleep for a few hours under a thick eiderdown.

I check out clearings.

I slog over one hill after another, in the rain – it is not without danger. For example, one day I hurtled into a guard post hidden by a curve of the road. A model of the type: on duty, a French gendarme, 10m further on, a German squad. My heart raced. Yet, I placed my feet carefully on the ground while gauging the copper – a faithful civil servant of the marshal, under German influence, certainly, but too well fleshed out to play the hero. He studied my papers then, thumbs in his belt, pointing to my saddlebags, he said the fateful words, 'What've you got in there?'

I opened them, placed a hand on my Colt, the other on the gammon ham, muttering, 'Don't say another word, don't move … this bomb will explode on impact and you and your friends will end up with as many holes as a colander!'

In Chorleywood this formidable gammon had appealed to me.

'You aren't going to bandy this baby about so near, Lieutenant, are you?' the incredulous explosives instructor said to me after having seen me stuff my back pocket with a good pound of plastic seeded with 100 nails.

I didn't let him finish. My gammon flew. We threw ourselves flat on the ground. A hurricane of iron pieces fell around our heads. The trees were stuck with steel points pretty well 100m away.

Smiling, I stared at my gendarme, 'If I get through, I promise you a message of thanks for you from the BBC – and the gratitude of General de Gaulle on Liberation. If not ...'

I never will ever see a copper roll his eyes in such a way again. He swallowed the lump that was blocking his throat and whispered, 'Is it true – de Gaulle?'

I whispered back, 'Yes!'

'And the message, what is it exactly?'

Without thinking, I said, 'Thank you, copper!'

He blinked a few times, signalled the *Feldgendarmes* who, as I passed, saluted me. I distanced myself slowly without turning round, my spine bristling with goose bumps. My saddlebag closed again, I was defenceless. What if my gendarme reconsidered?

No blast of bullets troubled the peace of the fields.

During six months of rambling behind the Atlantic Wall, I fell twice again into one of those Franco-German roadblocks. Twice, I survived. Thanks, copper!

Charles promised me, 'I think you'll get your money's worth with the *Diables Noirs*. They're expecting you near Ry.'

Along the apple-green banks of the Andelle, the whitewashed cottages glisten between two heavy showers of rain. Ry – a market town with brick houses roofed with slate, where Flaubert had Emma Bovary die of boredom.

At nightfall, I slide into an opening in the forest of Lyon. The hoots of a barn owl make me jump. A veiled silhouette comes to meet me. A hood is pulled over my head and I'm taken by the hand. We walk for about ten minutes. A door creaks, steps, twenty-one, I count them. My mask falls off, my eyes blink in the harsh light of bare bulbs. I find myself in a vaulted cave. Thirty people surround me, dressed in black and masked: the famous *Diables Noirs*! Between beret and scarf, thirty worrying pairs of eyes scrutinise me.Their boss, Raoul Boulanger, says to me in a loud, powerful voice, 'Welcome to Ali Baba's cave!'

Owners of a small sawmill, Boulanger and his brother joined the Résistance in the first days of the Occupation. They kitted out this brigands' hideaway in the chalk mines that run under the buildings. As good as gold, the *Diables* follow my weapons course, then have me visit their dormitories, an arsenal and even a gymnasium, lit and ventilated. It is necessary to feed this horde, dress them, protect them; the entire family and neighbours take on this responsibility.

One day, the bullet-riddled corpse of an overly curious gamekeeper, a Gestapo grass, was discovered at the foot of a tree. Commissaire Alie came to nose around. Unanimously the yokels, on being interrogated, swore that the murder was the deed of a mysterious man of the woods, a vagabond nicknamed *Fantomas*, as elusive as Gaston Leroux's heroes. Alie went through the forest, the fields and the sawmill with a fine-tooth comb. But, at the *Diables Noirs*, he drew a blank.

I send London a large order for weapons, clothes and blankets. My first parachute drop, near Boissy, is for them. Twelve parachutes deploy loudly under the stars; twelve containers of 200kg bounce over the meadow. The neighbouring farmer's cattle pull them into a grange.

Afterwards we comb the field and fill in the ruts. A Halifax drifting around for ten minutes above the clearing always brings the Fritz to you. In due course, Pierrot will deliver them to the required locations.

Staunton is never as serious – his British side – as when he utters the most outrageous things. One morning he shouts at me, 'Tell me then, big bloke,' he's hardly 1m 70cm in height, 'Would you know how to sink a warship?'

I go along with him. 'In Gibraltar, Crabb showed me how to do it. I can try.'

'Don't wear yourself out on it, I only need some limpets. The navy is begging us to torpedo one of these buggers, a submarine supply ship of 900 tons. It slips from the Seine into the Atlantic and provisions the U-boats. As a result, they stay at sea continuously. It's elusive and well armed – 88mm guns, quadruple Pom-Poms, heavy machine guns. Wrecked by an RAF Typhoon, it is being recast at the Normandy Quevilly docks. And guess who is putting the finishing touches to its installations: Hugues Paccaud!

In my arsenal, at Philippon's, I add final touches to two limpets, two slabs of 3lb of plastic with six magnets. Hugues watches me. I show him how to screw the flint wheels for delayed firing set for six o'clock. Casually he grabs the sticks, throws them in his haversack. My heart races, 'And the search – how're you going to cut it?'

'Pot luck! The sentries only search me once every three times.'

'And if it's this time?'

'*Bof*! Where there's no risk, there's no fun!'

And off he goes, smile on his lips, shoes well polished, wavy hair neatly parted.

After an attack, watch out for raids and roadblocks!

That night, I sleep with one eye open in anticipation of the blast – which never comes. When the curfew lists 5 o'clock I can't hold it in any longer, so I run to the victualling post on quay Jeanne d'Arc. Unusual atmosphere. Instead of crossing the Seine at the trot in order to clock in on time at the factory, the early morning labourers are milling about along the parapet, leaning over towards the water, where a swastika banner appears!

Those who are 'well informed' make the comment that: 'When it was all ready to go, it went on a trial run to Saint-Aubin then came back here for the reception. An admiral wrote out a cheque for 5 million to the director of the naval yards congratulating him on his "*schön Arbeit*"! Afterwards, they swill down copious amounts of champagne.' An old man shakes his head knowingly: 'And if it were a dirty trick of the Boches, just to screw the English, wouldn't they just have had their old tub submerged?' The atmosphere is all party but it's better to get back to the house – *Feldgendarmes* are spread out along the banks.

I send my 'cousin', René, off for news. Towards midnight, only the lower bank was awoken by a muffled explosion when, accompanied by a concert of rumblings and gurgling, the supply ship sank with all men and provisions on board!

The scuba divers from the Kriegsmarine went down. Verdict: a bomb placed on the exterior of the ship, quay side, sent it to the bottom. Consequently, the Admiralty had the sentries on shore duty thrown into prison to be shot – blind or accomplices?

The divers of the *Sicherheitsdienst* who went into the water a short time after sent the donkeys of the Génie maritime back to their dear research. The bomb was placed on the ... inside! The *Sicherheitsdienst* is the infallible arm of the SS; their head, Himmler, bears an implacable hatred of traditional weapons, first and foremost the navy! He demanded that the thirteen French workers on duty the day before be delivered to him; among them Hugues, who hasn't a hell's chance!

In the morning, when it went to embark, the crew didn't show the disquiet appropriate to the sight of their craft gurgling in the deep. Far from it! It is understandable: in the Atlantic, the solitary supply ship crew playing hide and seek with the RAF and Navy will soon be fish pâté! Two delighted petty officers even danced a little Bavarian *bourrée*. They were executed before the finale! As for the 'survivors', they were put on the first train to the Russian front!

Captain Staunton drafted a concise and even modest victory bulletin: 'Attention Colonel B. Stop. Your elusive unit sunk all hands and goods. Stop. Enemy losses: four killed, thirty-five presumed dead and five million bubbles. Stop. Ours: None. Stop. Raise a glass champagne to Vera. Stop.'

Our losses, none? But had he forgotten Hugues and his thirteen pals ...?

He awarded the dunce's cap to the Kriegsmarine for saving the guilty and exterminating the innocent in true Nazi style, on the basis of specious argument: 'The serrations of the breach oriented to the interior indicate without question that the explosion took place on the exterior.' Unless – 'the hull touching the quay, the blast of the explosion arising from the hold fretsawed the serrations first towards the exterior then, after having rebounded against that quay pushed them back towards the interior' – as, correctly, the *Sicherheitsdienst* concluded.

In the Kingdom of Hitler, might – i.e. Himmler, who takes pleasure in humiliating the squids – is always right. But for once the Kriegsmarine, surely second only to God in its maritime domain, wins the day.

The workers were released.

I do feel ill at ease when the Cerberuses controlling the entry point to the 'forbidden' coastal zone bark the eternal '*Papers, bitte!*' They are just as fussy as the grunts patrolling the town. The colour of my 'made in SOE' identity card is too pale, its cover too thin, I know that, Charles has often repeated so to me. I hold my breath. They go through every page carefully then give it back to me without commenting.

There's no crowd on the Le Havre station square. I recognise Roger Mayer as soon as I lay eyes on him, Staunton's deputy in the Le Havre area. He is standing as agreed under a Transat poster showing, pushing through the waves, the bow of the *Normandie*, which had been burnt in New York two years before.

'He's a gifted science prof. – so much so that he pulverised his laboratory with explosive of his own invention. Luckily, he was only in the test stage, not industrial production!' the boss confided to me.

Outside school, Mayer is compiler, editor and printer of the underground paper *L'Heure H*, which he delivers to letter boxes and sticks to walls. He makes false ink and paper chits attributed to the only publications certified by the German censor. He has taken on the duty of often taking his two little girls to their grandmother in Valence; there, he obtains ink that is impossible to find in Le Havre. The publishing of clandestine papers and keeping the infernal printing machines in working condition is all very expensive. He takes on private tutoring.

My task is to train Roger's volunteers. My zone of activities: the Atlantic wall, from Le Havre as far as Fécamp. The day after my arrival, Mauricette Hérault, my future 'sister', takes me to the town hall. At the sight of the *Entlassungsschein*, the repatriation certificate for health reasons, covered in swastikas, of her brother whose death has not been registered, a charitable civil servant gives me a full array of 'real' papers. Here I am, now René Hérault, resident in the forbidden zone, an invalided-out prisoner who is therefore exempt from the STO and worthy of compassion.

Roger Mayer lives in a villa on rue Picpus in the Sanvic district. His two daughters, although told off, straight off give me the nickname of Ton ton. Juliette, his young wife with an expressive face under a helmet of autumn-coloured hair and a sweet look, exhausts herself running to the market, the school and the kitchen range. Fatalist, she croons, 'One day, when you've got us all shot, we'll meet you again in heaven. We'll never get bored with you.'

The next day, when I load my bike in the Sanvic cable car, an obliging *Feldgrau* has it in his head to help me!

'*Ach*!' he exclaims, suspicious, '*Sehr schwer*! It's really heavy! What've you got inside that?'

I don't lie to him, 'My work tools, Sir.'

'Is that right?'

The hut is packed with workers, women and children. My stomach knots up. Before he says the inexorable 'Open up!', I mutter:

'I've also got some bottles of schnapps to give me courage!'

His face brightens; he sticks a finger in my chest, exclaiming, '*Ach,* crazy, big rogue, eh!'

As we ascend, we chat. At the top, again, he helps me. I shake his hand warmly. Hasn't he spared my life and ... that of a riot of mothers and kids.

Because a gammon in a funicular jam-packed with mothers and kids ...

To the north of Le Havre, pedalling on the little cliff road running along the coast, I imagine the journey undertaken by the commandos who carried out the assault on the Bruneval radar station last summer. They took the essential parts of the revolutionary mechanism and then blew up the rest and made their withdrawal by sea. A wild song pulls me from my reflections, '*Giovinezza! Giovinezza!*' the Fascist Alleluia, sung by a troop of *Bersaglieri*, just as incongruous as 'God Save the King' would be. These unfortunates appear out of a squall at top speed, looking like drowned rats, the plumes of their hats drenching them like sprinklers out of control. What are they up to freezing here, these poor buggers, instead of sharing the fate of their brothers caught by their millions in the ruins of the Duce's ephemeral empire? Agricultural prisoners, free as the English countryside air, they interrupt their *canto* resonating from their carts to let fly many *Buon Giornos*! all around. Only a big 'PW' for Prisoner of War on their backs distinguishes them from the local farm workers. They are also in the pub, whistling and drinking pints of beer. Some, beautiful as gods, have no need to deprive themselves by not taking the place of the farmer who has left his wife behind to get himself killed.

'You'll see the sea!' Staunton had said to me. Not since Etretat anyway; the Wall's flow of concrete masks the open sea but links the houses beside it. Blockhouses, bunkers, cannons, machine gun nests are ensconced on the cliffs, at their foot and in the caves. Behind this rampart, the people of the Pays de Caux – eastern Normandy – live a slow life; not many passers-by walk along the grey streets infested with *Feldgrau*. The shadow of Arsène Lupin no longer glides over the hollow spire.

As the leader of a group of resisters is a school teacher, I give lessons in a nursery school classroom to sea fishermen with weather-beaten faces, hunched over dwarf-sized desks. The silence is disturbed only by the rumbling of marching guard sections' boots climbing the bastions. I go back to Le Havre passing through Cany and the country roads.

Supplied with plastic, Roger no longer spends his nights putting together a mix of detonators; he dedicates himself to *L'Heure H* and gets me to contribute. What great evenings we pass together, ears vigilant, pasting copies on walls! He is keeping a vigilant eye on a factory producing oxygenated water for submarine batteries. He tells me: 'An engineer has promised to procure the plans for me. On your next visit here you'll be able to get your teeth into them.'

'See you, Roger!'

9

Rhine Gold

The *Entlassungsschein* opens all doors; it remains a moot point whether, on the way back, the guards checking the train from Le Havre salute me or not.

The next day is a fine one over Saint-Maclou; the slate roofs of old Rouen shine blue. Suddenly the alarm sirens, then the flak batteries, burst into life. Very high, beyond the little plumes of smoke marking the violent bursts of the German 88 Flak cannon, sparkling crosses draw out long white trails across the sky. Fortresses! It is only the US Army Air Force that bombs in daylight hours and from such a high altitude! Struck by a sense of foreboding, I grab the door. René Boucher shouts to me, 'It's forbidden to go outside during the alerts, and you know it! If you get caught …'

'Don't worry, the Boche have gone to ground!'

I rush down the five floors and jump in the saddle. Above my head, the flying crosses lay their minuscule eggs, which waver a few seconds in the air then disappear from view. One hundred and thirty Fortresses spray the town of Rouen. The bombs rain down. At rue Molière, on the quays, there is not a soul to be seen anywhere; it is a hell of explosions, columns of smoke at each corner of the street rend the air. Like an arrow, I cross Boëldieu Bridge surrounded by geysers. In Sotteville, a weathercock, a statue collapsing before my eyes, fly past me. I swerve at full speed into rue des Abattoirs capped by a blackish cloud. On my left, a block of houses vanish into thin air. Mère Ripol's café alone remains standing and she is planted on the footpath contemplating, alarmed, Philippon's garage is disembowelled and my depot open to the air. Behind its fretted iron shutter are spread out containers, parachutes, boxes of explosives and a panoply of machine guns, revolvers and daggers. Without bothering about the good woman, I rush to attack the shutter, hammering at it with a crowbar. Suddenly, behind me, I hear Georges Philippon gasping, 'Good, dear chap! You're in luck – we've had the same idea!'

We hammer, pull and drag. We hang from a steel shutter, which agrees to lower itself – at the same moment that the first German patrol turns up. The Ripol café opens especially for us. The owner tells us as she uncorks a bottle of Calvados from her private stock: 'It's my turn.' Not a word on what she must have just seen. The Cauchois are mean with their words: a blink and so it's understood.

'Provided your luck holds,' cries Charles when I describe our intervention. 'I need your scientific mind to put a lid on something that's turning the RAF's hair white on hold. If you succeed, you'll be praised to the skies – Evensen will tell you more about it.'

At 50, Birger Evensen is big, handsome, with a flat stomach, tanned face, neat beard under silver hair and the grey regard of a Viking – he is, after all, Norwegian. What's more, he is always dressed up to the nines, suit with sharp creases, shirt with an English collar.

In Nazi Europe, only three of the Norwegian Mustad firm's factories, famous for its hooks, manufacture nails for horseshoes. Now, on the Russian steppe, General Winter is freezing diesel and lubricants and the Wehrmacht has fallen back on using dung engines (horses); horseshoes are lost there in their thousands and nails for those horseshoes in their millions! Evensen, director of one of these factories, established at Duclair, distant suburb of Rouen, is pampered by the Occupier. They invite him to the round table intent on milking the most from French industries. Well-informed, he is Staunton's spy No. 1. His whole family is in our circuit: his son Sven is Pépé Newman's bodyguard and assistant; his daughter Liv, a college girl of 17, transmits messages hidden carefully in her skirts. Doyenne and mother of the family enriches her lavish Norwegian recipes with the double cream of Normandy in La Bouillotte, a beautiful house in the town of Duclair dominating a curve of the Seine.

Concise and methodical, Evensen unfurls a gigantic blueprint on the living room table. 'Here's the breakdown of the *Française des Métaux de Déville* factory that produces spare parts for landing gear for the Focke-Wulf 190 *Long Nez*, the best performing of the German fighters. It's a stronghold, impenetrable, in theory ...'

The blueprint is covered with a jumble of lines, rectangles, squares, circles that show the large halls, machines, pathways, rails, water conduits and those for gas and electricity. He mocks, 'You're already lost, eh? You'd have to be in the trade to be able to find your way around the forges, presses, ovens, embossing machines and the rigs spread out over acres of hangars. Fortunately, you won't be attacking these machines, only the hydraulic circuit that feeds and cools them. They need tons of water otherwise they overheat, seize up and break up! At the *Française* five pumps are working, fed by a bypass channel, great beasts – two bicylinders, a Champigneulles, and a Davey; three tricylinders, a Worthington and two Meiers. As a freebie, I offer you a large generator of 1,200 kilowatts. You smash up all that and a pretty pack of Focke-Wulfs won't have any wheels to take off with.'

One morning, I cycle along the cobbled street that encircles the filthy high wall of the factory. After crossing through three patrols, who seemed suspicious to me, I didn't delay. Behind the monumental entrance gate, the French watchmen, supervised closely by a squadron of *Feldgrau*, body search all the workers. Fortunately, the impregnable fortress has one weak point, which Evensen revealed to me.

On 10 October, a Sunday, as night falls, Philippon, his nephew, the Piontek brothers and Hugues are crouched behind Claude Malraux and me at the bottom of a dark cul-de-sac opposite the little door of a security agent's quarters that allows access to the workshops – the only single opening pierced through the encircling wall. The weak point …

'*Ein-Zwei*!' The 8 p.m. round passes in front of us stomping like an elephant. It disappears into the distance. I knock at the door, 'Police! Open up!'

A quavering female voice answers, 'My husband, who's not here, tol' me not to open to nobody!'

'You open up to the police, Madame! Especially accompanied by these gentlemen!'

In unison, Claude bawls out in a cavernous voice, 'German bolice! If yow resist, I vill shoot don you toor!'

The lock creaks. I force open the door with my knee and project the poor woman, arms stretched out wide, against her sideboard. I muffle the scream of terror she was about to make on seeing masked bandits. Seven men, seven bikes block the $10m^2$ of tiling.

'Little' Philippon ties up the unhappy woman, whose wails breaks one's heart. Sten and explosives sack on our shoulders, we dive into a cloud of dust tasting of coke and the deafening din of power-hammers, hissing steam, crunching of grindstones and sliding of gantries. Coils of steel brought to a white heat, forges glowing red, spluttering electric arcs and showers of sparks everywhere. I can hardly even make out the ceiling. From the entrance door, I'm disoriented. Georges shouts out to me, 'Don't panic, *mon ami*. We'll move along this wall, then the other ...'

We follow the wall, Indian-style. Hard at it at their benches, the workers don't even glance at us. We cross a large, second hall. We look at the blueprint: under the thin beam of the torch, a labyrinth without Ariadne's thread ... I approach a worker, a spectre in the night, tap him on the back. I imagine how surprised he's going to be at the sight of my Colt! He turns around; he looks at it – bursts out laughing, 'Ah, no, Lulu, you're not going to get me this time! If the foreman nabs you, you're in for it!'

A madman in hell? My mouth hangs open. But not Philippon, who grabs the man by the collar, brandishes his machine gun, growling, 'You f****** with us?'

Disconcerted, the man rolls his eyes towards the Sten that's reflecting sparks coming off the electrical arcs. Then he says, 'Shit, that's real! So you're not Lulu?'

'Lulu? Of course bloody not!' storms Georges. 'Who's this Lulu?'

'Lulu – Lucien – that's my friend, a real card! Just yesterday, he jumped me as a masked terrorist, like you, but with a cardboard revolver! Sorry, I thought he was at it again! I'm Bébert. What are you doing here?'

'Take us quietly to the cooling pumps and you'll see!'

Single file, we follow Bébert through two halls without attracting anyone's attention. A hidden door that we would've struggled to find opens up on to a canal where the waters are gurgling. Under a shelter, five large spirals buzz. It isn't an easy job to get the limpets to adhere to their casing! I go back over it three times to be fully satisfied. I adjust the delays to thirty minutes, time enough to do the generator and then get lost. At that moment, our guide fails, 'I'm not too sure where your generator is. Fuel isn't my thing. Emile, the head electrician, he'd know. But Sunday, he's not on duty. I do know a big engine, perhaps it'll do you?'

Unfortunately, it won't. It's only a small engine of 300kW. I hesitate to use the 3 kilos of plastic I've still got on that. Yet, as time is short to get the big beast, I take the decision to plonk them on the rotor bearing. God, was I inspired ...

The minutes disappear so fast that we are still grouped in the tiny kitchen when the pumps blow! The deflagration, so violent, shatters the windows and sends the earthenware on the dresser flying; it breaks as it hits the ground. A confusion of handlebars, pedals and men untangle themselves somehow or other. I find myself ejected into the street. Already my merry band of men are dispersing. Claude Malraux and I jump on to our bikes.

A hundred metres further on, we almost bump into two Germans arriving at full pelt, or rather tilt. Claude has the presence of mind to shout to them, '*Laufen Sie schnell*! There're terrorists over there!'

These *Feldgrau* aren't stupid. They come to a grinding halt, roll on the ground, and knee to earth, Schmeissers at the shoulder. We're going to be shot just like at a rifle range.

Suddenly, a patch of roof flies off like an exploding volcano; sheet metal spins round and round, in a roar; bursts of casting fall all around like rain! Our shooters take a header! A stroke of genius – those 3 kilos of plastic plonked furtively on a machine that didn't deserve it.

An hour on the road without a mishap and we reach Roumare and our safe house, a small country farm. The entire household is waiting impatiently for us in the large living room. The father reprimands us, 'We thought you'd never get here! Go on, get on the job!'

'On the job? To do what exactly?'

'To kill the steer, damn it. We've got a Marlin that we've kept hidden from the Krauts since 1940, but now the cartridges are useless. So you, with your popguns ...'

Without malice, the steer looks towards me chewing a straw. I advance, Colt behind my back, I shoot it right between the horns. It doesn't react or stumble. A second bullet, it hardly trembles. A third, its pasterns start to shudder. Only with the fifth bullet does it kneel and finally breathe its last. The farmer cuts its throat and splits the skin along the stomach. The blood, the guts, the bile and the dung spreads out in torrents. I'm handed a butcher's knife. All night long, Claude and I both cut it up and are bathed in blood. At dawn, The housewives who queue at the stable door are served. Then an out-of-breath kid emerges, 'An economic control team is searching the farm next to here!'

It goes without saying that clandestine domestic abattoirs are strictly *verboten*! Therefore, when the inspectors turn up, the place is clean – the steer has flown the coop, leaving no trace. Neither skin, nor drops of blood. The country folk collude to trick these inspectors. When the signal's given, the animals, the barrels, the distillery, all are moved from one farm to another. Foodstuffs, grains, potatoes evaporate. They're palmed off with a cheap wine that'd strip a tin kettle.

We regain our strength with the help of 14oz steaks, browned and simmered in cream, in a frying pan as big as a cartwheel.

Charles welcomes us to Rouen warmly, 'The RAF is very grateful to you. However, this sabotage has made the chaps here nervous. They've multiplied the road blocks and identity checks. I advise you strongly to stay indoors or to get a change of scenery. Bob why not go, for example, to Paris so they'll forget you. Look, I'll give you an R & R leave of absence. Come back refreshed!'

In Paris, the midday throng at Marbeuf station is unsustainable! Farewell to the pre-war Métro, in the time when gentlemen offered their seats to ladies and when soft leather benches in first class only welcomed the bottoms of the bourgeoisie. At a time when cars are asleep on blocks and diesel buses are rarer than fine days, occupied and occupier crush against one another.

I'm pressed against a very young woman whose curves feel harmonious on contact. My nose is attracted by a cascade of blonde hair where a chic perfume idles. A lock of hair casts a shadow over one eye and her eyelashes have deep blue mascara. Slim, she is faultlessly elegant: fitted houndstooth coat, straight blue skirt. My glance loses itself in the low neckline of a lace blouse. She surprises me, smiles indulgently.

That's how I meet Maguy.

That day, we have lunch in a black market restaurant, then she takes me to Ciro's, a piano bar, rue Cannou. The pianist plays his favourite tunes, Ellington, Basie, Django Reinhart. I'm astonished, 'I thought jazz was forbidden?'

'You're dated, René. Can see you've been a prisoner. You don't even know about Ciro's.'

I supress a smile. I know Ciro's – in London. Ann even fell under the charm of Stephane Grapelli's pizzicato, inseparable from Django.

I leave Maguy at her door, avenue Kléber. She offers me her lips, saying, '*A demain*!'

As if her mouth and '*demain*' – tomorrow – were a sure thing?

The following evening we got to Sheherazade, a nightclub where the caviar is paid for per seed, and the champagne per bubble. You don't dance there; the pious marshal has forbidden it – France suffers! Yet, the women paid by the cork, skirts split and fishnet stockings, are pushing officers with gilt-edged epaulettes to consume more. The thugs who make their living from the invaders laugh at their every word. Maguy watches me from the corner of her eye and whispers, 'You don't like them, do you?'

'And do you?'

She weighs her answer, 'I hate soldiers, all soldiers. This lot doesn't belong here. However, I'm ... half-German. My father, who occupied the Ruhr after the war, met my mother there. My mother tongue is German.'

A detail I keep from mentioning to Staunton or Buckmaster!

She is blonde, naturally. The Rhine gold, doubtless. I don't know what attracts her to me. The money I've got? I don't match up to the cosseted gentlemen who lure models with their chauffeur-driven cars parked in avenue Matignon, in front of Heim's couture house!

My delicious vacation comes to an end all too quickly. Workbench corner in rue des Abattoirs and my bike welcome me back.

In guise of welcome, Charles sniffs, 'For your next job, you'd better change! You stink of Shalimar, my word, and you're togged out like a lord!'

That's Maguy's fault. One morning she had patted my jacket, 'Pure Scottish wool ... haven't been able to find it for years now. Where did you get it? Mystery! On the other hand, what cut, provincial, old hat! You deserve better.'

Better: a Prince of Wales and thread-for-thread cut to the latest Parisian fashion by a little tailor among her friends, and from Faubourg-Saint-Honoré, whose needle is worth its weight in gold – without textile coupons, it goes without saying.

The next day, Charles calls Claude and me to a meeting in Philippon's garage, in front of a hamper of oysters, a dish of charcuterie, half-bottles of Muscadet, the lot supplied by Mme Ripol. 'I've got a problem, boys! Buck is asking us to f*** up two large power stations, one in Yainville near Jumièges, the other in Grand-Quevilly, categorised as priority targets. The RAF was first given the mission to flatten them. After having got lost twice in the chaos of the pisspot, its squadrons of Mosquitos threw in the towel. So, it's for us to do the dirty! Yainville is a piece of cake: at the smallest alarm, the guards throw themselves into the shelter, which has only one exit. One man armed with grenades and a machine gun will be enough to neutralise them. In Quevilly, it's another story. At the first threat, its garrison of 150 men take a position in a circular trench. We can only achieve it if the RAF supports us. Still, we've got to get it. Here's my plan, you'll see – genius!'

On a moody autumn evening I cycle to Quevilly. In spite of the blackout, points of light show up like a constellation, the station is visible a kilometre away. Better, a battery of lights sweep its perimeter regularly, literally pointing to it. It is surrounded by a high grilled enclosure, electrified, topped with barbed wire, a mined circular roadway, then a piece of waste land covered in potholes. I approach jumping over one hole after another between two projector lights. Reaching a good distance, I walk along it planting chains of thermite incendiaries along the way. These incendiaries have extremely powerful phosphoros, linked by fuse and detonator.

Genius is our dear Charles – he's convinced the RAF that if we mark it out, its bombers couldn't possibly miss the damned power station and the RAF won't dare slope off.

At 10 p.m., rolled into a fœtal position, I hold tight between my fingers the ignitors of my flares. Ear to the west, I'm listening for a celestial humming which, at first is hardly perceptible, then swells and swells. I prime the fuse, then, jumping from one crater to another, I bolt. When I reach the bush where I hid my bicycle, my 'fire pots' blaze up, illuminating *a giorno* the transformers, the cranes, a forest of pylons and cables. Machine guns hysterically open fire on the thermites, which just feeds the flames. Bursts of gunfire rumble mournfully in the bush of the wasteland. I jump on my bike, pushing down on the pedals. I notice the trails left by the fire of flak following the sound of the mosquitoes, fleeing at 600 an hour – above the impenetrable mattress of clouds lying along the bed of the Seine.

The pisspot has struck again!

And in Yainville, against all hope, the guards remain in their hidey-hole!

The next day, the RAF let us know, dryly, that they no longer thought risking the lives of teams on this basis was such a 'bright' idea. On the other hand, the War Office persists and signs: the industrial potential of Rouen remains categorised 'A, Top Priority', everything must be attempted to damage it at the very least.

'A block of kilowatts produced in Quevilly, enough to supply a substantial part of the industries in Rouen, is transferred under 90,000 volts to the transformation station in Dieppedalle on the right bank,' Monsieur Evensen explains to me after being called in as a reinforcement.

'There, the 20,000kw, 4m-high heavy plant transform the current to be delivered to the factories. They're an unusual type, obsolete, no others like them! No replacement nor spare parts are possible. Nonetheless, you must deal with these without delay. Traumatised by the last Mosquito raid, the Germans are getting ready to put them in safety under the cliff!'

I object, 'If they are guarded by a company ...'

'No! By French watchmen and German rounds. But don't be content with puncturing them! They'll be rewired and re-soldered in a few weeks. For everything to melt down, you'll need to set fire to ten tons of oil that they contain.'

'You can't exactly set fire to 10 tons of oil with a match!'

'Not 10 tons, Bob, 10 tons per heavy plant, 40 tons in all, half of which will be solidified, because the engines are operated in rotation, and what with the autumn cold ...'

One fine evening, from the sheer Canteleu cliffs, I sweep the Seine from Sotteville to the château of Robert the Devil, then aim my binoculars 100m lower down, a plot planted with large grey cubes topped with a network of cables. Evensen wasn't lying: ants in green are laying rail tracks that disappear into a cave at the foot of the chalk slope.

Sunday, 31 October 1943, in the freezing cold of the morning the plastic turns into stone. I put a few slabs under my armpits, between my thighs, and I go off to sit on my 'eggs' with a grog of Calva in the warmth of the Café Ripol. Once they are softened, I shape eight charges, enough to disembowel the transformers and their rotary converters. We rehearse the moves for the operation ten times, until even if we were blindfolded we could perform them as seamlessly and as prettily as a *pas de deux*.

At nightfall, one by one, Philippon, his nephew, les Piontek and Paccaud join me in the shadow of the sub-station's wall. An owl hoots, as if to announce the approaching drumbeat of the iron heels of the patrol, which halts a few feet from us.

It's 9 p.m.

His boss yaps, '*Hallo! Alles in Ordnung*?' ['Hello! Everything in order?']

In the night, the drawling voice of the watchman replies, '*Alles gut*!' All good, mate, don't freak out.

The patrol moves off. We've got an hour.

We jump over the wall. Quietly we approach the white building nestled at the foot of the cliff; the control room is the guard post. With a shove, I bust in the door. Sitting against a stove, the watchman, a middle-aged man in blue uniform, cries out 'Good God!' and makes a slight gesture in the direction of the leather holster hanging from his belt, then, catching sight of the Colt 45 muzzle pointed at him, he reconsiders. 'Little' Philippon sets down his weapon, an antique revolver Model 92, and wriggles into his chair, grumbling, 'Where're your friends?'

'On Sunday, there's only one! No relief until tomorrow!'

I didn't chose Sunday by chance! I retort like a shot, 'If you're called, if the telephone rings, if someone knocks, you'll reply normally, won't you.'

'He'll be good,' adds the 'young' Philippon, waving his Colt.

Effectively, the sight of bandits with masks and their machine guns paralyses the gentleman.

The transformers, grey behemoths mounted on copper bars, roar in the darkness, 'Danger; high voltage' signals the print. Blue phosphorescence flickers here and there. The large cubes, cloaked in black, are planted in concrete footbaths designed to collect escaping oil.

I kick off proceedings: between the cooling fins of the first, I stick a limpet that Philippon hands me. Then the well-rehearsed interplay of hands proceeds smoothly – the magnets of the second limpet clack on the rotary converter or transformer, adhesive fixes the tails of cordtex and the detonating fuse. At the corner of the footbath I place a thermite strung on to a cork float that I link to the explosive by 2m of incendiary fuse. If the incendiary holds firm in the rim, then kaboom – success! But if the explosion blows it away, it's bye-bye fire! In the central alley, Hugues and the Pionteks silently unroll 40m of a double master line of Cordtex.

While I'm dealing with the last transformer, the sound of boots resonates. Georges whispers, 'Shit! The patrol's early! Won't we be spotted? I'll run and save the kid!'

I jump in, 'Too late, wait!'

The sound of steps swells. I dread the '*Alles in Ordnung*?' that will surely follow.

But there's no halt ... the stamping of feet dies away.

'Oof!' sighs Georges. ' Just a passing company. That was bloody close!'

I leave the station last, after having pressed the four time pencils – chemical delay ignitors – and made sure that the acid ampules being properly crushed, the steel wire under tension retaining the firing pins would be fully corroded. I disengage the security pins correctly, I bolt the doors, portals and gates and I've thrown all the available keys in the Seine.

Afterwards, I mount my bike and make my getaway, pedalling slowly and reviewing all my actions. 'Let's see, did I correctly connect the incendiary fuses so they wouldn't overlap? Otherwise they will cut one another. Then there'd be no more fire. No, I left nothing to chance. I have checked everything.'

Fifteen minutes pass. Nothing. Stay calm – margin of error for ignitors, ten to twenty-five per cent. Twenty minutes – the anguish well known to saboteurs takes hold of me. I mull it over – how did I mess it up? Suddenly – eureka – the delays are calibrated to standard temperature – 15! Now tonight – it's freezing. Hence the delay ...

A flash of light tears the sky apart. The river is aflame. A thunderbolt goes on rolling. I look back. The flames twist within whirls of black smoke. I let out a long sigh.

Nose to the handlebars, I speed through the tiny roads of the slum districts, coming out into the Cathedral square like a whirlwind. It will soon be 11 p.m., the curfew hour, and hordes of spectators are spilling out of the picture houses. The cathedral towers are illuminated suddenly. A fracas ensues. At the corner of the square, flames rise, a cloud of reddish smoke, from the side of the *Soldatenheim*, it seems. Yells, orders, whistles blown. This smoke doesn't smell of lightning. It stinks of dynamite. It's surely an attack. So, in less than two minutes, the square is going to be surrounded, and those who hang around will be searched closely. Now, my bike's saddlebag is full of my 'work tools'.

Fear gives me wings. I throw myself into rue Saint-Romain, turn in front of Saint-Maclou, climb my five floors four by four. There's no way I'm paying for one of those bloody attacks that Orchard Court has forbidden us to commit! It's the credo of SOE – a well-judged act of sabotage is a harder blow to the enemy than the murder of a handful of *Feldgrau*. Above all, it doesn't result in reprisals. The blood of one *Feldgrau* shot always falls back on to the Résistance. The same *Feldgrau* who are being liquidated in their thousands by the Russians in their steppes.

The next morning, I arrange my easel in front of the window and open my box of watercolours. To Monet, the cathedral; I will be content with the roofs of old Rouen. Something to occupy me during the obligatory rest that follows such a Trafalgar moment.

On front page of the *Journal de Rouen*, the préfet, Parmentier, fumes – the bomb at the *Soldatenheim* killed two German 'female soldiers' and wounded several *Feldgrau*. In truth, the Kommandant smothered the story of the deaths of four other male soldiers; terrorists only target women, don't they?

In the course of a raid on a stationery shop, a policeman was killed. Further on, three lines describe the minor damage inflicted on an electric sub-station. Consequence: the préfet 'on the order of the authorities of occupation' decree that the playhouses, cinemas and bars will be closed until further orders and that the curfew is advanced to 8 p.m.

I deserve congratulations from Buckmaster – and from Captain Staunton: 'Evensen judged that the four transformers were good for scrap metal, and that before they are replaced the Allies will have landed. Therefore, I grant you a new leave permit.'

Immediately on getting off the train at Gare Saint-Lazare, I call Maguy. She answers in a voice as if she were dying, 'I've got the flu. I'm stuck in bed. I'm waiting for you at my place.'

'But, your parents?'

'They don't bite, you know!'

At Avenue Kléber, the lady who opens the door is the picture, just older, of her daughter. The bouquet of roses that I offer her makes her blush. She is adorable, but what a German accent! Lying languidly on her bed is Maguy. I sit down at her bedside. At that moment her mother announces from the vestibule, 'Darling, here's your uncle to hear your news.'

When the uncle appears in the doorway, my blood freezes. He is in his fifties, tall, upright, with a silver-haired crew cut and clear eyes like his niece, God did he look great … in his gold-braided *Oberst* uniform. He's a colonel of the Wehrmacht! A broad smile on his face, he shakes my hand. Maguy, innocence incarnate, converses in German, of which – based on the glances from the handsome officer – I'm the subject. I am not unknown to him, that's clear.

The next day Maguy says to me, 'What do you think of my uncle?'

'Charming! A real … gentleman who seems to adore you.'

'Oh, he likes you, too.'

'I see. You've described me as a nephew – presentable?'

'Not at all, simply such as you are! As he would do anything for me, he could be useful to you ... couldn't he? Whatever happens, come back to me quickly, for New Year's Eve.'

The 'couldn't he?' doesn't stop whirling round in my head.

Charles is waiting for me confidently: the thousands of tons of weapons and equipment en route from Germany to Le Havre that cross the Seine on board giant self-propelled barges are causing problems for headquarters. There's a strategic bottleneck – a set of big model locks that they pass through at Léry-Poses, at the confluence of the Seine and the Andelle, near Pont-de-l'Arche, 25km upstream from Rouen.

Armed with a fishing permit and a set of the latest rods, I set up my tackle under the Côte-des-Deux-Amants, in sight of the lock and a section of the Wehrmacht that guards it. I get their assent with the help of bad brandy.

This time, doing things quietly is not going to be possible. Two sentries are on guard permanently in front of the works. Got to bring them both down with a Welrod bullet, that silent pistol that only fires one bullet at a time. I will take one myself; Hugues, the best trigger of the team, the other – at night it's a challenge. If we miss the target, the Germans will line us up instantly in front of the machine guns. Fall back into catastrophe! Charles weighs the pros and cons.

'It's doable. New Year's Eve. As for me, I'll be in London. I'll not be there more than a month, I promise you. Time to recuperate.'

It's his stomach: in spite of high doses of bicarbonate, he suffers from heartburn, followed by severe cramps. At times, he's doubled over, hands held tight against his stomach.

'Claude will take care of management, you – direction of operations,' he continues. 'No problems?'

'None, Claude and I are thick as thieves. By the way, why is he back in again while his brother, André, the 'great' Malraux, isn't taking part? He stays cloistered in a château in the Dordogne, as far as I know. He only comes out for cocktails in Paris with Cocteau, Guitry, Arletty, Rebatet, Brasillach, doesn't he?'

'André and I have been very close – don't trust appearances, don't forget his Spanish War! The Gestapo have him in their sights so he has to keep a low profile. But neutral he will never be! When the hour arrives, he will be Gaullist, with panache because he likes to be in the spotlight. Yet, he's done better! He has made Drieu-la-Rochelle, among the most anti-Semitic pro-Nazis, godfather of his second son, while Roland, his other brother, belongs to a network in Corrèze! The Malraux family cannot be judged like common mortals. His grandfather was killed, apparently, by a blow from an axe. His father, hero of the Great War, ruined by the crash of '29, committed suicide. André got stung for taking the Buddhas from Angkor temple, then got the Goncourt Prize for literature. Afterwards, he played the clown in Moscow in the Thirties. Finally, he "lent" me Claude – some months ago!'

My new turn in Le Havre and along the Atlantic Wall coincides with an inspection by Rommel. I avoid getting too close to him. A single incident, I skid on the greasy road surface in front of a German barracks; fall at the feet of a sentry who kindly comes to my assistance. Just at that moment my Sten gun decides to poke its nose out of my bag. I just manage to hide it. Then I have to disengage myself from the 'kind' German, who while dusting me down presses me to go with him to the infirmary to treat my scratched knees.

My combat groups have multiplied. They dream of nothing but booting out the Krauts on D-Day. I start my fifth month in France – it's one in the eye for the Cassandras of SOE who only expect agents in the field to survive a few weeks. Not me – I've got that famous sixth sense.

This parachute drop, routine, to be received on 20 December. Easy peasy …

Afterwards, Christmas – champagne, candlelit dinner with the shine from flames reflecting in the ash hair of Maguy!

10

Final Mission to Rouen

It is the night of 21 December. I catch a gypsy working for tips at the Monseigneur making his violin weep so close to Maguy's ear that he brushes against the back of her neck with his violin's bow, far too close for my liking! I lift my head, threateningly. Suddenly he misses a chord; the moaning of his violin comes to a stop in a tearing screech. After that, the orchestra, violins, tambourines and balalaikas get in a muddle. I fix a black glare on the man, who melts away into the infinite sky and the blinding sweep of the searchlight at the Sotteville railway yard. The discordant tambourine and the balalaikas become the telescoping wagons and squealing wheels, and loud speakers that bawl and shout!

I wake up all at once. Here I am back on the frozen patch of ground where at midnight I kicked the bucket. Am I still alive? To make sure, I gently try to move. I cough, I spit, then I sit up and scan the horizon …

A huge red moon is about to set. The *Feldgendarmes* have disappeared. Nevertheless, I hold no illusions. They've raised the alarm, they await me at each crossroad. An idea is forming: at the crossroads, probably, but perhaps not along the railway lines! My breath is a rattle, but at least I'm breathing. I stand up and take a small step, then two. I fight my way past the barbed wire around the yard. Here I am, wandering among the comings and goings of locomotives. I pick up an abandoned lantern at the foot of a shed, balancing it with the ease of an old railway man. I face north, shouting loudly, between two attacks of coughing, 'Hello!' to the French workers and '*Guten Morgens!*' to the *Reichsbahn* agents.

Two kilometres further on, the railway runs alongside a workers' district that is waking up slowly. Its hard-working men are everywhere on the streets, all heading towards Rouen. I gradually blend myself into the crowd.

Seven kilometres further on, I spy the threshold of the Boëldieu Bridge, no police check. I'm getting out of breath, I cross it gasping. Climbing rue des Carmes up to Saint-Maclou is a real struggle. Afterwards, I climb the five floors, crouching over step after step, before falling exhausted in the arms of my 'cousin' Madeleine, who hoists me into my bed shrieking at the top of her voice.

On 24 December, lungs on fire, I spit lumps of blood. Madeleine has washed me, shaved me, wrapped me up and put a mountain of pillows behind my shoulders, saying to me, 'You've got to be presentable. You have a visitor.'

While listening to the BBC, I think of Fernand, shot already a year ago. By eliminating Darlan, he cleared the way for the general, who only had a bunch of old Vichyist big shot punters – those 'lily-livered sons of whores,' as Eisenhower called them – and instituted a provisional government in Algiers.

'Park's friends are thinking of the former pupils of the Orchard and wish them very happy holidays,' the voice from London suddenly declares.

'The pupils,' 'the Orchard?' Boomerang effect: my thoughts fly off to Eliane, Eric, Diana, Pierre as well as to Staunton, whom I imagine in a select restaurant in Bond Street stroking a glass of old whisky with his grey eyes – and a lovely young thing asking nothing more than to be tasted herself, too. Damn Charles!

Claude Malraux comes in. He precedes our old doctor, Delbos, a doctor in Flaubert's fashion, waistcoat adorned with a watch chain, pince-nez, jowls and a Gallic moustache yellowed by snuff. He's an optimist: 'You'll be up by New Year's Eve … Nonetheless, I wish I could locate that blasted bullet you've still got somewhere in your body. No point in sending you to a radiologist as the Gestapo must be lying in wait for that kind of thing. You weren't in a position to let me have a go at taking it out by natural means, anyway.'

At that moment, to my utter astonishment, Charles comes through the door, all smiles! 'As you can see, I didn't leave, big man. In fact, I almost came to a sticky end! Thirteen evenings – one after the other I stamped around a field near enough to Amboise without getting a glimpse of a Lysander tail. The fourteenth and last night, full moon, a lookout shouted, 'There's Krauts all around!' Every man for himself, you know … fortunately no damage! The next moon will be the one. I'm taking you to be looked after in London!'

In the Café Mas, place des Ternes, Henri Déricourt is waiting for us. He's head of air operations, managing 'black' plane pick-ups; the ones that drop and collect SOE agents in secret. A fine kid with a charmer's smile, clear regard, tousled hair. 'A damned good pilot,' Charles tells me. 'Air shows, aerobatics, mail service, test pilot. He needs to be that good to judge if a pocket handkerchief of a field is long enough, has enough light soil and is open enough for a colleague to risk his life in the dark without knowing it!'

Henri sets up our rendezvous. 'Gare Montparnasse for the Express departure from Angers, 6 January at 11 a.m.'

When I surprise Maguy in avenue Matignon, she explodes, 'Not only do you leave me without any news but you come back to me like the living dead. You're skinny, pale, hollow eyes surrounded by dark rings – enough to put the fear of God into me! So, what's happened to you?'

'Bad bronchitis ...'

'Obviously not looked after properly! In the back of beyond, that really doesn't surprise me. I'm going to send you to a good doctor.'

So he can discover the jackpot! No way, so I cry out, 'I know an excellent one. I'll make an appointment this evening, I promise.'

Trapped, the only thing I can do is call Jean Ducroquet, a friend since forever ... who is flabbergasted. In a couple of words I explain what's happened. He's got the solution, 'The Résistance network in the Faculté de Médicine that I belong to is headed up by Doctor Delors, my thesis mentor, a super gastroenterologist. You couldn't do better. He's quite a character, you'll see.'

The home of the 'character' is on the first floor of a prestigious building, place d'Iéna. It's full of owls, in watercolours, in oils, in bas-reliefs, in statuettes, tapestries, ashtrays, paperweights, letter-openers, clocks, vases and lampbases. The 'professor' is a frail little man with no shoulders to speak of. An immense forehead sits above a triangular face, flat, lit by endlessly blinking eyes – the face of an owl!

He exclaims with a high voice, 'Fascinating aren't they, these birds? They've been hunted, exterminated, crucified on farm doors simply because they're awake when we sleep! An abomination. Perhaps I was an owl in another life – and I'm still one, aren't I? Right, go behind the screen. Let's see, the scar shows the bullet touched the intestines. You're a miracle, young man! But where the devil did it go? If you evacuated it naturally, the paper to the Académie des Sciences – after the war, of course – will make me famous!'

After having moved the screen, he exclaims, 'Alas, no, not this time! Here it is, in the Douglas pouch, a fold of the abdominal lining between bladder and rectum, where it must've fallen after its course through your body! A unique case worthy of being commented upon anyway. Now we come to my fees.'

I evaluate the armchairs, the Louis XV commodes, the tapestries, the wainscoting, the golden wall-lights, the crystal chandeliers: I expect the worst.

'I don't have a price,' he goes on, 'You'll pay me when you're in London – in a message letting me know your fate! "Douglas thanks his doctor". It'll be a pleasure to see you again!'

The goodbye is the prelude to a friendship that lasts until his death.

With care I announce to Maguy that my company is sending me to Turkey for a month, no longer. It's a heartrending separation; body to body bathed in tears. Does she believe me? I feel bad and annoyed with myself. Turkey, no problem, but a month? I know so well that the timetables of the 'black' planes are unpredictable!

On 6 January, applying the security orders learnt at Beaulieu, I arrive at Gare Montparnasse a good hour in advance to reconnoitre the platforms. There are no more *Feldgrau* than usual, no suspicious loiterers. To kill time I go down the toilets. Just as I'm putting myself at ease, a cavernous voice freezes me, 'Hands in the air, Bob? You're done!'

My heart races, my blood congeals – he knows my name, this French *Gestapiste*! Who sold me down the river? Trembling, I glance sideways. On my right Vallée, on my left Grand-Père, grinning, 'We're not the Gestapo, fortunately because, with your thing in the air ... people just never check their backs enough, you see, kiddo!'

Arm in arm, we go to meet Déricourt and Charles, who are waiting at the door of a first-class wagon. The compartment reserved for German officers is occupied, six of them nattering and smoking non-stop. The next one is empty. While we choose our seats, a sixth passenger appears. He greets Déricourt like an old acquaintance before addressing a 'bonjour' to everyone in the carriage. He's about 40, tall, well built, tanned, profile of a bird of prey. He certainly catches the eye! Grand-Père remarks, 'A compartment of British officers beside a compartment of Krauts, nobody would believe us.'

Charles observes the newcomer carefully. 'My word,' he breathes, 'It's Robert Benoist!'

Benoist? All school kids like me who scrawled Bugattis on their exercise books know this racing driver – a real legend! Between the two wars, he took all the great prizes, including the 24 Hours of Le Mans.

'He's mad not to use make-up to disguise himself,' adds Charles. 'His photo still appears in sports newspapers.'

After having jolted 20km from Angers, the Le Mans bus dropped us at the station of Tiercé market town as night fell. There, it disgorged countryfolk, the men in cloaks and women loaded with shopping baskets, and among them, a dozen or so fashionable tourists. In our brand new trench coats or sheepskin jackets, carrying almost cubic suitcases in blue or red leather that will fit through a Halifax parachute jump hole, God do we stand out! An incandescent redhead in high heels and fur coat punctures the darkness of the night.

Under the round eyes of the locals and in single file, this pretty crowd follows Déricourt who, in the middle of the village, forks off into a little country road. This evening no German has the bad taste to put their nose outside, thank goodness! After an endless walk, we come into a field. As if she had read my mind, the young redheaded woman says as an aside to me, 'My hair colour is to deceive the enemy. The Gestapo wanted notice describes me as blonde, you know. In fact, my name is Henriette. Here's Marius, my boss.'

South African, Marius speaks French that is impossible to describe. Two French colonels, defectors from Vercors, introduce themselves: 'Ely, Valette d'Osia'. The disguise of the latter is worthy of the Count of Paris – beard and black glasses, square helmet, trench coat, golfing breeches! A third colonel, called Limousin, 'in the Résistance', he clarifies, disappears into the countryside.

'There's a choice of LZ – either the Vieux-Briollay or Soucelles,' explains Déricourt to us. 'It's a doddle – 3km long of which 900m are landable. A minimum for the Hudson, a transformed twin-engine that'll fly you. Don't expect Pullman seats!'

A troop of apparitions race along on the frozen 'doddle'. At times a glitter, a sparkle – someone pulls on a cigarette hidden in the crux of the hands. At each drone, we are petrified. Unruffled, Déricourt comments, 'From the noise of the engine – a Heinkel. Hold on, this time a Halifax

– behind a patrol of Messerchmitts. Patience! Your Hudson won't show before midnight.'

Charles Fatosme, one of his adjutants, takes charge of me, the lame duck that I am. He swathes me in a blanket, makes me sit on a block, brings me some coffee. A real nanny.

Midnight, no Hudson. The hours roll past. I get the feeling my feet will never come back to life. At 5 a.m. Déricourt announces, 'Finished for tonight! Let's separate into two groups. Charles, Bob, Marius, Henriette and Robert, go to the village inn, it's pretty sure to be empty this time of year. I'll take charge of the others. En route!'

As a reply, Benoist grumbles into the night, 'Look Henri, there's no Robert! I'm Lionel, I've told you 100 times!'

The inn looks out on to the main street, halfway to the station. 'Lionel' knocks on the door; it opens. Confused exclamations follow, then our friend cries out, 'Come in, you lot! We're at home here. Let me introduce you to Fernand, the boss. In 1918, you see, I was a fighter pilot – he was my grease monkey.' Then adds philosophically, 'Drop the "Lionel", he'll never get used to it!'

At midday, surprise! Four of the five tables of the little dining room are occupied. One by travelling salesmen, the second by French railway watchmen, the third by some *Feldgrau* and the last by Miliciens in black, sinister, bearing an armband stitched with a silver gamma. It's an explosive mix – especially when Fernand, rejuvenated by the war, moves aside for Benoist with an 'after you, Cap …' that he swallows in a cough.

Yet, since he had explained in poignant terms the car breakdown that in the middle of a winter's night made us end up in his inn, the welcome is benevolent: '*Bonjour*', '*Guten Tag*' and '*Bon appétit*' and '*Prosit*'.

The sky is in mourning – operation postponed. After two nights spent in the warm, Fatosme, upset, rushes into the inn, 'Déricourt has just been arrested! Be ready to scram at the first sign! Roads and trains are definitely watched. We'll have to avoid the roads.'

In the evening, who's that pushing through the back door with a bag at his feet? We wait. Déricourt in person, more casual than ever, 'It's my round. Have I got a story for you – at Vieux-Briollay, the village where I'm staying, a pensioner has been stabbed. As she was dying she said, "Baudoin killed me!" Baudoin is the name I use in these parts, would you believe it? The gendarmes jumped on me. Only way out: tell them the truth with a promise of a BBC message. Since then they've caught the real Baudain, a tramp. And now, the gendarmes are our guardian angels!'

I don't doubt it but no Hudson will show up before the moon starts to wane.

When I surprise her, Maguy jumps for joy and melts into my arms. She doesn't give a damn for the reasons that push back my departure. 'You've got two weeks in front of you? I'll use them to get you back on your feet. You're still so pale!'

She pushes me to take slow walks on her arm in the Bois de Boulogne, around its frozen lakes and along Avenue Foch. I glance furtively at No. 84, fief of *Sturmbannführer* Boemelburg, who is dedicated to hunting down SOE agents. In that fine house, they are grilled before being gassed, infected or shot in the death camps. I shudder.

'Are you cold?' enquires Maguy. Maternal, she knots her scarf around my neck. If only she knew!

One week later, we have another *adieu* just as heartbreaking as the last.

On the way to Montparnasse Station, I bump into my friends, Vallée and Gaillot, on a Métro train. I exclaim, 'We're going to take the same train again!'

'No,' replies François, grim-faced.

'But Déricourt is waiting for us!'

'Exactly, he stinks of corruption, your Déricourt! We saw him in the company of German officers.'

'Are you sure? Charles and Benoist, who have been in his hands several times with no problem, swear by him!'

'Henri's taking them for a ride! Irrefutable proof has been communicated to London. So, we're leaving via Spain. You'd do better to come with us!'

'Sorry, friends, I've got a boss, Charles. It's for him to decide. Anyway, even if I did go with you, with my dodgy lung, I wouldn't get far.'

One by one they hug me fiercely, to raise my spirits, 'Let's hope you weather the storm okay,' sighs François. 'See you soon on the Champs Elysées – and not a word to Déricourt, huh?'

Their silhouettes melt into the crowd. I remain stuck to the ground, arms hanging down, totally thrown. What if it's true?

'I'm short of two!' worries Déricourt when the departure whistle blows for the Angers train.

I take the plunge: 'I bumped into them – they prefer to go via Spain.'

'Did they say why?'

'Having frozen through two moons for nothing, they'd had enough of the "pickups".'

Henri, the fine talker, remains silent for a long time then says, giving me a heavy look, 'Is that all?'

'That's all.'

On the wall of my pink bedroom, a chubby-cheeked cupid aims his miniature bow at a water nymph in her birthday suit. The roses, satin eiderdown, lampshade and bidet decorate a four-star Angiers brothel; their owners are on leave. The owners are on leave. Farewell, Tiercé. 'Once is enough!' decreed Déricourt. How did he manage to get this 'house' reserved exclusively for Henriette, Marius, Benoist, Charles and me? It's a mystery.

On the evening of our arrival, his team took possession of the bar. His second, Rémy Clément, describes his hedge-hopping exploits between the Franco squadrons when he delivered planes to the Spanish Republicans. Formerly of Aeropostale, Dumesnilis relives his stop-over in the slums of Cap Juby, in the middle of the Sahara, which he shared with Saint-Exupéry. Benoist reminisces about the Great War. Henri teaches us to play liar's dice. Armed with an angelic smile and a clear, innocent regard, he lies as easily as he breaths and swipes the winnings.

Of course, I put Charles in the picture regarding François' revelations.

'Hot air!' he retorts. 'Robert went via Henri's hands twice, me once. And we're alive. So he's clean, I'd bet my right arm!'

Charles and Benoist being my spiritual fathers, their words – evangelic – quieten my anxiety. Robert takes me under his wing, 'After the war, I have plans for you. I'm going to take you on at my racing stable.'

I sleep like a log. As I'm too weak to cycle the 20km from Angers to Soucelles, Charles takes on the weight of the work – on a tandem. The moon goes from red to platinum. The frozen clumps of the LZ melt away under our boots. Midnight passes. Henriette is ironic, 'It's one in the morning. No plane just as usual. Shall we go sleepy-byes?'

Henri cuts in, 'Yes, but in London, dear heart! Just listen!'

To the north a slight rumble could be heard. A black cross spitting flames flies over us. Déricourt's torch blinks. In reply, lights glimmer in the sky. Fatosme, Clément, Dumesnil take off; on the plain luminous points appear. A meteorite supplied with a blinding headlight dives on to us so brutally that I see it, literally, crashing into the planet! At the last second, it straightens its course, bounces. Brakes squeal. The silhouette of a twin engine can be made out. A moment later, a Hudson swerves and stops, door open, right under our nose. It engines howling to waken the dead and … all the Boche around! Gerry Morel appears at the opening in RAF uniform. He shouts dryly at Déricourt. Covered by the storm evoked by the propellers, the slanging match turns bitter! Alarmed, the pilot sticks his head out of his window hammering at the cockpit's sheet metal, and howls, 'What the hell. Let's get out of here, Goddammit!'.

When Morel tries to seize Henri's collar – Henri resists like the bloody devil – his helmet flies off. Clément gallops off into the blackness – whether the Gendarmerie is on to it or not, an RAF helmet found in a meadow would make tongues wag!

Back, helmet in hand, he calls Henri, 'If they want you in London, it's perhaps to award you the DSO!'[1]

'I couldn't give a f*** about their gong! Don't try to get me aboard, Gerry – my men are behind me! I refuse to leave my team behind and just abandon my wife. And anyway, there are six bikes and one tandem to get rid of, aren't there? You lot, get in,' Déricourt shouts at us. The minuscule door is taken by assault.

'Everybody in the front!' roars the pilot.

Eight men and Henriette squeeze in like sardines against the partition of the cockpit. Two thousand horses are unleashed; its whole membrane trembling, the Hudson leaps forward, jolts, accelerates and then finally points it nose to the stars. I cry out in relief – too soon. Streaks of light zigzag through the darkness of the night, explosions shake us, tracer rounds reach for the plane, and beams add to the chaos. The plane dips its wing, and starts to swerve wildly in every direction. My stomach bounces from toes to throat. Benoist says, 'The sniping between Henri and Gerry got our captain in a right tizzy! He headed straight for Angers and its flak!'

The plane having refound its equilibrium, I murmur to Charles, 'Do you still think Vallée's suspicions are just hot air?'

'I'll get all that cleared up in London!' he grumbles.

1 Distinguished Service Order. Highest British military decoration after the Victoria and George Crosses. Reserved, in principle, for senior officers, rarely awarded to junior officers and very exceptionally to foreign officers.

'As a matter of fact, why did Gerry disguise himself as a squadron leader?'

'Think – the Hudson gets hit, the team and he then jump. The Boche catch on the ground. A major of the infantry in an RAF team would be a bit suspect.'

11

Violette

'Your meal is sublime!' Charles goes into raptures kissing Jeannettee Déricourt, known as Jeannot, on both cheeks. 'Especially when it's known you can't find a single *herbe de Provence* in the entire country! How did you manage to imitate thyme?'

'That's my secret!' she simpers and blushes while waving her plump fingers, loaded with rings. She is round, heavily made up and with hair redder than Henriette. Her accent has a whiff of garlic as much as the West End flat where today Déricourt is offering lunch to his 'faithful' friends, Charles, Robert and me.

I thought he was a goner when, at dawn on 5 February, our Hudson landed at Tangmere, the base for 'small aircraft' pick-ups near Portsmouth. Morel jumped out first and went straight to Buckmaster, who was waiting on the tarmac in a state of excitement. The 'exchange of views' this time was less tumultuous than the last, but just as tense. Buck, who was expecting to see Déricourt behind Gerry, was none too pleased! To welcome us back, he pasted a third-rate smile over his funereal expression. I whispered to Charles: 'So?'

Old compaigner, in twenty-four hours he had got to the bottom of the whole episode, 'So: Frager – network chief in our section – told Buck that a double agent in the *Abwehr* he was dealing with had sworn that Déricourt "loaned" mail, plans, photos, etc, which came into his hands to the Gestapo to be photocopied. His suspicions were corroborated by Yeo Thomas, the famous "White Rabbit", and spokesman for Churchill with the Résistance bigshots, Jean Moulin among others. Also, the security service, which keeps a watch over the viability of SOE, got mixed up in it. In spite of his protestations, Buck, who has more faith in Déricourt than in the Holy Virgin, was put on notice to repatriate him, *manu militari* if need be. As a result Morel, whose mission had been baptised "Knacker", was armed – just think! He didn't dare make use of his popgun fortunately; Déricourt's men would have riposted. Morel having come back empty-handed, the super-snitches deduced that Déricourt was guilty and gave him a black mark. However, Benoist and I remain sceptical.

'On 9 February at midnight, the young Lysander pilot who landed at Azay-sur-Cher, with the mission to take delivery of a passenger, saw with stupefaction a ball of fur emerging from the shadow behind the listed "Joe". The "Joe" was Déricourt and the ball of fur: Jeannot, wrapped up in a castor coat and perched on needle sharp heels. "I will not abandon my wife!" Henri had sworn.

'And,' concluded Charles, 'he pleaded his innocence so well that the judges reviewed their copy and let him go. He will soon return to France; Buck needs him too much. While waiting, it is Jeannot's bouillabaisses for us!'

Harley Street, a super chic thoroughfare in the West End, is lined with private hotels sporting gleaming bronze plaques, behind which, London believes, fashionable doctors lie in wait for patients dripping in gold. The secret services' approved MD who welcomes me is wearing a monocle and Savile Row suit. He listens to my tale while nodding his head and, without listening to my chest with the stethoscope nor radiographing me, gives his diagnosis, 'Your cold bath checked the haemorrhaging. Otherwise, well, you'd no longer be in this world.'

'And the treatment, doctor?'

'Time – let time do its stuff, young man ...'

'And you,' I ask Charles, 'where did you get with the pains in your stomach?'

'Stress, old chap, stress. According to Harley Street, after a month's rest I'll be as good as new. Therefore, I've decided to do a parachute jump.'

I'm astonished – Charles always claimed he was too old for 'throwing himself out of a plane in mid-air'.

'So you've got young again all of a sudden?'

'No, I've been thinking – it's stupid to be dropped on to a LZ 300km from Rouen, then go through half a dozen or so checkpoints with loads of money and documents in my pockets when I can be dropped from a bit higher than the ground and land where I need to be, or almost! Come on, let's go to my place and drink to that.'

The 'my place' of Major Staunton – he's just been promoted – is off Curzon Street, a smart Mayfair road; it's a 'serviced' flat, with a maid in a lace apron and ageless Chivas served on a silver platter by a butler as tight-arsed as Park.

Charles receives officers, journalists, businessmen and pretty, classy women there. In quartermaster's uniform, Ann doesn't look out of place in such circles – she has shortened her skirt by 2in, belted her pea-jacket, worn diaphanous nylons. The only spot marring the tableau: her nails coloured with grease spots left over from the submarine she's scouring.

Subbed by Charles, I sometimes lunch at Ciros with Grapelli, sometimes at Prunier or L'Écu de France, society watering holes for English gourmets and VIPs of the Free French: Schumann, Jean Marin and Pierre Dac who, having escaped through Spain, battle Pétain from the microphone of the BBC. He can certainly allow himself the pleasure – at Verdun he had been left for dead as a Jew. The artists of our country who have chosen the path of 'blood and tears' can be counted on one hand – Jean Pierre Aumont, Joséphine Baker, Gabin and my friend Lynen. The others live off the Continental, the Nazi firm that spearheads the French cinema. Goebbels regulates the 'triumphal' *nach Berlin* showings of writers and artists who don't spit on the sauerkraut.

Charles shares with me the rumours he has gleaned regarding the Déricourt affair: 'I discovered just by chance that a whole load of networks have been infiltrated, like the *Interallié* of the IS that was sold by a French woman nicknamed "La Chatte". Today she'll be holed up somewhere in England. Others, too many to mention, escaping all checks, have been penetrated by the Gestapo or the *Abwehr*, sometimes by both. Take *Prosper*[1] for example: that was a massive operation extending from Belgium to Poitou. A deluge of arrests. As a result, at Buck's insistence, it is claimed, Bodington took himself off to France to judge the scope of the disaster.

1 *Prosper* was a Parisian network broken up brutally by the Germans in 1943, leading to the arrest and deportation of hundreds of people.

Jean Claude Guiet

Wanborough Manor, where Bob started his SOE induction. Credit: Mark Yeats

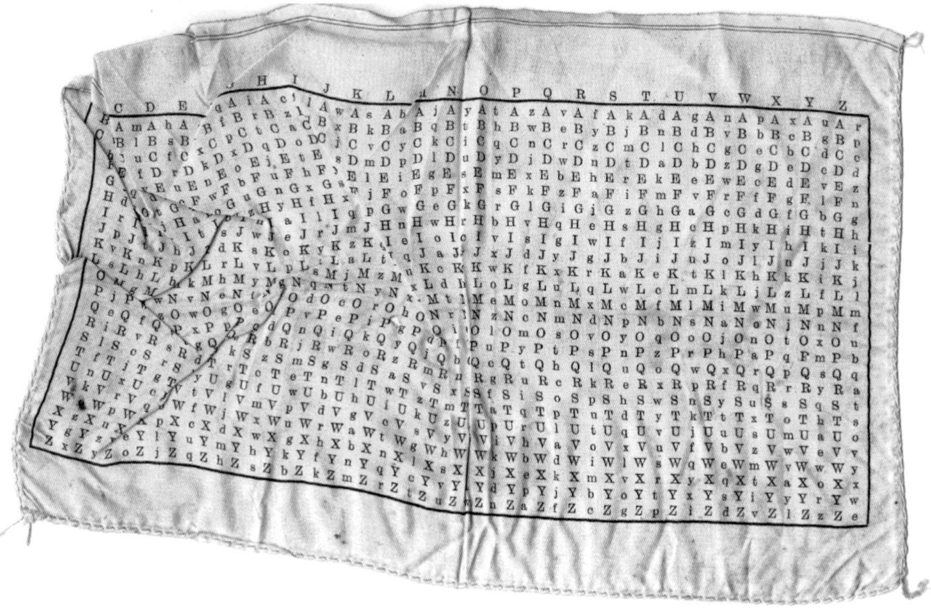

Agent's double encryption silk for messages to London.

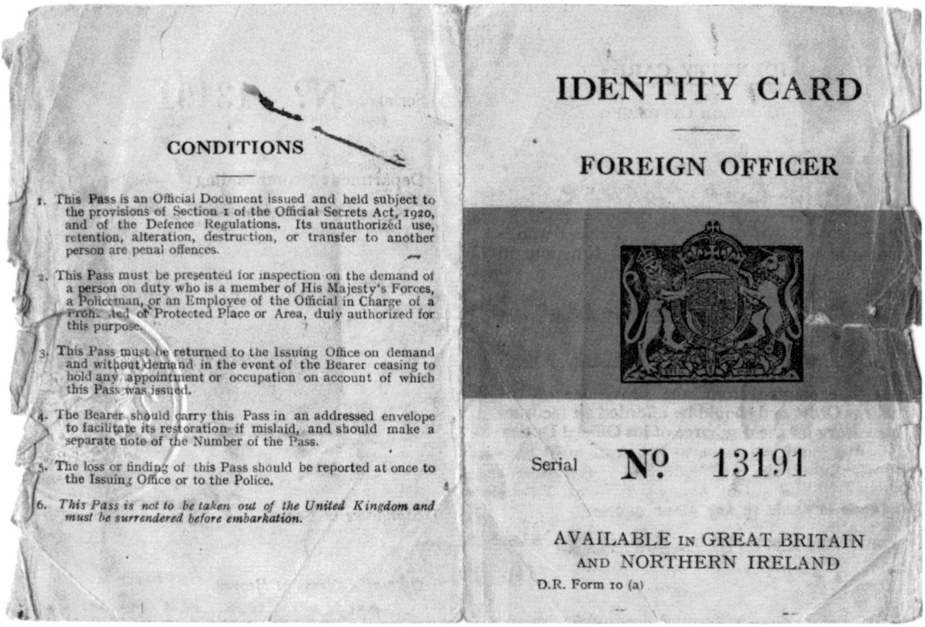

CONDITIONS

1. This Pass is an Official Document issued and held subject to the provisions of Section 1 of the Official Secrets Act, 1920, and of the Defence Regulations. Its unauthorized use, retention, alteration, destruction, or transfer to another person are penal offences.

2. This Pass must be presented for inspection on the demand of a person on duty who is a member of His Majesty's Forces, a Policeman, or an Employee of the Official in Charge of a Prohibited or Protected Place or Area, duly authorized for this purpose.

3. This Pass must be returned to the Issuing Office on demand and without demand in the event of the Bearer ceasing to hold any appointment or occupation on account of which this Pass was issued.

4. The Bearer should carry this Pass in an addressed envelope to facilitate its restoration if mislaid, and should make a separate note of the Number of the Pass.

5. The loss or finding of this Pass should be reported at once to the Issuing Office or to the Police.

6. *This Pass is not to be taken out of the United Kingdom and must be surrendered before embarkation.*

IDENTITY CARD

FOREIGN OFFICER

Serial No 13191

AVAILABLE IN GREAT BRITAIN AND NORTHERN IRELAND

D.R. Form 10 (a)

Bob's Identity Card from the War Office for a foreign officer exterior (above) and interior (below).

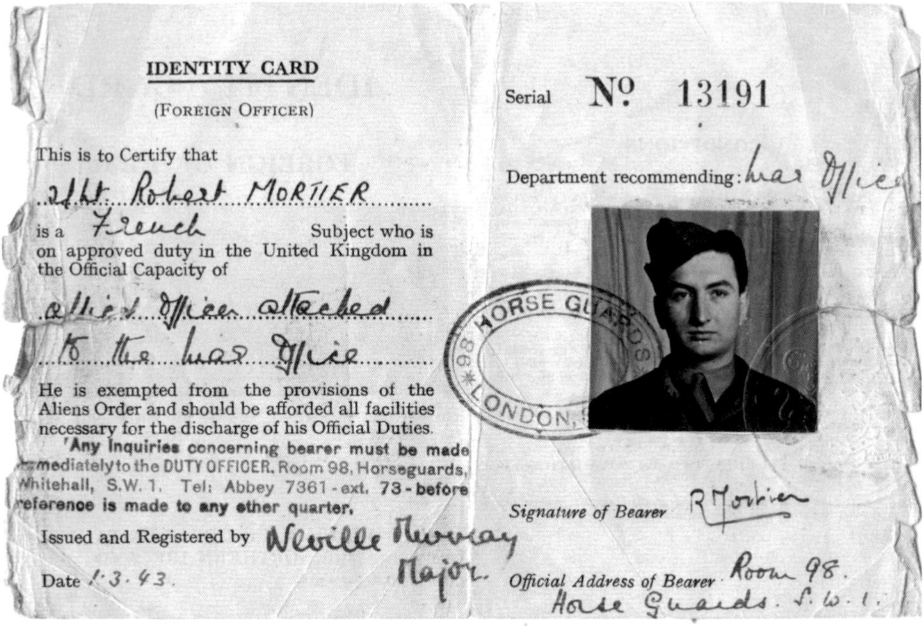

IDENTITY CARD

(FOREIGN OFFICER)

This is to Certify that

2/Lt. Robert MORTIER

is a French Subject who is on approved duty in the United Kingdom in the Official Capacity of

Allied Officer attached to the War Office

He is exempted from the provisions of the Aliens Order and should be afforded all facilities necessary for the discharge of his Official Duties.

Any Inquiries concerning bearer must be made immediately to the DUTY OFFICER, Room 98, Horseguards, Whitehall, S.W. 1. Tel: Abbey 7361 - ext. 73 - before reference is made to any other quarter.

Issued and Registered by Neville Murray Major.

Date 1.3.43.

Serial No 13191

Department recommending: War Office

Signature of Bearer R Mortier

Official Address of Bearer Room 98. Horse Guards. S.W. 1.

Operation: PORTER - 2 - 18.5.43
Christian Name in the Field: PACO
Name on Papers: Robert MOLLIER

[illegible]

MISSION

You are going to France, together with PEDRO, as the advance guard of a Coup de Main party who are to attack the lock gates at GIGNY.

You will be parachuted to a point

9 km. W.S.W. of POITIERS
1½ km. E.N.E. of LA TORCHAISE (In fork of road).

There will be no reception committee, but you will make your way at once to the following safe house:

M. ou Mme. GATEAU,
Commissaire Priseur,
19 bis, rue BONCENNES,
POITIERS.

The password, which MUST be given, is: "Mon ami Pierre m'a dit que vous pourriez me presenter à sa cousine".

You will stay here until the 25th, when you will go to meet BOB (whom you have already seen here) at the rendezvous which you have arranged with him, namely:

at 2 o'clock in the afternoon. He will give you a safe house in the vicinity of your target.

METHOD

1. You have been given a cover story and papers in the name of Robert MOLLIER, which you will use for your normal life in the field. To cover your personality as an agent you will use the name PACO.

2. When you have reached the vicinity of the target, you will proceed to carry out the three following orders:

i. Investigate the grounds suggested to you here for receiving the party at the beginning of the June moon.
ii. Investigate the route between the said dropping ground and target.
iii. You will reconnoitre the target itself for two things:

(a) the manner in which it is guarded,
(b) the answers to the questionnaire you have been given here.

COMMUNICATIONS

1. You will refrain from contacting any other members of the organisation apart from those whose names you have been expressly given.

2. You will arrange with BOB that he meet you on or about the 30th May, so that you may pass your information to him regarding the target. He is in wireless communication with us.

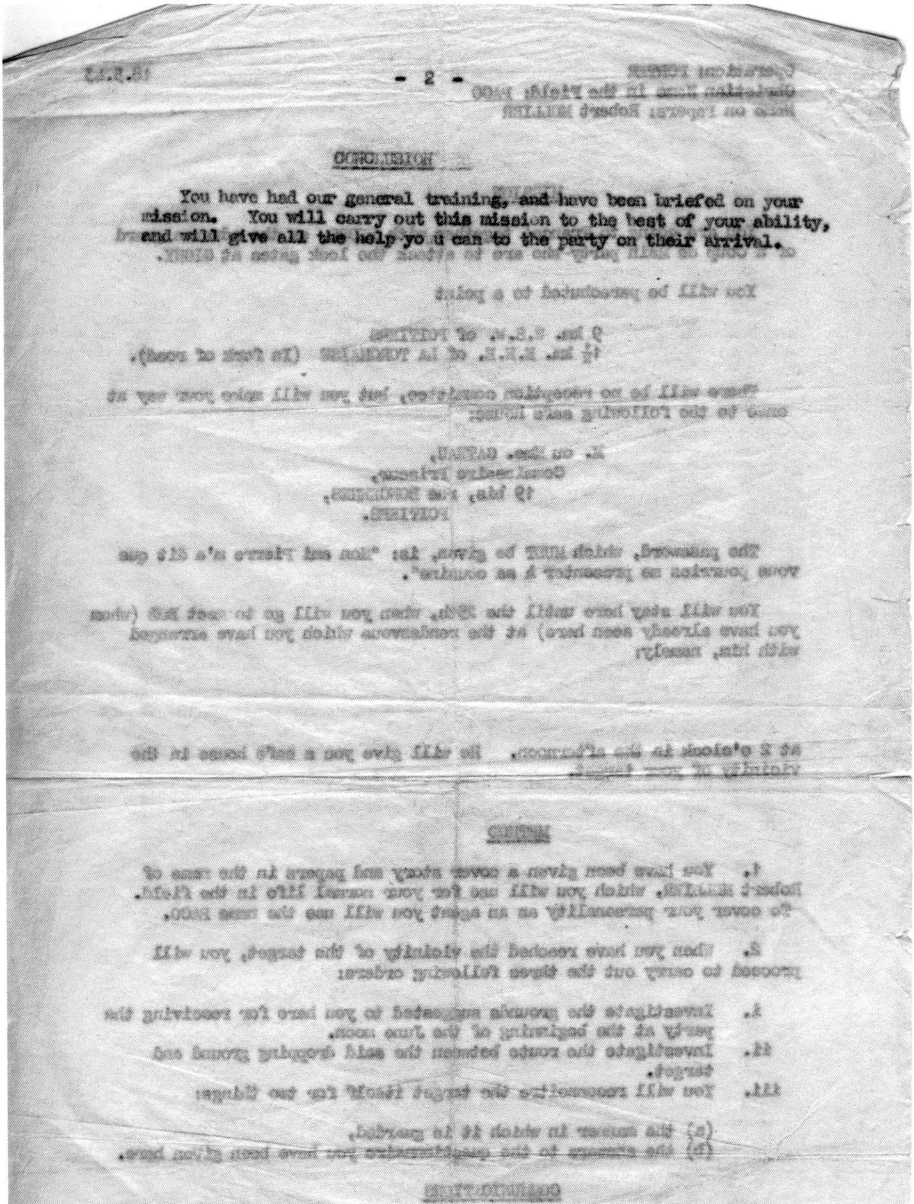
You have had our general training, and have been briefed on your mission. You will carry out this mission to the best of your ability, and will give all the help yo u can to the party on their arrival.

(Left and above) Bob's instruction for Operation Porter.

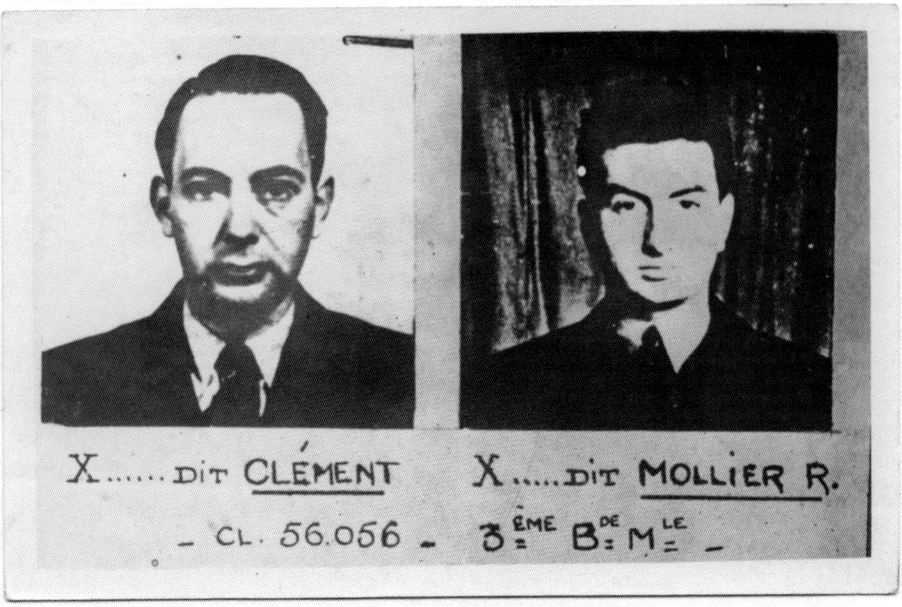

Wanted poster for Bob and Phillipe Liewer, taken by Violette Szabo from the wall at Rouen Station in April 1944.

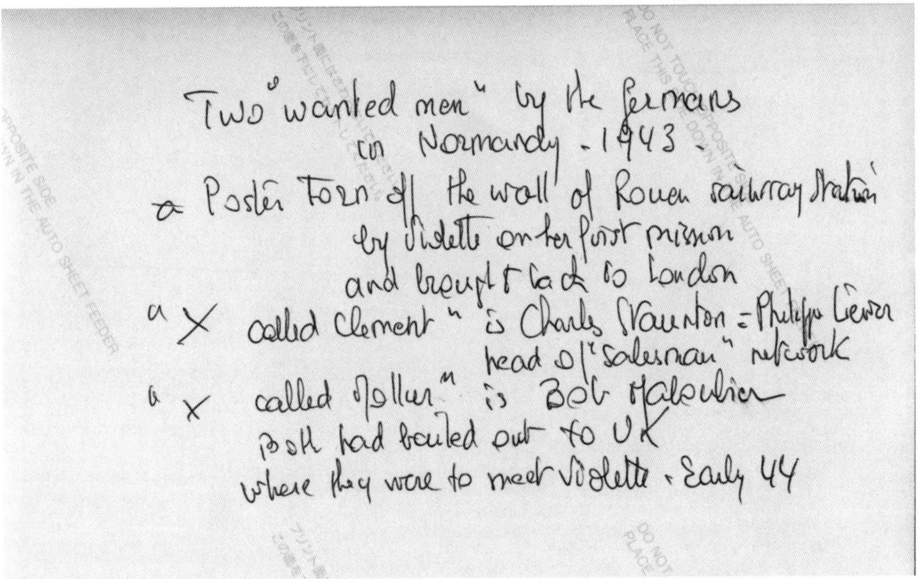

Two "wanted men" by the Germans
in Normandy - 1943 -
a Poster torn off the wall of Rouen railway station
by Violette on her first mission
and brought back to London
a X called Clement" is Charles Staunton = Philippe Liewer
head of "Salesman" network
a X called Mollier" is Bob Maloubier
Both had bailed out to UK
where they were to meet Violette - Early 44

Handwritten notes on the recovered poster above..

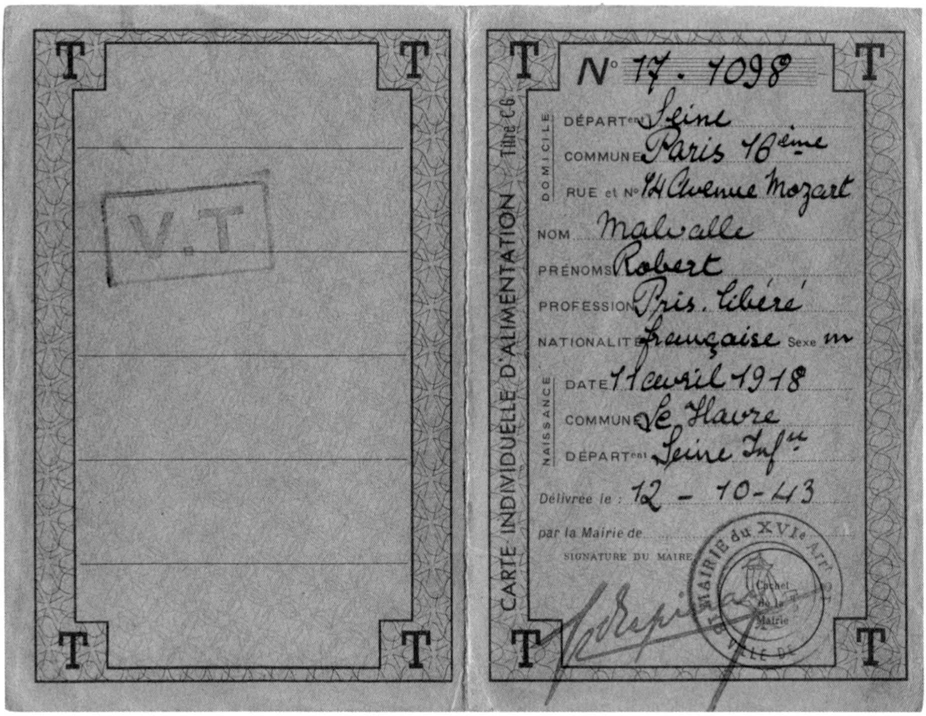
T
T
T
T
V.T
T
T
T
T
CARTE INDIVIDUELLE D'ALIMENTATION Titre C6
N° 17. 7098
DOMICILE
DÉPART^ent Seine
COMMUNE Paris 16ème
RUE et N° 14 Avenue Mozart
NOM Malvalle
PRÉNOMS Robert
PROFESSION Pris. libéré
NATIONALITÉ française Sexe m
NAISSANCE
DATE 11 avril 1918
COMMUNE Le Havre
DÉPART^ent Seine Infre
Délivrée le : 12 – 10 – 43
par la Mairie de
SIGNATURE DU MAIRE
MAIRIE du XVIe Arrt
Cachet de la Mairie
VILLE DE

(Above) Bob's French Identity Card.

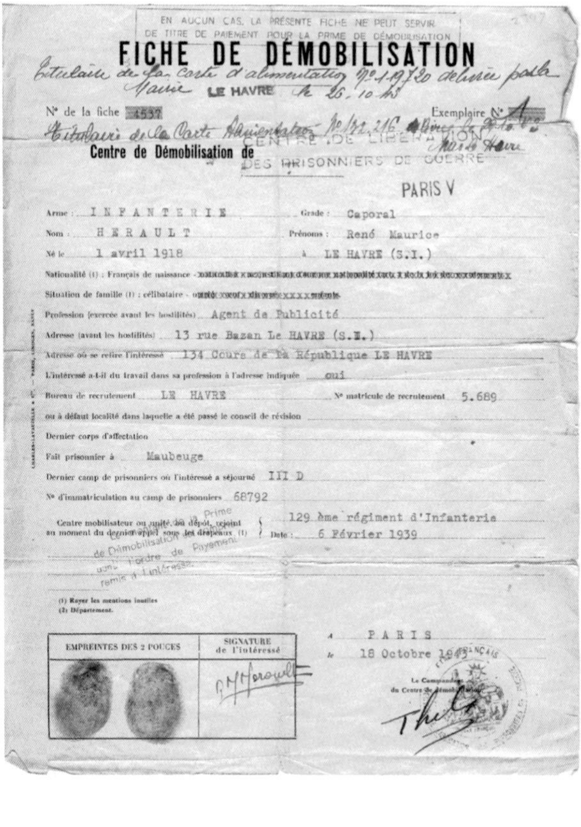
EN AUCUN CAS, LA PRÉSENTE FICHE NE PEUT SERVIR DE TITRE DE PAIEMENT POUR LA PRIME DE DÉMOBILISATION

FICHE DE DÉMOBILISATION

Titulaire de la carte d'alimentation N° 1.19720 délivrée par la Mairie LE HAVRE le 26. 10. 43

N° de la fiche 4537
Exemplaire N° 1

Titulaire de la Carte d'alimentation N° 122.216

Centre de Démobilisation de CENTRE DE LIBÉRATION DES PRISONNIERS DE GUERRE

PARIS V

Arme : I N F A N T E R I E — Grade : Caporal
Nom : H E R A U L T — Prénoms : René Maurice
Né le 1 avril 1918 à LE HAVRE (S.I.)
Nationalité (1) : Français de naissance
Situation de famille (1) : célibataire
Profession (exercée avant les hostilités) Agent de Publicité
Adresse (avant les hostilités) 13 rue Bazan Le HAVRE (S.I.)
Adresse où se retire l'intéressé 134 Cours de la République LE HAVRE
L'intéressé a-t-il du travail dans sa profession à l'adresse indiquée oui
Bureau de recrutement LE HAVRE — N° matricule de recrutement 5.689
ou à défaut localité dans laquelle a été passé le conseil de révision
Dernier corps d'affectation
Fait prisonnier à Maubeuge
Dernier camp de prisonniers où l'intéressé a séjourné III D
N° d'immatriculation au camp de prisonniers 68792
Centre mobilisateur ou unité, ou dépôt, rejoint au moment du dernier appel sous les drapeaux (1) — 129 ème régiment d'Infanterie — Date : 6 Février 1939

de Démobilisation ... de Payement ... remis à l'intéressé

(1) Rayer les mentions inutiles
(2) Département.

EMPREINTES DES 2 POUCES	SIGNATURE de l'intéressé

à PARIS
le 18 Octobre 1943
Le Commandant du Centre de Démobilisation

(Right) French movement permit.

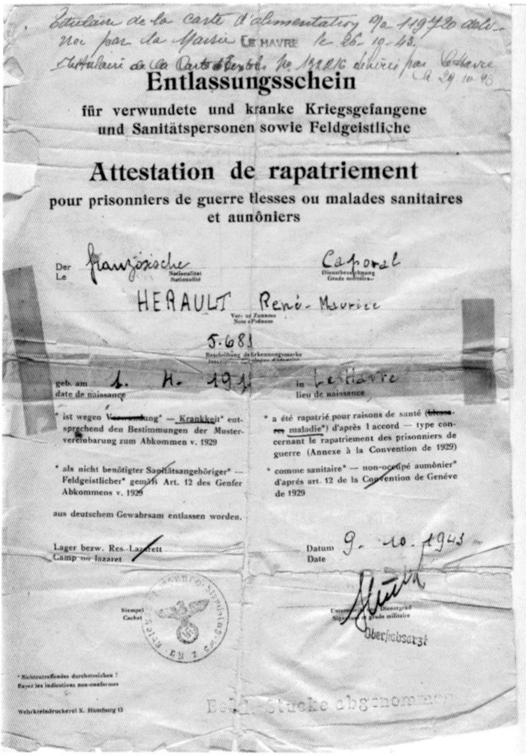

Titulaire de la carte d'alimentation No 14920 délivrée par la Mairie LE HAVRE le 26-10-43.
Titulaire de la Carte Textile No 13206 délivrée par Le Havre le 29.10.43

Entlassungsschein

für verwundete und kranke Kriegsgefangene
und Sanitätspersonen sowie Feldgeistliche

Attestation de rapatriement

pour prisonniers de guerre blesses ou malades sanitaires
et aumôniers

Der / Le Französische (Nationalität / Nationalité) Caporal (Dienstbezeichnung / Grade militaire)

HERAULT René-Maurice (Vor- u. Zuname / Nom et Prénom)

5.681 (Beschriftung der Erkennungsmarke / Inscription de la plaque d'identité)

geb. am / date de naissance 1. 4. 1911 in / lieu de naissance Le Havre

* ist wegen ~~Verwundung~~* — Krankheit* entsprechend den Bestimmungen der Mustervereinbarung zum Abkommen v. 1929

* a été rapatrié pour raisons de santé (~~blessure~~, maladie*) d'après l accord — type concernant le rapatriement des prisonniers de guerre (Annexe à la Convention de 1929)

* als nicht benötigter ~~Sanitätsangehöriger~~* — ~~Feldgeistlicher*~~ gemäß Art. 12 des Genfer Abkommens v. 1929

* ~~comme sanitaire* — non-occupé aumônier*~~ d'aprés art. 12 de la Convention de Genève de 1929

aus deutschem Gewahrsam entlassen worden.

Lager bezw. Res.-Lazarett / Camp ou lazaret

Datum / Date 9. 10. 1943

Stempel / Cachet

Unterschrift / Dienstgrad / Signature / grade militaire

Oberstabsarzt

* Nichtzutreffendes durchstreichen !
Rayez les indications non-conformes

Wehrkreisdruckerei X. Hamburg 13

Bekl.-Stucke abgenommen

A set of false papers in the name of R. Herault. With the help of these papers, a complete range of identity documents was able to be delivered via the mairie of Le Havre. These included the crucial certificate of residence in the 'forbidden' coastal zone (opposite page, bottom): an invaluable asset.

Titulaire de la carte d'alimentation No 17-7098 delivrée par la Mairie de Paris XVIe le 12-10-43
Titulaire de la Carte de Textiles No: 48612 delivrée par Paris XVIe le 15-10-43

Entlassungsschein

für verwundete und kranke Kriegsgefangene
und Sanitätspersonen sowie Feldgeistliche

Attestation de rapatriement

pour prisonniers de guerre blesses ou malades sanitaires
et aumôniers

Der / Le Französische (Nationalität / Nationalité) Caporal (Dienstbezeichnung / Grade militaire)

Malvalle Robert (Vor- und Zuname / Nom et Prénom)

16.007 (Beschriftung der Erkennungsmarke / Inscription de la plaque d'identité)

geb. am / date de naissance 11. 4. 1918 in / lieu de naissance Le Havre

* ist wegen ~~Verwundung~~* — Krankheit* entsprechend den Bestimmungen der Mustervereinbarung zum Abkommen v. 1929

* a été rapatrié pour raisons de santé (~~blessure~~, maladie*) d'après l accord — type concernant le rapatriement des prisonniers de guerre (Annexe à la Convention de 1929)

* als nicht benötigter ~~Sanitätsangehöriger*~~ — ~~Feldgeistlicher*~~ gemäß Art. 12 des Genfer Abkommens v. 1929

* comme sanitaire* — ~~non-occupé aumônier*~~ d'aprés art. 12 de la Convention de Genève de 1929

aus deutschem Gewahrsam entlassen worden.

Lager bezw. Res.-Lazarett / Camp ou lazaret

Datum / Date 2. 10. 1943

Cachet

Unterschrift / Dienstgrad / Signature / grade militaire

Oberstabsarzt

* Nichtzutreffendes durchstreichen!
Rayez les indications non-conformes

Wehrkreisdruckerei X. Hamburg 13

Bekl.-Stucke abgenommen

Another set of false repatriation papers attributed to R. Malvalle.

CERTIFICAT DE TRAVAIL Mod. 1
délivré sous la responsabilité de :

Monsieur ....
Qualité : ....
(l'Employeur indiquera son titre, la raison sociale et l'adresse de son Établissement)
....
....
....
A .... le 24 NOV 1943 1943
Signature et cachet du Responsable :

MAIRIE DU HAVRE Seine-Inférieure

J. 37280-43 (8) T. S. V. P.

Work permit.

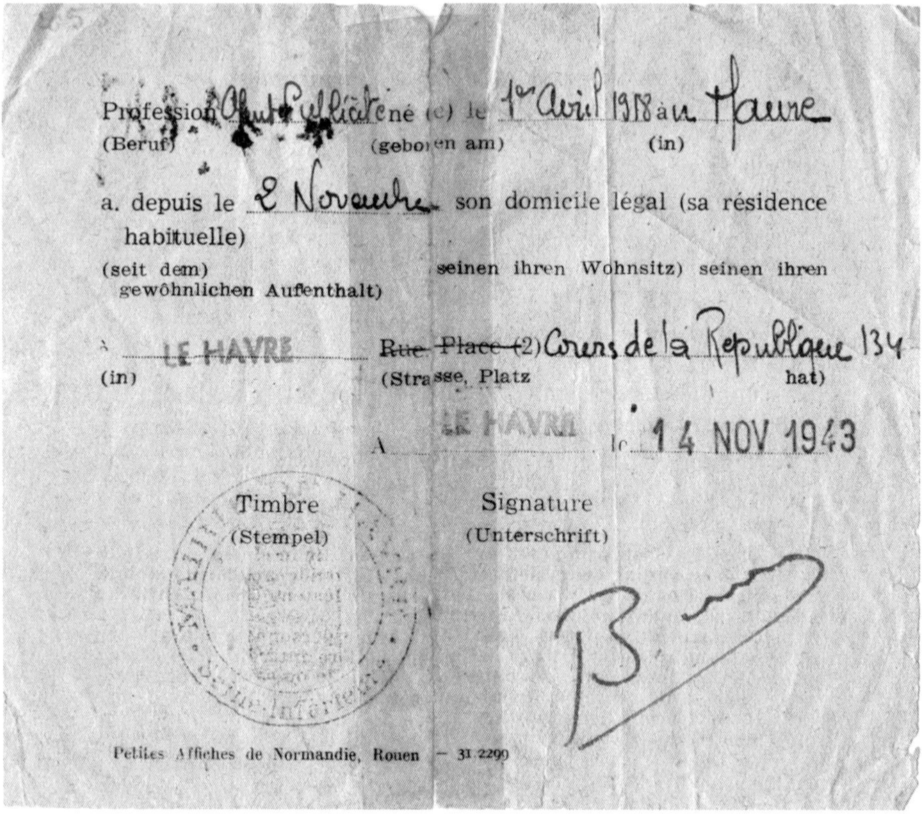

Profession Chef Publicité né (e) le 1er Avril 1918 au Havre
(Beruf) (geboren am) (in)

a. depuis le 2 Novembre son domicile légal (sa résidence habituelle)
(seit dem) seinen ihren Wohnsitz) seinen ihren gewöhnlichen Aufenthalt)

à LE HAVRE Rue Place (2) Cours de la Republique 134
(in) (Strasse, Platz hat)

A LE HAVRE le 14 NOV 1943

Timbre
(Stempel)

Signature
(Unterschrift)

Petites Affiches de Normandie, Rouen — 31 2299

Proof of residence.

Membership Card

Name Mortier R.

Address as in Club Register

Expiring 24.4.44 No. 1867.

Secretary.

Chesterfield Officers' Residential Club

8, Chesterfield Gardens, W.1.

Membership card for the Chesterfield Officers' Residential Club.

Marine parachutist training centre in 1940 - location unknown.

(Above) Parachute drop on 25 June 1944 at Sussac, the largest to take place in France. 72 Flying Fortresses dropped 864 containers of stores into Colonel Guingouin's territory.

(Left) Bob in London during the war.

Photo taken in Sussac July 1944. In front, left to right: Bob Maloubier, Radio Lannou (BRCA), J.C. Guiet (SOE), Jacques de Gueilis (SOE), Andre Simon (SOE), Jacques Dufour (SOE), Doctor MacKenzie (SOE). At the back, left to right: Colonel Charles (Maquis), Commandant Fernand (Maquis), Commandant Thomas (BRCA), Radio Lacouture (Maquis).

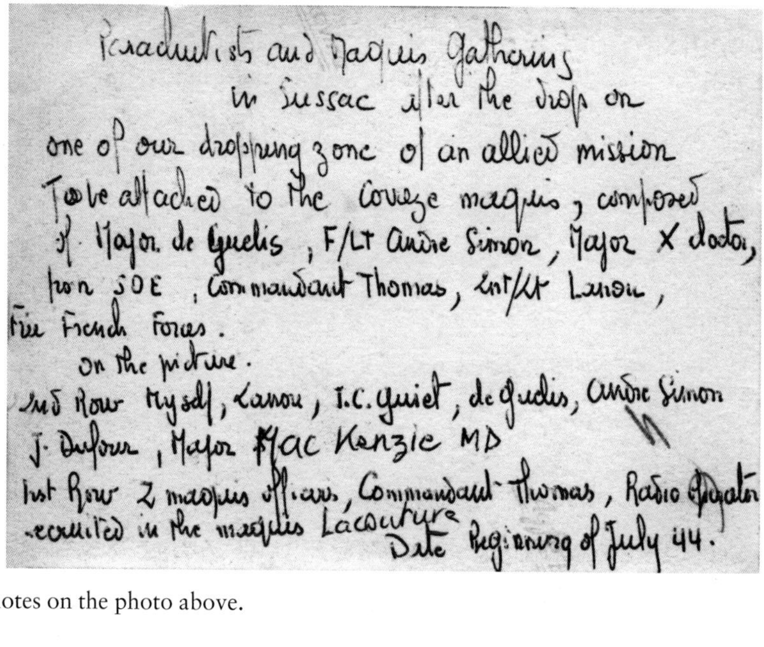

Parachutists and Maquis Gathering
in Sussac after the drop on
one of our dropping zone of an allied mission
To be attached to the Correze maquis, composed
of Major de Guelis, F/Lt Andre Simon, Major X doctor,
from SOE, Commandant Thomas, Ent/Lt Lanou,
Free French Forces.
On the picture.
2nd Row Myself, Lanou, J.C. Guiet, de Guelis, Andre Simon
J. Dufour, Major MacKenzie MD
1st Row 2 maquis officers, Commandant Thomas, Radio Operator
recruited in the maquis Lacouture
Date Beginning of July 44.

Bob's notes on the photo above.

Bob as Captain Robert Mortier in British uniform as a foreign officer.

(Above) Jean Claude Guiet receiving the Croix de Guerre, Phillipe Liewer and Bob are fourth and fifth from the left.

(Left) Bob receiving his Croix de Guerre.

(Left) Bob in uniform about town.

(Below) Bob in London after the war.

Picture of Bob taken by Max Danton in front of the Roll's Royce of one of his best friends, Edgar Bensoussan. All now deceased.

He stayed three weeks under Déricourt's leadership. Sent to a suspect rendezvous, his radio op, Agazarian, disappeared. On his return, Buck got rid of him. Where to, nobody knows.'

'You astonish me! The No. 2 of the service with knowledge of all its secrets, its agents, its circuits, their codes, going to play cat and mouse with the Gestapo? And if they trap him and make him sing that would mean the SOE in its entirety would fall!'

During the first days of spring in London, a light rain of bombs, nothing more. A devastating ack-ack defence and fighter raids at night cools the Luftwaffe's ardour. However, one evening, my district's station, Gloucester Road, is on fire and when I get back to my place, my landlady, an old girl, dry as a prune, yaps, 'Lieutenant Mortier, four unexploded bombs have been detected in the garden. Go down immediately to the shelters!'

She hates her French and Canadian lodgers, who are flippant about the blackout, skip their scheduled watches on the roof (with a supply of sand to put out incendiary bombs), bring home visitors of easy virtue, and – worst of all – waste water. I've barely got in my bath before I hear, 'Lieutenant, you're over your limit.' The limit is 8in of water, which doesn't even come up to my navel.

I groan, 'Your bombs, Miss Martins, can sort themselves out. I'm going to sleep.'

Hardly had I closed my eyes than she knocks on my door again. I grumble, 'I've just told you, Miss, that your bombs ...'

A male voice answers, 'It's not Miss Thingummy, it's Robert. I'm outside. I came back from Ciro's and found a pile of stones where my building was. A Kraut bomber and he didn't bungle it!'

So I share with Benoist – my spiritual father – my room, my razor, my toothbrush. 'I'm used to this now,' he jokes. 'A year ago, with my brother, my brother-in-law Wimille, and Grover Williams, an English pilot friend of mine, I put together a circuit. Worked well until the day the Gestapo got me. I found myself stuck in a front-wheel drive with three of these chaps on the boulevard des Italiens. It took a corner so tightly that the guy guarding me was thrown towards the opposite door. I managed to shoulder-barge the door open, rolled myself out on to the road and fled through the passage des Princes, where I beat the 100m record. Second mission – my wireless op – a crazy football fan, went to the matches with his radio strung on his bike! He was spotted and killed. I got away that time too.'

In the morning, I give him a shirt, socks and underpants.

'Thanks. I'll give them back to you after the war! Don't forget, on liberation go to the Automobile Club of France in place de la Concorde. I'll be there!'

Charles returns from Manchester enchanted: 'I'm converted to parachutes! Better still – at Ringway I recruited a "courier" for our future operations. D-Day, you know, we might often find ourselves separated. This way we can keep in touch.'

'What's he look like, your carrier pigeon?'

'You'll see him tomorrow, at the Studio Club.'

From the entrance of the Studio Club, a private club in Knightsbridge, you can see Harrods. Charles is leaning on his elbow at the piano bar, beside him, a young, petite woman, slim, in a simple and chic, black dress with a round neckline. Wavy chestnut hair surround her delicate face and high cheekbones. Charles smiles to himself: 'Here is our courier: Violette.'

She puts aside her long cigarette holder, stands on the tips of her toes and, in a cloud of Guerlain, kisses me on the cheek. The boss continues, 'We'll need her. Churchill is counting on us to prevent the Krauts from blowing up Le Havre port on D-Day. Buck has just informed me. Quays, locks and cranes are mined. Your objective, the cable exchange box, housed in a sewer under the Grande Poste footpath. Access through a manhole cover ...'

'Weighing 100 kilos – and under the eyes of the Krauts?'

'Mayer has everything worked out. You'll be disguised as a sewerman, helped by real sewermen. We'll look into all that later. Let's go and have dinner. Here, the South African wine is undrinkable. On the other hand, the director of the Regent Palace, a friend, filled up with Bordeaux before Dunkirk. The Saint-Estéphe is like velvet and half the cost it is in Paris.'

Violette is limping slightly. 'A sprain while parachute jumping at Ringway in December,' she explains. 'In plaster, too. Course interrupted for two months. A good thing, I guess, as it meant I met Charles.'

By the pale glimmer of the veiled street lamps we go back up Piccadilly. Suddenly, appearing out of the gloom, a woman accosts us. Platinum blonde, skirt split right up to her bum, balancing on stilettos. It's one of the streetwalkers who a short while ago did the summer season in London. The debacle of 1940 pinned her to this road paved with gold since the Yanks conquered it. She says with a fine Belleville accent, 'You want to make a foursome, darlings?'

'No thanks, they're too fat so I'm looking after them!' answered Violette, tit for tat.

'Shit, you slogging away, too? Excuse me, old thing, I'll leave you to it!'

Charles burst out laughing, 'Ah well, you've just earned your stripes!'

On 6 March, he tells us, 'I'm on for the next moon. You follow me in a month.'

A few days later, at Robert Benoist's farewell dinner, Violette shines in a midnight blue suit and a star's make-up. I say to her, 'You should be on the big screen!'

'For a while I thought so, too. I've had a few test shots at Arthur Rank. It seems one of my profiles didn't quite work out!'

When we were saying our goodbyes, Charles gives Benoist a little scolding, 'This third mission, Robert – at your age – is it a good idea?'

'At my age? The age of my arteries is 20, like you, little chap!'

One weekend, Violette's parents welcome us in their little home in Stockwell, a suburb in the south of London. Her mother, Reine, is plump, dark, with astonishing bright eyes. Her father, Charles Bushell, is a small dry man, all muscles and nerves, with thick black hair.

'I was driving a military lorry on the Somme in '16,' he recounts with a mocking smile. 'Going through the market in Pont Rémy, I saw her, Reine, 19 years old, a cracker! I almost crashed into a stall. We waited two years. We got married just at the end of the war. Result – Violette and her four brothers.'

He forgets to add that, as he has itchy feet, they were born on both sides of the Channel and alternate from one language to another, although he never could pronounce a word of French himself. On the other hand, he's a dedicated bodybuilder: exercises for the whole family, Violette serving balls to the boys.

At the end of the meal, Reine feels a troubling need to confide in someone so she takes me to one side: 'When Paris fell, *mon Dieu*, how I cried. 14 July, when the first Free French paraded before General de Gaulle, I said to Violette, "Go and invite one of these poor exiles to dinner. At our table, he'll be in a little bit of France." She came back with a handsome legionnaire, Etienne Szabó; his family is of Hungarian origin. Love at first sight on both sides! Got married five weeks later; lightning honeymoon before Etienne embarked with de Gaulle for Dakar in the month of August. Afterwards he was sent all over Africa, liberating Gabon, Eritrea and Syria ...'

'But how many months were they separated?'

'A year, Bob, a full year! Interminable for them both – so madly in love with one another. So, finally, after taking Damascus, he came back. It was like a second honeymoon, they were overjoyed ... but also felt let down: just one week! Then he set off again to war. So, to be worthy of him, she joined up. When he was under siege at Bir Hakeim, she was pregnant. Crazy with joy, he only dreamed of seeing his child being born. The War Office telephone, "He's coming." She made herself really beautiful, waited for him, days, weeks, months. Tania, her daughter in her arms – finally a letter! "We regret to inform you ..." Etienne had been killed at dawn during the assault at El Alamein. He was buried in the sand there, simply. A Legionnaire dies light, you know ...

'Violette remained shut away at home for months, devastated, without words, her daughter in her arms. She refused to see anyone at all. Finally, she let herself be convinced to re-enter the world, to mix in the whirlwind of the war years. She saw her friends again, made new friends. And so she went out with administration officers, Harry and Jack, full of life and fun – until they were sent to somewhere in Italy.

'Some time later she was summoned to the Ministry of Pensions. Just like so many war widows, she thought to herself. An elegant gentleman welcomed her, kept chatting until he said that her profile corresponded to a certain category of personnel for a certain "very special" service. Would she consider taking part? Coming back down to earth she replied "Yes!" before he could finish his sentence.'

On 7 March, Charles meets us again, 'I'm leaving this evening for Hasell's Hall. The next night I shall drop into Normandy. In a month's time, it'll be your turn.'

On 12 March in the morning, a loud knocking at my door, I hit back, 'There's no alert, Miss Martins! Leave me in p ...'

'It isn't Miss Martins, Bob, it's Charles!'

He comes in, white as a sheet, his face tense and says, 'Here, read this!' waving a text in capital letters full of typos:

TOR 1028-12 MARS1944.

BLUFF CHECK. STOP – CHECK REEL. STOP – NR 73. NOUVELLES DE ROUEN : XLAUDE MALRAUX DISPARU PNESONS ARRETE PAR GESTAPO. STOP. OPERATEUR RADIO PIERRE ARRET. STOP. SI CLETENT ENCORE AVEC VOUS. NE LE ENVOYER PAS. STOP. DOFTEUR ARRETE. STOP. DIX HUIT TONNES D'ARMES RAMASSEES PAR POLIFE. STOP. PNESONS CECI DU ARRESTATION D'UN FHEF SCTION QUI A DONNE ADRESSES. ADIEU.

So Claude, Pépé, and our old doctor have been taken! Without counting Georges Philippon, because the 18 tons of arms mentioned couldn't have been seized anywhere except from his garage! And the saga doesn't end there!

'This message is signed "MacIntosh Red", code name for the radio op for Roland Malraux, in the Dordogne, emphasises Charles. Catherine, Claude's companion, slipped through the net; she managed to join Roland, afer travelling 600km. I was supposed to jump directly into the arms of Alie, who seized the message slips, Peter's codes, the DZ maps. A German operator was playing the keys on his radio set.'

'And Buck didn't notice something amiss? We were taught that a radio op's touch was recognisable among thousands!'[2]

'That's what they say. So, the listening service signalled him one day that the touch of Norman, Prosper's radio op, was hesitant, confused, as if he was sending under constraint. He had even omitted his security checks. Buck just ignored it; he even explained it to Penelope, his secretary: "Rubbish! He's just under pressure, that boy. A real gentleman like him would commit suicide rather than submit." And, for a month, the SD has taken delivery of our weapons, money and even men, completely free. God keep us from valiant knights of Oxford! As for our network, it's well and truly infiltrated! I'm going to take stock in situ.'

'You're crazy! Your portrait will be plastered all over every street corner!'

'Ah well, I'll disguise myself as Peter Pan and I'll make use of a Tinkerbell.'

2 The security checks correspond to the typing errors left deliberately by the agents. Messages without these checks were interpreted as having been sent by the Germans or under their control.

12

The Late Salesman

The life that I have
Is all that I have
And the life that I have
Is yours.
The love that I have
Of the life that I have.
Is yours and yours and yours.

Violette merely had to recite this verse a single time for it to remain engraved upon her heart forever. It isn't a banal poem but her code poem, key to a cipher for her personal messages. The cipher is an exact science: a single letter in error makes the message indecipherable. Now, our Violette has an irritating tendency to spell French words in English. Result: she produces gobbledegook. Charles sent her straight away to Leo Marks, the crypto genius of His Majesty's Secret Service. Leo was too puny and short-sighted to be a combatant, much less a fighter pilot. But specifically, figures were his thing; the son of a second-hand bookseller of great renown, he teaches chess and is an addict of pure maths and rare editions. When he sees 'this little brunette thing full of mischief and delightful smile' appear, he falls under her charm. Without reflection, he suggests as a cipher base this poem from deep within his heart and which he hadn't shared with a living soul. Almost miraculously, the French words form themselves on Violette's lips:

La vie qui est mienne
Est tout ce que je possède

Et cette vie qui est mienne
Est à toi.
L'amour qui est mien
Dans la vie qui est mienne
Est à toi, à toi, rien qu'à toi.
Cers vers, elle les chiffre aussitôt, à la perfection.

With these verses she makes a perfect cipher immediately. 'Surely, it's a lucky break!' exclaims Leo. 'Let's try the next one.'

A sleep I shall have
A rest I shall have
Yet death will be but a pause
For the peace of my years
In the long, green grass
Will be yours, and yours and yours.

Vi translates line by line, without hesitation:

Me viendra le sommeil
Me viendra le repos
Mais la mort ne sera qu'une pause
Car la paix de ces ans
Dans l'herbe verte et haute
Sera à toi, à toi, rien qu'à toi.

She feels as though she has been transported away, far away to a corner of the desert, where under a mound of sand now erased in the desert wind, and with neither epitaph nor verse, lies Etienne. Holding back the tears, she murmurs, 'Who wrote it?'

'I don't remember.'

Leo would never have admitted that these words had come to him of their own accord as he embraced the love of his life while she lay dying in his arms.

On 5 April 1944, a Lysander takes off from Tangmere, carrying Staunton and his Tinkerbell, Violette, of course. The day before, she embraces Tania to her heart, her daughter of eighteen months, humming: 'Maman will come back quickly and she'll bring you a dolly from Paris, imagine that!' Tania smiles at her, opening her big eyes. Wonder of wonders – no false departure this time. The plane lands on the LZ without incidence, not far from Chartres. When they get out, Charles and Violette are embraced by Rémy Clément, who has succeeded Déricourt. Two hours by bus, they get out at Gare d'Orsay, where Violette bumps into her first *Feldgrau* and doesn't bat an eyelid.

Within a week, she becomes accustomed to the tide of grey-green, hideous banners marring the most beautiful façades in Paris, the vélo-taxis, the ration cards, the black market and the yellow stars that the Jews must wear.

'Up and ready for your mission,' Charles concludes.

He has already described her mission to her, 'As Buck has decreed that I am forbidden to stay in Rouen, I will stay in Paris and you will be my eyes and ears in Normandy.'

He escorts her to Gare Saint-Lazare as far as the half-Wehrmacht, half-French police cordon filtering the travellers. From the quay, Violette turns and waves to him one last time.

I spend four weeks on courses at Special Training School No. 17 – an institute for higher learning in industrial demolition – taught by a Colonel G.T. Rheam, ex-director of London Electricity, and a team of top-class engineers. From dawn to dusk, they stuff my head with the industrial structure of a modern nation, enumerating everything that such a nation counts as sources of energy, factories and machines, then I'm taught to dissect them. I visit blast furnaces, coking plants, steel works, power stations, railway stations and locks. I learn how to dynamite anything; I burn plastic by the kilo, all day long. Each night we execute a simulated attack. Clouds of dust caused by detonations haunt my sleep. I get the feeling that my ears will never stop humming. In Brickendonbury, plastic is all one ever dreams of, speaks of and smells.

The day of my return to London, I get a telephone call, 'They're back!'

As soon as I arrive at Knightsbridge Studio Club, Violette – she must have been watching for my arrival – performs a dance step that makes her beautiful dress in fine red and black tartan bob and dip around her. A moment of bravery in a French haute couture house, I didn't doubt. Women in uniform or dreary outfits devoured her with their eyes. I murmur to her, 'Where did you steal this masterpiece?'

'Chez Molyneux, rue Royale. I would never have imagined owning something like this ... And Charles bought me three!'

'I wonder what Vera will have to say when she finds out!'

'She already knows,' cuts in Charles. 'And you, do you know who was the director of Molyneux before the war? No? Well, it was Yeo Thomas, the "White Rabbit" who, I've just learnt, has been taken by the Gestapo during his third or fourth mission. Violette, for her part, fulfilled her contract so well that she has earned her ill-gotten goods.'

'Sure, but if you were to tell me what's been going on down there, that'd be good?'

'Ah well, Salesman is dead – 100 of our lot have been arrested, among them Peter, Claude, Mayer, the Boulangers. However, my landlords, the Franchterres and yours, the Bouchers, as well as Evensen and the members of your team have not been apprehended, with the exception of Philippon, who was among the first to be picked up. A member of the Dieppe cell may have brought a spy to Micheline's, our dead letter drop in rue des Carmes in Rouen. The Gestapo set up a police trap.'

'How did you find that out?'

'This Mata Hari you see before you. On leaving Paris, she seduced a major in the Rouen *Kommandantur*.'

'Stop. I did not seduce him. He took my case without asking me, and as my carriage was full to bursting, he offered me a seat in the Wehrmacht officers' compartment. An unhoped for piece of luck to travel in total safety, isn't that so? The major, Karl, a *Junker* of the old school, spoke such good French that, fearing he might question my accent, I hardly said three words. These gentlemen plied me with chocolate and cigarettes. I refused the Schnapps. On arriving it proved really difficult to distance myself from my faithful admirer. I promised to call him. He's still waiting.'

The next day she posted herself in front of Saint Maclou, very close to the lodgings run by René Boucher, my 'landlord'. When he came out she intercepted him. He took her to the Francheterres, who took her to the Evensens, who told her that Denise Desvaux was picked up at her home along with Peter; that she had played innocent swearing they knew nothing of this lodger who had simply been introduced to them by mutual friends. The major who had interrogated her had believed her, or pretended to.

'He was a gentleman,' she reported. 'He told me in no uncertain terms that, "we no longer shoot the men nor imprison the women."' In fact, it was Karl, Violette's admirer.

'In short,' concluded Charles, 'your mission was a walk in the park.'

'You're joking? During the return flight, I really thought my last hour had arrived, remember!'

On the departure LZ, near Châteauroux, two Lysanders landed one after the other. Dumesnil put Violette in one and Charles in the other. 'Never put all your eggs in one basket, eh!' While Charles' plane flew off, the engine of Violette's Lizzie started spluttering; the pilot struggled with the throttle lever until he turned round. However, this misfiring troubled him to the point that he flew straight over the town! A remake of our flight over Angers. Fireworks, racket up there in the sky. Violette was shaken about, thrown in every direction. She hit her forehead on a corner and was knocked out.

'When I came round the Lysander was at a standstill on a landing strip equipped with lights. Suddenly, I noticed a tall, blonde German standing under the wing. He motioned for me to get down. Then I realised the awful truth – hit by flak, the plane had landed on the first airfield available, a German one! I thought about Etienne and fury overcame me, he would never take me alive, this Jerry! Sure of himself in front of a weak woman, he hadn't even drawn his pistol! I jumped on him grabbing for his throat. Taken by surprise, incapable of deflecting my blows, he hurled "My God! You're crazy?" with such an inimitable Oxford accent that I stopped to get a better look at him. It was my pilot, head bare. In my defence, I had never seen him except helmeted, in full flying suit, and in the dark! The plane had indeed been hit, a shell burst in a tyre; he had to make a forced landing which, on one burst wheel, resulted in a ground loop spin! The pilot had jumped from the cockpit to go and sort out the damage. I had seen nothing – I had been woozy for a couple of hours, at least. We weren't on enemy soil but at Tangmere! But it's just a joke compared to what our people caught by the Gestapo are suffering!'

'We're with them all in spirit,' murmured Charles. 'And there's some truth in what your Karl said to Denise. We'll see them again. But show Bob your war trophy.'

She unrolls a small poster. Two sinister-looking faces and a message: 'X ... called Clément – X ... called Mollier', with a reward on their heads from the 3eme brigade mobile, a French anti-terrorist unit attached to the Gestapo. The image doesn't flatter us but there is a resemblance.

'I pulled them off a noticeboard at Rouen station. The walls of the town were covered with them. Buck was absolutely right to keep you out of there, Charles! I give you this poster as a gift, Bob. And then a lighter for you.

In Paris, I did some shopping: some earrings for Vera, a cigarette case for Buck and a lovely dress for Tania. I cleaned out the Trois Quartiers. And before that I had a staggering encounter. Who did I see coming out of rue Saint Florentin – you'll never guess ... Jack Peters, one of the two officers I was going out with in London less than a year ago!

'My foot! I recognised him immediately, even disguised as a middle-class Frenchman, blouson and Basque beret. Better still, he winked at me, then afterwards when he brushed past me, he whispered "God bless you" and disappeared.

'If you're sure you're right, your Peter is an Intelligence Service agent, that's all!'

'Let's get on,' cut in Staunton. 'Salesman is dead, Bob and I are blown in Normandy. At the present time Buck no longer needs the teams that have been put together. Similar, the circuits operating in France only ask him for assistants, saboteurs, wireless ops, especially wireless ops. Today, we are unemployed – it's every man for himself!'

Violette remains impassive. 'Sod that! We are a team, I feel it, I know it!'

'God is listening, girl. While you're waiting, Orchard Court is about to propose a new mission to each of you. And you ought to accept it!'

I was called to a meeting first. Buck gave me his pastoral smile. 'Hello Mortier. Do you know the north of France? Laon, for instance?' – he pronounces it *Laounne* – 'No? So much the better, you won't be recognised. I suggest you parachute in blind. Your liaisons will be assured by a radio op shared by several networks. You'll only have to recruit a group of partisans and, on D-Day, as their leader you will sabotage the communications links. A mission tailored for you! Think about it for a week, no longer.'

Think about it? The north of France, the forbidden zone, even more sensitive than the Atlantic Wall, is already crawling with Nazis. Imagine it on D-Day ... as for depending on a joint wireless op, that's multiplying the risks by ten! I salute Buck, smile fixed to my face and I run to confide in Charles. He comes out with his habitual humour, 'He's not tailoring a mission for you, he's digging you a grave! At least demand your own wireless operator!'

As for Violette, she says: 'Don't fret, you'll cut it!'

Five days later, Charles calls me, 'Violette was right! It'll be confirmed to you tomorrow at ten o'clock at the Orchard.'

That morning, Buckmaster smiles broadly at us all, 'Here's a mission that fits you like a glove: in the Limousin, a certain Colonel Guingouin, who's been dubbed "First Resister of France", commands a veritable army and deserves our interest. Here, just read his biography!'

Orphan of a father who died in the Great War, and a ward of the state, Georges Guingouin was a hard-working boy and an avid reader of Proudhon, Engels and Karl Marx. A diehard communist teacher, he fought well in 1940. He withdrew before being captured, got back to his village, dug out a hideaway – 'like the Boulanger brothers, see?' – 'Comrades' joined him. However, he 'deviated' at the time of the indestructible German–Soviet friendship; he dared to take on Vichy and the occupier while Jacques Duclos, leader of the Party, implored the Nazis to let *L'Humanité* be published. At the beginning of 1944, the 'Préfet Rouge' commands several thousand badly equipped partisans, because, from Moscow where he took refuge, the secretary general of the Communist Party, Maurice Thorez – who deserted in the first months of the war – is spreading the word that de Gaulle is the sworn enemy of the communists, as much so as Hitler, and they should be wary of him. Consequently, the Marxist chiefs of war refuse to be 'infiltrated' by the agents of France Libre, who will be sure to land in among the containers. However, without sponsorship, no parachute drops! The lion's share instead goes to the Armée Secrète, reputed to be apolitical, and the Organisation de Résistance de l'Armée.

'In order to get his hands on the weapons that he claims de Gaulle is denying him, Guingouin has made a play for us,' explains Buckmaster. 'He vanished! And suddenly a Colonel Charles appeared on the scene, like you Staunton! He poses as the head of a "neutral" Maquis willing to collaborate with the English, that's to say, with us in SOE, but not with the FFL. This Charles, one of those faithful to Guingouin, of course, is supposed to be a smokescreen, but we can see straight through it. Guingouin dreamt this con up to grab some weapons behind the general's back, so he wouldn't have to worry about the Gaullists trying to deflect his troops from the final objective: to take power in France after liberation!'

'But how can he be unaware that Koenig is actually chief of the French Forces of the Interior,' says Charles, astonished. 'He heads the Résistance organisations, the agents of the BCRA, SOE and OSS [Office of Strategic Services] and thus has the right to scrutinise the logistics: provisioning, transports and such like. And let's not forget above all that the money weapons and aircraft are all dispensed by Churchill. Of course, OSS would like go it alone but it isn't autonomous yet. De Gaulle owns nothing. Have faith in Churchill, whose hobby horse is the subversive war, to settle the distribution. All that Koenig, an unconditional supporter of the general, can do is give his opinion.'

'Therefore, Staunton, from your arrival, you get around the angelic digressions of Colonel Charles and you deal with Guingouin. You evaluate his numbers, and you order from us whatever is needed to arm them properly. You, Bob, take charge of training, guerrilla activity and management of parachute drops. And believe me, you won't be unemployed! By the way, Maingard, the head of our circuit in Indre, bordering Haute Vienne, has an inside source – a young man from the region who has his contacts within the Maquis. Jacques Dufour. He has even been attributed the commission of sous-lieutenant. He will take care of the reception with a 100 per cent British team near Sussac, a village about 40km from Limoges, you ...'

I cut in, 'That's fine for Violette and Staunton but I've got an accent!'

'Fine, I'll make you Canadian. Your wireless op is a young American from OSS of 19. He is of French origin; Jean-Claude Guiet is his name. He was studying French at Harvard.'

To test this novice, Charles invited him to lunch in Soho at Rose's, a small café owned by a little Breton woman who serves lavish steaks, without ration tickets! This is an admissions test in the form of an ambush – the steak is horse meat! Now, to take a bite from the rump steak of Man's finest conquest is a sacrilege both for the English and the Yanks. The young American arrives chez Rose, freshly ironed, teeth white from chewing gum. Violette says as an aside to me, 'He's a rather fine kid. Let's see if he fits the bill.'

The 'fine kid' eats his sirloin without flinching.

Jean-Claude grew up in Jura. In 1940 his family emigrated to the United States. In 1943, a headhunter from OSS netted this very young francophone GI. He followed the same training course as we did but in the American STS.

At a bourgeois house in Wigmore Street, not far from Orchard Court, the French Section has opened a lodging house for agents: bedrooms, snack-bar and a lounge where we can meet up in the evening. There we play pontoon (later to become blackjack in Las Vegas), gin rummy and poker. The French Canadian agents of the section are from all parties. Among them, the d'Artois, a case of love at first sight in the STSs, marriage expected. They dream of liberating the 'Old Country' hand-in-hand. I disabused them, 'I've known others just like you, kiddy-winks. Don't have any illusions!'

Violette's gaze is filled with melancholy when it rests upon Sonia d'Artois, so pretty, hardly 19, the age that she was when she and Etienne ... She nestles Tania's head in the crux of her shoulder and hugs her tight. Tania never leaves her side. She is a doll, only 2, hair done the English way that she shakes like small bells. She climbs under the table, babbling. Every man who bounces her her up and down on his knees and stuffs her with sweets she calls 'papa'.

The conducting officer for Jean-Claude is Ted Fraser, a great beanpole of a confederate captain with a caricature of an accent. In London, he's lost. Of France he knows nothing, especially not the language. Of Paris he only knows the Eiffel Tower – as a postcard.

OSS has no francophone cadres to speak of! Thanks to President Wilson who, in 1919, decreed that it was unworthy of an American gentleman to listen at doors and so abolished his secret services. Without antennae, America didn't catch a whiff of the Nazi peril. Only in 1939 did Roosevelt charge William Donovan, one of his pals from law school who became a millionaire, to put together a spy network pronto. Donovan, nicknamed 'Wild Bill', was a good choice. The most highly decorated hero of the Great War, he was connected with Claude Dansey, the soul of the Intelligence Service. Nevertheless, in 1944, OSS still hadn't caught up with SOE, so contented itself with putting agents at the disposition of Churchill's 'fourth arm'. It only parachuted two or three teams into France from Algiers, and without great success.

Violette goes to relax for a few days at Wormelow, a hamlet near Hereford, a medieval town where she spent a part of her childhood, 'When I was little, I dreamt that I would ride through it wearing a medieval headdress on a beautiful white palfrey!'

Charles wishes her happy but short holidays, 'Go and play Lady Godiva if you wish. However, be ready to jump off your nag at the first call. You've got a plane to catch!'

13

12

No D-Day for Das Reich!

One evening in June, overcast and windy, we take to the air – not aboard a Halifax of the RAF but a Liberator of a US Army Air Force squadron formed over a few months for clandestine parachute drops. Its teams had already adopted the nickname of 'carpetbaggers', from the name given to the first candidates for election sent into the English rotten boroughs to tackle the teething problems there.

Charles grumbles, 'Bad omens! These tender feet are going to let us loose over the Alps – or in Spain!'

'Don't cry, it's a miracle we're on board!' retorts Violette.

She's right. After having lunch we're knocking the ball about on the tennis court of Hasell's Hall, where we were staying ... when the net suddenly disintegrated in an apocalyptic racket! A reddish cloud envelopes us. When it dissipates, only a crater is left on the court and, at the bottom end, a cylinder wrapped in steel wire and string. Violette shouts out, 'A bomb!'

'A duralumin bomb that didn't explode? More like an auxiliary tank, my girl! And let loose by one of those f****** American fighters that just flew over us. A few metres further and we would all have passed over! Enough tennis for today. Let's go and play ping-pong!'

Our B-24 rises into the air, pierces one layer of clouds and then a second. Progress: two nights previously we had to turn back and land!

Violette suggests a game of pontoon. The game drags on because the aircraft dances about and the cards slide all over the place. She wins the game just as an order is shouted, 'Kit up!'

The trap opens up, a squall sweeps in. At reduced speed, the bomber sways, veers then veers again, still turning. Charles makes for the cockpit, shouting at us, 'I'm going for news!'

A few moments later, he rejoins us disillusioned: 'We're over the right DZ. No beacons. We're going back.'

The calm of old troops. Parachute under their heads as a pillow, everyone hunkers down in a corner and dozes off. When, on the approach to Tempsford, the engines decelerate, the flaps creak, it seems to me that I only dozed for a few minutes. I say to Charles, who's getting out of the cockpit, 'In this dirty weather, you couldn't've seen much!'

'Yes, I could – through gaps in the clouds, I noticed a fair amount of wake on the sea.'

'The navy, for sure. It's on permanent Channel patrol, you know!'

It takes a matter of half an hour to reach the manor and then our bed. Charles, Jean-Claude and I occupy the little dormitory, Violette a private bedroom. The day is hardly dawning when someone knocks on our door and a voice calls, 'Seven o'clock. Up, gentlemen!'

Charles thunders, 'But we didn't ask to be woken!'

'Sorry, Sir, there's a note on your door, "Wake up call without fail at 7 a.m.!"'

'I get it! It's that she-ass, Violette playing tricks! She'll pay for this!'

Two hours later, the she-ass enters noisily shouting, 'This time it's not a joke! The ...'

Her words are cut off. She beats a retreat under a torrent of curses, pillows and boots while crying out, 'It's true! I swear to you on Tania's head ...'

We finally wake up at midday. Hasell's Hall is in turmoil. At the bar round after round is being drunk. The Allies landed in Normandy at dawn! The newspapers bear huge headlines screaming 'D-DAY!'

On this longest, most celebrated day of the twentieth century, 140,000 men led the charge on the sands of France, 5,000 ships ploughed the Channel, 2,000 aircraft flew over it, among them one unarmed Liberator in which ... we hit the deck and slept.

This 'Day', I lived through it ... and saw absolutely nothing!

On the night of June 7, I'm hanging out under the stars crooning 'I'll be Around', a Mills Brothers' tune that Violette hums all day long. She had jumped first, behind Charles; Jean-Claude and I were dropped on the second pass. Voices can be heard from the ground. A profusion of lamps, torches and headlights pierce the darkness. Discretion, thanks a lot! Let's hope the Germans aren't patrolling the area!

Suddenly, between two valleys I can distinguish a clear patch – and what looks like lapping waves. I quickly review in my mind the sequence of actions I need to take to avoid drowning should I land in the water: get out of the harness, hang by the straps, let go of everything on contact with the surface so the parachute doesn't become a shroud. The combined pick and shovel, pistol, munitions, compass and first aid box are so much ballast. But it is rising too fast towards me, this pool. Without the time to even lift a finger, I am swallowed up – by the high wheat, which, swaying in the breeze under the moonbeams, looked like waves!

Men in leather jackets drippng in shoulder belts and bands of cartridges throw themselves on me, lifting me up, embracing me. A big bloke with a long angular face under wavy black hair comes up to me, 'I'm Jacques Dufour.'

Charles and Violette follow him. A retinue of Maquisards pushes us towards a line of black tractions that in town were only known as the Gestapo's vehicles. We hurtle at top speed, lights blazing, along a winding road: Tyres howl, gears clash, breaks squeal. Behind, bumper to bumper, a procession of cars follows right on our tail. Charles sighs in my ear, 'In Rouen we only had the Krauts to fear! Here, death awaits at every S-bend!'

Coming out of a more or less controlled skid, we come to a stop in a cloud of dust and against a shop window.

'Do you always drive so fast with all lights blazing?' comments Charles evenly to the driver.

'You think so? Yet, this evening, I kept my foot off the floor so as not to frighten the little lady! As for the headlights, it's months since the Jerries last set foot in the place.'

A smiling woman in an apron comes out of the shop, 'Welcome to Sussac! I am Madame Ribiéras. You're lodging at my place.'

A crowd of Maquisards follows us into the grocer's without ceremony. When Violette climbs out of her overalls and appears in a casual suit, emerging as if from a chrysalis, she's a hit. Jean-Claude throws an antenna across the shelves and keys a message of safe arrival.

In the very early morning, we prepare to greet the 'authorities'. A reedy man dressed in linen emblazoned with five stripes makes his entry, 'I'm Colonel Charles, head of the Maquis and ...'

All smiles, my major cuts in, 'Of which Colonel Guingouin is the big boss ... Delighted to meet you!'

'Colonel Guingouin? No, he isn't ... By the way, do you know him?'

'Of course. Who, in London, doesn't recognise the first résister of France? My mission is to get up to date with him ...'

'But I can very well ...'

'Sorry, I have my orders.'

For the sake of peace and quiet, the colonel grumbles that he 'will try' to get in touch with Guingouin. 'But that will be difficult, he moves constantly from place to place, you understand!' Yet, he authorises me to familiarise the Maquisards with our modern arms. The first stage: a clearing full of swarthy men wearing red scarves. Desperados of the International Brigade, like at Matifou! My 'airborne' carbine with a folding butt, my Colt .38 and the Marlin machine gun fascinate them. They only have obsolete Lebels, a few Stens and a tired-looking French 24/28 light machine gun. They're strung along an improvised shooting range covered with bottles in shards and grand-cru labels.

'They come from the wine cellars of collabos' châteaux,' explains their *jefe*. 'Don't worry, we already drank them, *hombre*!' He only lets me leave after having clasped my hand three or four times to his chest and giving me crates of these venerable bottles. Standing before one of them, Charles goes into raptures: 'A Napoleon Fine – 120 years old! Must kneel before it.'

'Guingouin isn't on the move,' Dufour reveals to us, 'but holed up in La Villa, his HQ, a hamlet about 3km from Sussac! Charles is his eye on the ground, you see! Le Grand is going to stand back a bit, believe me. Gives him the time to check you're who you say you are, English, not Gaullists – and to obtain the green light from the Party!'

On the other hand, many Maquisards came to see the 'English'. Charles makes a face when confronted by the riot of stripes they're wearing. Dufour defends them, 'Do you see graduates of Saint-Cyr here? They sit on their arse in front of their fire yowling: "*Vive le* Maréchal!". The squaddies who are going to be killed in their stead nicked their stripes. Natural, don't you think?'

The next day I do the rounds looking for a field good enough to be a DZ. On my return, Violette's sombre expression puzzles me, 'Something wrong, Vi?'

'No, nothing. Well, yes ...'

In the afternoon, she had gone out on to the village square after sending her coded messages. At that moment, in a cloud of dust, a lorry stopped in front of the church. Some Maquisards placed a bundle rolled in a tarpaulin down on the paving stones. Housewives came forward and lifted a piece of the tarpaulin, revealing a livid, bloody face. The curé appeared at once, tracing huge signs of the cross in the air, and then said to Violette, 'Again a poor child dies for nothing! Ah, these stupid accidents which kill more than the Germans do, I've seen so much of it! Just think, they drive around, machine guns on their knees and on the fenders of lorries driven at ungodly speeds, skidding and ending up in ditches. The machine guns go off by accident. It's me who buries them!'

At dinner, even Charles is delighted to uncork his century-old Fine but doesn't manage to cheer her up. 'Look, just taste some of this nectar, my girl! Tomorrow be seeing everything through rose-tinted specs on your trip!'

Tomorrow, 10 June, she has to get to Pompadour, a market town in Corrèze held by the Armée Secrète. From there she will establish contact with Nestor, head of the circuit covering Corrèze and Dordogne. To reach Pompadour, some 50km away to the south-west, she needs to cross the Nationale Paris–Toulouse route. That bothers Charles. He badgers Dufour several times, 'It's a prime north–south main route! Are you certain that the Germans don't use it?'

'Affirmative, *mon Commandant*! I often cross this RN20 through Salon-la-Tour, which straddles it. It's my hometown, born there, all the inhabitants know me! Any hitches, they'd warn me, see!'

'Shouldn't you do a quick reconnaissance first?'

'Useless! The Fritz, the Milice and the GMRs haven't risked going there for months.'

'The GMRs, what's that?' asks Jean-Claude.

'Mobile gendarmes who back up the Germans, although less and less. Last year, one of their sections delivering ration cards to Sussac fell into Guingouin's hands. He sent them back to Limoges, naked! Their colleagues mounted an ambush on the route, killed three Maquisards and got two prisoners. The Maquisards waited for them on the way back and killed seven of them! Since 6 June they have realised which way the wind is blowing; they're deserting, joining the Maquis.'

Charles gives up, 'Fine! But don't drive like these mad buggers! Don't bring her back to me rolled in a tarpaulin!'

At 6 a.m., her cup of coffee in her hand, Violette strikes a model pose, back arched, legs akimbo. She slips on her gabardine suit: 'Less practical than trousers for running in Maquis country! But in London they told me "French women don't wear trousers, you'll draw attention to yourself."'

'Don't worry, you'll be a sensation in Pompadour!' grins Charles, who, addressing Dufour, adds to his recommendations, 'You've got a spare wheel, a jack, enough petrol? And drive slowly!'

Violette reaches her arm out to Charles and then Jean-Claude, then me. When the traction takes off, her Sten on her knees, she gives us a big smile, throwing us kisses.

We spend the day in the countryside seeking isolated houses. Colonel Charles had assured us that he was well protected from bad surprises from the Milice, GMRs and Germans by a network of PTT telephone operators, sounded the alarm as soon as they even blinked, but my Charles had grumbled: 'Young women telephonists as safeguards, I don't think much to that! So, one false note and we're caught with our pants down! I quite simply apply Beaulieu's teachings: to live happy, let's live hidden – and let everyone do their own thing.'

For him and Jean-Claude, he chooses an isolated cottage. Further on he comes to a halt in front of a a picturesque mill straddling the Combrade, which gives out a nauseating stink. He doesn't take exception to it. The miller's wife, a middle aged matron in full bloom, enlightens us: 'As there's no more grain to mill, we've taken to maggot farming instead, for the fishermen.'

Under a sloping roof of sheet metal broiling in the sun hang some very, very old quarters of beef crawling with waves of white larvae. The stench is appalling.

'It's perfect!' exclaims Charles delighted. The Fritz would never come looking for you here!'

'You soon get used to the smell,' adds the good woman. 'Look at my little things – three kiddies with pink cheeks, they don't look unhappy, do they? The cooking, that's what does it; it's my forté!'

For supper, Madame Ribiéras serves us the delicacies of the country, tender potatoes simmering in an ocean of double cream under a golden crust. As she digs her knife in, a car brakes noisily outside. A young man covered in mud crashes in. Out of breath, he babbles, 'I'm Barriaud, a childhood friend of Dufour, I live in Croisille, 6km from here. As I was going to Salon-la-Tour, he stopped to give me a lift this morning in front of my dad's general store …'

He had tied his bike somehow or other to the flank of the traction. Dufour was driving carefully. They had driven through hamlets, La Porcherie then Lamongerie, from where the road descends at a gentle slope towards a tunnel under the Paris–Toulouse railway, at least a kilometre from Salon. From there, a straight line, then a curve. A farmyard hides the first houses of the village.

On coming out of the curve, Dufour cries out: '*Merde*! The Fritz!'

Posted at the entrance to the market town, a helmeted sentry, machine gun around his neck, lifts his arm at the sight of the Citroën. Without losing his cool, Dufour waves in friendly fashion to the German while whistling between his teeth. 'Run, I'll cover you.'

'I pushed out the door and sent my bike flying,' went on Barriaud. 'I ran like crazy towards the tunnel. Bullets were whistling. I hid in a thicket. The Fritz continued to fire for a long time, a very long time. I heard the sound of tracked vehicles along the route, then an isolated burst of rifle fire. I waited hours. Nobody! I came back through the woods.'

'Can you take us to the tunnel?'

'Of course, but better wait till tomorrow, don't you think? If the Germans have raised a barricade ... In the dark ...'

Before dawn, as we get ready to leave, a lorry halts in front of the shop. Dufour jumps out, covered in earth, unshaved, hollow eyes.

'Where's Violette?' yells Charles.

'She was taken.'

'What? You abandoned her?'

'No, I did what I could! It was her who ordered me to come and warn you. Let me explain ... Past the tunnel, an old woman cut across the road with her sheep. She didn't say a word to me, the bitch! And at the entrance to Salon, a German! As I was dressed in a black blouson and beret I could pass as a *milicien*, so I addressed him in a friendly way and I calmly got out to give time to my passengers to get away. He only started shooting when they jumped out of the car. I gave a burst of fire back before rolling into the gutter. I was going to take shelter behind the farm when, in the opposite ditch someone started firing: it was Violette, who was shouting, "I got one of them, I'm sure!"

I told her, "I told you to get away."

She replied, "I wasn't going to just leave you. I'm a good shot, you know!"

I got really mad: "Against a regiment, a fat lot of good that is! Get over here behind this building!"'

Bullets rattled against the wall. A burst of fire cut a woman in two as she was taking a cow to the stable. The fugitives threw themselves into a steep field. They climbed, opening up two parallel trenches along the way in the wheat, an ideal target! Corns fell like rain around them and on to their necks. A bullet grazed Dufour's back. They reached the end of the field by zigzagging.

'Behind the apple trees, up there at least 300m, is the railway, and after that, it's the Maquis!' whispered Dufour. They were getting close to those apple trees when suddenly Violette's ankle cracked. She fell to her knees groaning, 'I can't walk on that foot any more! It's the old sprain gone again.'

'Grab on to me, around my neck! We'll get there!'

'No. I'll delay you and we'll both be taken. Save yourself!'

'Never!'

She got up on her knees. Her clothes were covered in earth. Curls stuck to her forehead in sweat; she was grimacing from pain. Her eyes flashing, she hissed, 'Get out of here, idiot! Someone's got to warn Charles that the Germans are here! I'm a lieutenant of the British Army, don't you forget it! I'm giving you an order!'

'I obeyed her,' Dufour goes on. 'I galloped until I reached a farm that overlooks a bridge over the railway. Suzanne, the farmers' daughter – the Montintins – a childhood friend, saw me as I got there. A German car arrived at full pelt. She quickly lifted up a pile of kindling with her fork, and I slipped underneath it. One of my feet was sticking out so she sat on it. From my hole, I saw Violette standing in the car, a command car with its hood down. An officer offered her a cigarette – she flicked it away and spat in his face. In a rage, he put his hand on his pistol. He stopped himself with a bitter laugh, and scanned the forest beyond the bridge. "You can always search!" mocked Violette. "My friend is far away by now!" The car turned; two SS remained on guard on the bridge ...'

'You said SS? You certain of that?'

'Absolutely – the Panzer Division Das Reich.'

'The Das Reich? There's none worse! We've got to get Violette out of there!'

One hundred per cent British in all circumstances, my major knows how to keep an Olympian cool. But that morning, as he calls Colonel Charles, he is close to exploding, I cen tell. 'So then, what happened to your '100 per cent impenetrable' rampart of lady telephonists, Colonel?"

'It's that – at night they sleep, got to!' And then, 'these SS, they're coming from the Corrèze. It is therefore for the Armée Secrète to give the alert!'

'Telephonists, Armée Secrète or not, this day, they are in Limoges – and they've got Violette! And I certainly have no intention of sleeping! I intend to do everything possible to save her. Bob and I will need help. Have you got any assistance in town?'

'I've got all the men needed! I'll put them on to it.'

'Do it! As soon as they've located Violette, we'll get over to Limoges and strike our blow.'

Not content with getting annoyed with the little colonel, my major mouthed off copiously to London,

'How did Das Reich leave Montauban going north four days ago and nobody in Orchard Court cared to give the alert?' He has seen red!

While we're pacing up and down the square like caged lions, a concert of blaring horns and singing suddenly shakes the village. A strange procession of Maquisards appear braying the 'Marseillaise', capering about in front of an armoured car bearing swastikas, but from its tower the Tricolore is flying. Where have they come from? They explain: the car was holding the rearguard of a column that went around our Maquis without knowing and us not knowing either, along the *départmentale* road leading from Eymoutiers to Limoges. Wheezing, it fell back, lost sight of its unit. On a curve in the road, it forked off on to the Sussac road and came out in the town of Sainte-Anne-Saint-Priest, without warning! There, one of Guingouin's battalion leaders, Pierre Magadoux, was on guard. If he felt let down or overly surprised, he kept his cool. He opened fire. Exposed on his tower, the German sniper was killed on the spot and then Magadoux attacked. The rest of the crew surrendered. Two SS, great big Aryans with golden hair, who, just like vanquished barbarians, are dragged behind their captor triumphant all the way to the forum of the great Sussac square. Dazed and battered, they are abused but the crowd, which chants, 'Shoot them, shoot them!'

My major suggests to the colonel in a smooth voice, 'Before shooting them, shouldn't you question them? They surely have a great deal to tell, don't you think?'

Magadoux frowned, 'The thing is, nobody around here speaks German ...'

'I do.'

In the haberdasher's, they disclose more than was necessary to this major, who is more abrupt than a *Junker*. Tapping his boots in the Prussian way with his stick covered in leather, he attacks them in perfect German.

The Das Reich is one of Hitler's favourite toys – 3,000 vehicles of which 600 are armoured, 14,000 men, two grenadier regiments, the Deutschland and the Der Führer; all commanded by an iron general, Lammerding. And yet, the Red Army fixed them in Kharkhov – the Red Army and the Russian winter. Afterwards, the Das Reich headed to Montauban, to supress any turbulence or attempted landings in the Entre-deux-Mers region, from left or right.[1] Three days ago, von Rundstedt, great chief of the Western Front, entrusted it with the mission to crush the Maquis of the Centre, that bloody thorn in his side: 'Without consideration, right! Strike the populations with terror until they lose their taste for resistance!"

To save thousands of tons of fuel, the *Das Reich* had to be transported by rail. But, on the night of 7 June, at the head of a tiny army of railway workers, Tony Brooks, one of the youngest in SOE, blew up all eighty-two available wagons, 104 trains and kilometres of rail. As a result, the *Das* Reich had to take the road. The Maquis were waiting. *Sturmbannführer* Adolf Diekmann – head of the 1st Battalion of Der Führer, the scout party – took twelve hours to reach Brive, a journey of less than 100km, and lost twenty-four SS men en route. In reprisals he had shot, covered in petrol and burned about forty hostages, among them three women.

On 8 June, the division splits into columns – one goes towards Limoges, the others towards Brive, Tulle and Guéret that the thinking heads of the French Communist Party (PCF) had commanded their troops to occupy without informing Koenig. Guingouin had cancelled the 'aberrant' order of storming Limoges, 'Veterans of the Eastern Front and street combats, these SS are going to have my badly armed and barely toughened Maquisards massacred, and then the population. A massacre – and for nothing.' The chief of the Francs-tireurs partisans (FTP) in Tulle occupied the town for a few hours – the time it took for 500 *Panzergrenadier*, supported by a squadron of tanks and by militiamen, to sweep in and hang ninety-nine of the town's inhabitants from its balconies. On that same day came Rommel's call for help; Lammerding orders his columns to return to Limoges at top speed, to be ready to pounce on Normandy en bloc.

1 '*Entre deux mers*' means between two tides. The region is situated between the Garonne and Dordogne tidal rivers. The Das Reich divison was defending both rivers from invasion forces potentially coming upriver from the sea.

That very evening, the chief of the 3rd Battalion and Diekmann's best friend, Helmut Kämpfe, turns up in Guéret – too late. The garrison has subdued the rebellion. So, impatient to join Lammerding, he dispatches two scout riders, imperiously salutes Müller, the unit's doctor, pushes the accelerator to the floor of his 'salvaged' Talbot Grand Sport and, leaving the convoy on the spot, speeds off in a cloud of exhaust fumes. Suddenly, a van surges in front of him. A riot of men jump out. Before being able to make a gesture, he is relieved of his Luger and thrown in the vehicle, which disappears into a road off to the side. A few minutes later, his astonished grenadiers discover the Talbot, empty. No trace of struggle, not one spot of blood, not a cartridge on the asphalt. This brave among braves, the most decorated of the division, who had previously bumped off a string of Popovs far tougher than these tinpot guerrillas, surrendered without fighting? *Unmöglich*! The mystery just adds to Diekmann's fury. He is already appalled by the outrage these French pygmies had inflicted the previous day on two of his titans!

Gerlach, an *Obersturmführer* charged with organising the billeting to the north of Limoges, takes to the road without a care in the world,with his chauffeur as his only escort. Not far from Peyrilhac, an ambush! The two SS are seized, disarmed, slapped, kicked and stripped. They appear in their underwear before the ferocious Maquisards. The verdict: death. They are thrown in the back of a lorry at the corner of a wood – the Bois du Roi. Terrified, the chauffeur takes the guards by surprise and runs off into the thicket. The guards open fire, shooting burst after burst, massacring him ; meanwhile the *Obersturmführer*, forgotten, scampers off like a hare. He gets back to Limoges by climbing along a railway and appears, still in his pants, in front of Diekmann. But he doesn't even know where he was captured. He remembers a fork in the road, bits of a name caught on a sign as he flew past in the lorry ...

The next day, 10 June, towards midday, the rumble of boots is heard outside the *boulangerie* in Salon-la-Tour. Yvette Bessoule, the daughter of the baker, pricks up her ears. That very night, the Das Reich had swept into the town; the inhabitants dig in at home. Samel, a brave father of five children, had thrown himself headlong at one of their barricades; he was with the Maquis of Terrasson, but sometimes came to town to see his family. At lunchtime, a fusillade erupts, so close that the plaster crumbles from the walls and flies on to the plates. A long time after, the father risks coming out on the threshold of his shop and at the foot of his shop window, splashed with blood, is the body of Samel, riddled with bullets. A grenadier forces him back, '*Verboten* to touch the body! He must stay and rot there, as an example!'

In the afternoon, the sound of boots anew; Yvette lifts the corner of a curtain: six SS surround a young woman. She is dressed in elegant clothes, but muddy, torn, good for the dustbin. In spite of her drawn features and gammy ankle, she is pretty. Curiously, she doesn't seem afraid, rather detached, a half-smile playing on her lips. Her clear gaze pans the façades. She limps along; the soldiers slacken their pace to hers.

Only that evening do the villagers dare to come out on their doorsteps. Far to the north a stream of smoke is rising; so high in the sky that one could take it for the anvil of a cumulus.

Saturday is when cigarettes are sold and distributed by the tabac in Oradour-sur-Glane. This 10 June, the schoolchildren have been summoned for a medical visit. At midday, two trams have already disgorged a crowd of citizens come from Limoges to buy food from the farms. The cafés are full. It's a beautiful day. At the beginning of the afternoon, the access routes to the market town are suddenly swamped by Germans, SS of the Der Führer. They push before them men gathered from the fields, force open doors to houses, pull out the inhabitants. A boy of 17, Martial Brissaud, hides so well that he evades the search and manages to get away. When the SS present themselves at the front door of the school, Roger Godfrin, a very smart little chap from Lorraine (in 1940 Oradour had welcomed about thirty school pupils from Alsace-Lorraine), aged 8, slips out through the back one. He crosses the Glane and disappears into the woods.

Diekmann roll calls the villagers on the town's drum. The villagers assemble without suspecting anything much; routine checks, they've had so many of them over the last four years. The SS bawls out, 'I know that you're hiding weapons! Bring them out!'

Panic: Oradour had never been a hideout for the Maquisards! Nevertheless, two men reluctantly hand over their antique hunting guns.

The officer then separates the men from the women; some of the SS lead the males by groups into the four corners of the town. The women, and the children hanging on to their skirts, are pushed into the church. Pressing their babies to their breasts, consoling their crying little ones, the mothers gather together by instinct in the choir. Grenadiers place a crate on the altar and withdraw, unrolling a sort of black ribbon, locking and bolting the door. Outside, a grenade explodes. Is it a signal? Everywhere bursts of gunfire crackle. An apocalyptic detonation follows; the crate placed on the altar explodes. It tears apart the women and children, pulverises statues, pious images, stained-glass windows. A short time after the door opens, the sun comes in. The nave resonates with plaintive moans. With their backs to the light, the silhouettes fire long and indiscriminately on the pile of dead and dying, who are united in this final, interminable burst. Afterwards, they steadily pile up the bodies on the benches and kneelers, sprinkle the whole lot with petrol and phosphorus. A flame gushes forth. They beat a running retreat, carefully close the door behind them.

Miracle – one woman manages to flee! She will bear witness.

While this has been happening, the men have been killed, their bodies burned just like those of their female companions. The SS finally dynamite each house and burn the rubble, so that only blackened ruins remain. The gigantic plume of smoke that rises can be seen 50km away.

Diekmann supervised the event from his 'headquarters' established at the Masset farm, beyond the Glane but in well in sight of Oradour. He can brag, 'I purged Oradour of its terrorists!' Terrorists, there weren't any among 145 women and 207 children – nor indeed among the 190 men. On the other hand, he ended up signing the death warrant for his friend Helmut Kämpfe, whom one of Guingouin's men, Sergeant Canou had so shrewdly hidden away. Not considering himself a judge before the law, the Préfet Rouge had been content to keep him in the cooler. But when the echoes of the butchery of Oradour reached him, he stuck the butchers' brother-in-arms in front of the firing squad.

At twilight on this damned Saturday, the door of the prison in Limoges closes on Violette.

Three days later, there is an arrival from Limoges: a stocky man with a square face, a crew cut and sharp eyes. It is Major Baptiste, who 'rules' the town. He describes to us how: 'I have a traction stashed in the garage. Sometimes, after dark, I go out on a raid. As I pass the end of a street, I take potshots at the Krauts on café terraces and make my getaway through the backstreets, never spotted, never caught! But, apart from that, I haven't wasted my time. Your friend is in prison. Better than that, she has been seen coming and going through the Champ-de-Foire to the Gestap', rue Louvrier-de-Lajolais, two hundred metres from there. She is not in handcuffs nor chained, just surrounded by two cops in civvies. Here's the scenario – I drive slowly close to them; two of my guys gun down the Fritz and jump with your Violette into my traction. End game: I get out of town though an unguarded exit. I know them all like the back of my hand. How does that grab you?'

My major is sceptical but diplomatic, 'Between the prison and the Gestapo, there's surely a whole bunch of Germans. In the full light of day and an open space, you won't benefit from the element of surprise that you have with your raids, I fear. It would be better to remove the two guards quietly, Welrod, for example.'

'What's a Welrod?'

'A totally silent pistol that fires breech locked, a single bullet at a time. But Bob knows how to fire with two hands and whole thing will be done at close range. As a precaution, you could cover him if he were to miss one of the Fritz?'

'No problem. He will be doubled by one of my guys who knows how to use a revolver. I've got my Sten and I'm not one-armed! What does it look like your Wel ... thing?'

I produce a blackened steel tube supplied with phosphorescent sights, 'Do you want a demonstration? Okay just one. Each shot uses rubber baffles that smother the detonation.'

Delighted to hear nothing but a fuzzy 'phut', Baptist exclaims, 'Ah, if I just had a dozen of those! I'd do for every last one of those vermin!'

'And the reprisals wouldn't make you popular!' retorts my boss. 'Sorry but we've only got two. Go and time the route. Keep an eye out for the point of attack, prepare your lines of retreat and come back quickly to get Bob!'

Baptiste comes back three days later, in despair – while he was putting the finishing touches to the plan Violette was taken to Paris. We guess her destination: the oratory, 84 Avenue Foch, dedicated by *Sturmbannführer* Boemelburg and *Hauptführer* Kieffer to the agents of the SOE Section.

That evening we drown our sorrows in the 100-year-old Fine, which, until then, Charles had only used a drop of at a time. Bitterly, he says, 'I dedicate it to Violette. And we'll empty the bottle!'

14

The Hour of the Préfet Rouge

When Charles reproaches himself for having sent Violette to her death, I cut him off, 'Remember that Major Karl, from Rouen: "We no longer take it out on women!" We'll see her again alive and well, believe me!'

He digs his heels in, 'I don't trust any Nazi, no more your Karl than the others!'

'Why did you save those two SS, then?'

'Them. Bah! Robots! It's the thinking heads, the dogmatics who manipulate; those are the ones I want to crush!'

He is no longer the phlegmatic Major Staunton speaking but an implacable judge. Then suddenly his regard softens; the crisis passes.

The V-1, Hitler's supreme weapon, which was to raze to the ground Perfidious Albion, ran into a snag. It didn't even dent the morale of the English. As for the Das Reich, harried by the Maquis in Dordogne, in Limousin, in Poitou and in the regions of the Loire, by the time it arrives in Normandy the Allies are already anchored there solidly; it will not dislodge them. Nevertheless, it will get there in time for Diekmann to join Kämpfe, his brother-in-killing, in the hell reserved for SS men. It isn't known which who bumped him off, Tommy or GI. It doesn't matter; justice was done!

One evening, after having put it together ad hoc, I station one section of the Maquis in ambush on a deeply embanked section of national route 20, north of Uzerche. I apply to the letter the directives of the guerrilla manual: I successively align a 'bell' up the road to signal the arrival of a convoy, then grenadiers, a Bren light machine gun. I position my Bazooka alongside this, in battery.

I preach, 'Above all, let the convoy engage. Nobody shoots before me! Afterwards, fire at will, for only one minute and the withdraw quickly before these old foxes who know the score encircle you. Got it?'

'Got it, Captain!'

The undergrowth is bathed in the aromas of humus. A beetle and a few ants proceed on their way under my nose. My Bazooka is lodged firmly on my shoulder. A familiar humming begins to grow, no end of vehicles. So, shall I treat myself with a Tiger this evening?

A state-of-the-art military motorcycle appears.

Suddenly: tac-tac-tac! A Sten spits – too early! The leading tank brakes hard, out of the range of my Bazooka. Its tracks squeal over the asphalt loud enough to burst your eardrums. The lorry tyres hold the note. A concert of yelling follows: '*Achtung Terroristen!*' Machine guns sputter, cannons and mortars thunder. Head tucked in, I decamp, crashing through the scrub.

Back at the camp they get a dressing down and the guilty fellow makes his act of contrition: 'Sorry, boss! Next time I'll wait!'

The next time, the following evening, he does. We strike full centre. If the Tigers may be off the menu but three lorries give up the ghost, and doubtless a dozen or so *Panzergrenadiers* with them.

'Bravo!' says my boss. 'However it won't stop Lammerding sending his machines by rail. Sending them by road is just throwing petrol down the drain! I expect they'll make use of every little bit of railway they can to save fuel. The Krauts will only risk repairing them by day. You've got the night, then, big fellow, to blast them to hell and back – like Penelope.'

Sending a metal rail bridge flying is child's play I often practised at the Hartford superior demolition school: 4lb of scissor plastic at each extremity, 5kg of dynamite underneath and the whole shebang explodes like a giant propellor.

Each night, I send three or four towards the stars, but the Krauts get them back in working order the following day. At break of day, an armoured train emerges from Brive or from Limoges. It unloads a company of grenadiers armed to the teeth, pros who set up in one go an entire impregnable line of defence. A workshop train follows with its crane. The juniors of the *Reichbahn* throw the girders, then the rails over the breech, solder, rivet and it's all done! These trains are now out of our reach; they roll in convoy. The armoured train, a steel caterpillar bristling with cannons and machine guns that we nickname 'the Casserole', has such thick skin that it resists bullets, grenades and maybe even Bazookas. It pushes a platform wagon in front loaded with pitiful hostages crouched down, doomed to suffer the wind, cold, machine guns and to be torn apart by the first mine on the line. Charles swears, 'One day, I'll get that Casserole!'

On short intact lengths between Limoges and Uzerche, at risk of bridges patched up and raids on the Casserole, the haphazard local circulars continue to run, used by the villagers but never even a single German; on the edge of Maquis country his life wouldn't be worth a fig!

So, the *Reichsbahn* re-establishes circulation as quickly as I cut it? I decide to strike a grand blow. One morning, at Masseret station, a bus is parked. I politely invite the travellers to get out and I run to booby trap the line in an embanked curve a kilometre away. I come back. The mechanic and I launch the locomotive and then hastily set off ourselves; when it comes to the curve at full speed in a thunderous roar, a geyser projects it against the rubble. The wagons capsize, stack up and block the section. I am bathed in euphoria – the *Reichsbahn* will surely take weeks to clear this Himalaya of iron!

It is clear in thirty-six hours – I'm disgusted.

'You were stingy with the material, dear chap,' decreed my boss in a condescending tone. 'My turn to play. Listen to me ...'

We mine the routes between Masseret and Saint-Germain-les-Belles, then send down two trains, one after the other. With their throttle valves wide open, the two locomotives tear along, one behind the other. The first high jumps into a trench in a curve, speeds along the shoulder then breaks up. The wagons land crazily on top of the disembowelled locomotive. Shortly after, the second locomotive hurtles into the pile of battered wagonsand scales what has become an actual volcano of iron crashing down in torrents of steam and dust.

Planted on a bank much like Nero before the fire of Rome, Charles shouts to me, 'Ah, if only Violette could see that!'

Might these fireworks have woken Georges Guinguoin? For here he is, in Sussac! He's a big bloke of about 30, gangling, dressed in a canvas-type 'colonial' uniform with sleeves and trouser legs too short for his long limbs, his unruly hair escaping from a crumpled beret. Behind thick, iron-rimmed glass, his gaze is frank and engaging, devoid of malice. A face that expresses belief like that I saw in the face of Fernand Bonnier. He has nothing of the bogeyman depicted in the Vichy newspapers. He can even find the right words to move us, 'I know only too well how the disappearance of your friend distresses you both. I too have lost so many of mine! We shall wreak vengeance, I swear to you!' Behind me are men who demand only that. But they lack weapons.

Major Staunton seizes the bull by the horns, 'Our Prime Minister is aware of that, Colonel!' – as if he had lunched the day before with Winston. 'My missions consists of supplying you with all that you lack – if you agree to concentrate on the objectives fixed by London, of course ... '

'Of course! I pursue the same ends as you: to hunt the Boches out of France, Major!'

Colonel Charles is dethroned: in Guingouin's shadow, he is only allowed to nod in agreement. The real boss has taken over command.

Very late in the night, Jean-Claude, Charles and I finish off coding an interminable message. I'm dead tired. Before going to bed along with my blokes, I grumble, 'You do realise, Charles, that you've just ordered 200 tons of weaponry, enough to fill eighty bombers, which'll take months to parachute the whole bag of tricks – if the weather remains fine. The war'll be over before then!'

'The matter is far too complex for the single little grey cell that makes up your brain, dear chap. Your second-rate little night-time parachute drops are done! I see the bigger picture. Find me a giant DZ, sort out the caches for stock, gather together any kind of transport you can. Let me deal with the details.'

'Eighty bombers, a detail?'

The Das Reich passed. National route 20 is deserted. Germans, *miliciens* and the mobile reserve groups (GMR) have gone to ground in town. Only the Casserole persists, repairing the damage done unremittingly by Penelope. The *Feldgrau* no longer venture out of the towns. Presumptuous, the Maquisards don't give a damn. My Charles, though, is worried about it.

'The Krauts still haven't surrendered any weapons. The proof – Montgomery, who ought to have easily taken Caen as soon as he landed, was just marking time! And, in the south, their divisions and aircraft are still there. If I were them, I'd take it out on the Maquis from the centre who are the bane of their existence. I fear this is just the calm before the storm! Could you at least teach your fellows who are assembling all over the open terrain to camouflage themselves?'

One afternoon in June, instead of wasting ammo, I force a Maquis battalion the size of a large company to walk in line along the road and not in disarray in the middle of the roadway as is usually the case; then to throw themselves into the gutter on the blow of a whistle. The ranks protest, 'What's the point? The vermin haven't got a single flier anymore.' At that moment – does Charles have second sight? – I notice some planes in the sky. I whistle like the damned. Someone grumbles, 'It's the English, see!'

'Or maybe butterflies with swastikas?'

My 200 men consent to crouch – protesting – in the ditch, but make no attempt at hiding the red scarves they all wear – around their necks or as turbans like pirates. Seen from the sky, they must look like giant poppies!

Messerschmitts and Focke-Wulfs dive on to us, so low that I can see the face of the pilots. Bursts of gunfire and bombs chop up the field in front of me. I huddle as best I can at the bottom of a hedge. Brushing the length of my thigh is a viper, tongue tasting the air, raising its pretty triangular head. Its golden eyes, two topazes, question me. What do you think you're doing on my turf? Rocked by the wind from the explosions, she poses her head on my fly and goes to sleep, leaving me – bomb or no bomb – paralysed, not daring to move a muscle! The last bomb explodes half an hour later, the viper wakes up, gives me a final look and slides away through the dead leaves. Thank you viper! Fearing your fangs, I forgot the hail of bombs and bullets.

We escaped without a scratch. However, the bombs turned over the field bordering the road and ruined the hamlet of Amboiras a few hundred metres away. The closest farm had just one piece of wall remaining. Suddenly a silhouette gallops towards us waving its arms. It's a kid who's laughing like crazy, 'These whores of Jerries used me for a target while I was pissing against the wall and didn't stop firing at me. I didn't dare move. Around me, the wall fell, but not me!'

So, by taking it out on a youngster stuck against a wall, the killers neglected an entire company, even though they were lit up in red. The people of Amboiras having made a dash for the fields at the first sounds of the bullets, the rain of fire had claimed no victims – except that the bulls, cows, pigs and chickens remained locked away.

Charles had forecast correctly as usual: the Maquis suffered several raids, one of which took Sussac as a target. Madame Ribiéras's grocery took a hit. However, with a burst from a Bren gun, a Maquisard brought down a Focke-Wulf!

On 21 June at 8 a.m. on the DZ of Le Clos, the largest I could find, there are three mountains of green branches and reddening dead leaves. They spit out three columns of greasy smoke, smoke, which spreads itself across a sky as blue as the southern seas.

At 9 a.m., silvery bursts of light appear, leapfrogging over the hills – P-38 Lightning fighters of the US Army Air Force. Fuselages sparkling, their auxiliary tanks hanging from wing points sharp as a knife. My boss laughs: 'Watch out Bob! You escaped them at Gaynes Hall. This time they're not going to miss you!'

In the north, a cloud of black points indicate a procession of B-17 Flying Fortresses travelling three abreast, holds wide open. Soon, in batches of thirty, their containers are released, dancing prettily under the multicoloured canopies. A symphony as on a sheet of music until some of the parachutes don't open and ten cylinders of 200kg crash howling like Stukas!

'Watch out – look up!' Panic-stricken, gatherers disperse, zigzagging between the steel caissons hitting the ground and bombarding the field with the debris of weapons and equipment. And it's only the beginning: all over, other flying torpedoes dive whistling! Everyone for themselves! To top it off, one of them, full of weapons, crashes, lighting up the powders. Barrages of red and green tracers skim the ground. Everyone hits the ground except those clumsy labouring oxen being used to gather in the materiel. One of them suddenly lets out a blood-chilling cry: the bullet that had just grazed its rump made it absolutely nuts! Clinging to the reins, its driver swears loudly at it. His minotaur ignores him, charges at a triple gallop, sweeps all before it, finally plunging into the woods, trampling open a gap for itself. We hear branches cracking, or perhaps bones?

The Clos is now simply a Waterloo, strewn with parachutes, container wrecks, weapons in bits, a ragbag of sacks, bits of uniform, dressings – and nearly 800 containers still miraculously intact! My major is delighted.

'Aerial rodeo, bombardment, corrida, we've had the whole shebang!' guffaws Charles. 'And now this lot on the house! You see, there's some good in this war!'

The Préfet Rouge is in the seventh heaven: Major Staunton has presented him with the largest parachute drop ever delivered to the Maquis. Better still, he has promised him a second one for 14 July! Let's hope that the bedlam that is the Clos field will be cleared up in time!

Guingouin charged me with the formation of units divided over the hundreds of hectares. Gilles, a young and jovial captain, gets me a 21cv Hotchkiss that was top of the range – before a *gazogène* engine that reminds one of a Wild West steam train chimney spoilt it. With my little spade, I fill its boiler up with 50kg of charcoal, I activate the blower. By the time I've taken a bath in the millcourse of the windmill, enjoyed a solid little meal prepared with love by the miller, my little 'tinpot', is at full pressure! Open to the fresh air, my cabriolet lends me the aura of a playboy. Better still, as I depart, the emanations of coke cover the smells of carcasses.

On the evening of 7 July, I receive at Le Clos the Inter-Allied missions announced by Buck. At midnight a sprawling shadow appears nearby, crying out, 'Hi, Toto!'

Unmistakeable! 'Bissett, no way? Is it really you?'

'Of course, and not alone!'

Two sets of laughter I'd recognise anywhere! Nobody laughs as loudly as André Simon and de Guelis: 'It's really us! Judging that, if we got captured what we might spill to the Germans no longer has any value, Baker Street is letting us play in the final. Suddenly I have the pleasure of finding two of my recruits again, you and Staunton. I enrolled him in Nice in 1941. Here's Mackenzie, our doctor, then Thomas, commandant of the BCRA, then Lannou and Edgar, our wireless ops.'

Simon chimed in, 'We are *Tilleul*, one of the Inter-Allied missions let loose just about everywhere in France. They all bear the name of a tisane, *Verveine, Camomille* or *Bergamonte*. Tisanes parachuted into fine wine country, can you believe it?'

When you know how André likes his drink, you can understand his sourness. On his head is the decorated helmet of a squadron leader. As he looks so good my boss will send him to sing the praises of the Maquis in the adjacent towns. Perched on a bistrot table in Châteauneuf, Eymoutiers or Masléon, he'll be a hit!

On 14 July, we receive 400 containers released by three dozen Fortresses. This time the parachutes all open, or nearly all. We're not subjected to bombing, nor hassle, but we don't lose anything for waiting ...

During the night, having set the Cantal ablaze, 2,500 SS, Caucasians and Tartars occupy Meymac, at the doors of the Maquis. At their head, General von Jesser, another Lammerding. Elsewhere, a battalion of Waffen SS, 200 Milice and the 95th Regiment of Security threatens Linards! At the Clos, the endless stream of ox-drawn carts and lorries follow one another day and night. Yet, the DZ is far from being empty when the Germans attack our outposts in La Croisille, less than 8km away!

On the 17th they occupy the château of this town, La Vialle. So as to delay them, even if for a short time, I shower this château with a haphazard attempt at a burst of shells from a 3in mortar – a sophisticated heavy support weapon for the infantry that we've been furnished with, probably in error, as only a specialised team can use it. By chance, an STS had one of these mortars and I had tried it out.

The next day, the Tartars of von Jesser assault Mont Gargan 5km to the south; Guingouin's Maquisards fight like lions. My desperados of the International Brigade defend the cemetery of Saint-Gilles tomb by tomb.

'They've got guts,' Charles tells me, 'but they're fighting one against three. The SS are going to swamp them then come after us. These SS, you've got to take them quickly. All the roads leading to Sussac must cross briefly over one or other bridge. There are six or seven of them. You know them, of course. Go and cut the ground from under their feet, so to speak. Take Dufour with you.'

I stuff the tinpot with explosives and drive towards a quarry stone bridge over the Combade. We cram into its abutments 40lb of ammonal, a nitrate of alumina, a slow 'sapper' explosive – its shockwave blasts at more than 3,500mps – but one that is able to set off a seismic chain reaction. Just as I am putting the finishing touches to my charges, a light armoured vehicle appears on the opposite bank. In the time it takes to say 'oof', its tower pivots and the mouth of its machine gun spits out fire. The bullets miaowl around us. A delayed explosion is no longer on the cards. A ten-second Bickford wick should do the job. I light it then we scamper under the bank. The bridge explodes in front of the tank which, lost in a cloud of dust, keeps firing blindly.

I fire a steel-furnance hell from my mortar. Well before Châteauneuf, a fusillade splutters, shells explode. Maquisards crouched in trenches shout to us, 'They're advancing!"

Second objective: an armed concrete bridge. Hard as steel, concrete is a nightmare for the saboteur. You've got to trim it to the plastic. We make up two puds; we roll them from one parapet to the other; they cut clean through the concrete span – which balances gracefully in the still intact metallic sheathing, as if in a hammock. At the moment that we, walking the tightrope, are fixing a string of charges to the recalcitrant irons, some *Feldgrau* appear opposite and we fire point-blank. Then we beat a hasty retreat, while the remains of the bridge, at last, go poof!

We head for Châteauneuf. Forty kilos of nitrate reduces a venerable arch to rubble. However, as I omitted to treat the tramway rails, they remain, forming an elegant arch astride the river. The Krauts have the good taste not to get mixed up in it this time.

Before the old banger, out of both coke and breath, gives up the ghost in front of Charles' house, two other culverts bite the dust. The boss says to us: 'It was in vain, my children, they broke through. They forded the rivers. Guinguoin held them heroically. But what chance does he have against three hardened regiments? From now on we have to observe the law of the guerrilla – lose ourselves in the natural world around us, let the storm pass. Tomorrow, you will blow the last two bridges still intact for me and then meet up with me at Vassivière, 30km from here. Guingouin will find us there. Don't tarry along the route, I'm counting on you to receive the reinforcements that Buck has promised me and which won't go amiss in the liberation of Limoges!'

The next day, 19 July, Caen falls, the route to Paris is open. As for me, take care of the Domps bridges.

On the 20th, the SS Tartars take 'La Villa', Guingouin's command post. They make a bonfire of buildings, carts and lorries; they spread out over the roadway all the Maquis treasure, ten tons of victuals, 20 tons of weaponry and equipment, they flatten them with the caterpillars of the armoured vehicles. Then they withdraw. The Préfet Rouge, Guingouin, has killed or wounded 345; he lost 100 men. A victory!

15

The SS Never Dies!

I baptised her 'La Marquise', the lady Pascale, manager of the Vassivière manor standing on an island in the middle of a lake, because she lives only to be happy and controls her world with a rod of iron. She will only serve the upper crust. George Guingouin – *un colonel*! – this perfect gentleman Major Staunton, and the cultured Jean Chaintron, one of the big shots and brains of the Communist Party – thin, crew cut, engaging smile and eye gleaming with intelligence, a brilliant conversationalist! He is close to Thorez, who pulls the strings with the USSR, founder of the Algerian Communist Party, political commissar during the war with Spain, liberated from Vichy prison – thanks to a bishop, it appears. A Jesuit deep down, he knows how to mask with a modest veil his visceral Marxism and his role as Moscow's eye near Guingouin. For Georges is in trouble with the Central Committee! Anti-Nazi at the time of the Hitler–Stalin idyll, he afterwards refused to give in his notice and do penitence in the Puy de Dôme and, on top of all that, he contravened the order to put Limoges to fire and blood. A dangerous deviationist; his account is good.

On 20 July, there is a failed attempt on Hitler's life. The Führer is safe but 3,000 officers, among which are some excellent generals, will be condemned to being shot, hanged or having their throats cut. Add to those, Rommel, machine-gunned by a Typhoon. A purge in the style of Stalin, and a blessing for Eisenhower!

Accommodated in the outbuildings, I'm not part of La Marquise's evening bridge games. For the fourth, she calls 'her' curé. My evenings are spent on the surrounding DZs.

On the night of 2 August, Ted Fraser, the big southerner and Guiet's conducting officer, rolls on the ground. His mission: to put Limoges's aerodrome back into action once the town has been liberated. Baker Street plans ahead!

Eighteen strapping chaps follow, all with blond hair shimmering under the moon. A Viking invasion? No, it's an Operational Group, or OG, of the OSS. I billet them at the Château de la Vialle that the SS have left in a good state. To my eyes, four stars! I share my lodgings with maggots and I have the River Combade for a bathroom, don't I? Not my Yanks; they demand soft beds and hot water! No doubt overstimulated by the Cahors wine, their libidos are on the loose. They focus their attentions on the the girls from La Croisille whom I have hired as maids, particularly the smalls of their backs. But the girls are ladies; they're not going to give it up for 'Lucky' ciggies. Scandal at the manor and in the market town! I tell Captain Larson, who commands these hyper-sexed men, to make them them to keep their paws to themselves. Why are these Vikings in deep France, anyway?

In 1942, the US Army made up a battalion of parachute skiers manifestly intended to be sent to Norway. The OSS fished in this breeding ground for our future OGs, who were trained at various places in the US, England and even in Algeria. No better way to attract spies, right?

'Absolutely, since it was a gambit set up to convince Hitler that we were going to land in Norway,' Ted explains to me. 'Once Overlord was go, what were they to do with these chaps? Of course, engage them on the first theatre of operations offered – France. They were sent all over in small groups. The big boss is Colonel Prince Obolensky, an ex-officer of the Tsar's Guard, you know. Now he's the prince of hotels in Hollywood, a bit of a playboy, well up in Washington. A dandy, a pretty boy, acting tough, he was dropped in Sologne.'

On 9 August, nineteen French SAS[1] commanded by a young lieutenant, Lemaire, also land. 'Lee', a team of Jedburghs, follows, composed, like the Inter-Allied, from Allied officers. One is Captain Viguier, a Free French, the other, Captain Brown who introduces himself arrogantly as 'from the US Cavalry', all the while swearing like a trooper because his wireless op and he crashed some kilometres away, and their wireless, having plummeted, wrapped up in its parachute canopy, is in pieces.

1 SAS – Special Air Service, unit of parachutists with a mission to operate behind enemy lines.

I take delivery of wirelesses, batteries, quartz, codes, confidential mail and money on the private DZ that I sorted out in a Sussac clearing – so skimpy that, describing it for London for ratification, I shamelessly doubled its area. Triangular, it is pinched in between two routes, a ravine and the cemetery, but it's so close by!

On a beautiful star-filled night, three parcels are to be parachuted down to me. The village wheelwright's tip-cart will collect them. I stand gaping beside his mare. There is a roaring to the north, a shadowy cross visible against the Milky Way, the recognition signal … Soft thuds, one, two, three – five – ten parachutes deploy. The wheelwright grumbles, '*Merde*! more than expected! I dunno how I'm going to shift all this lot.'

He is interrupted by dull shocks accompanied, on the cemetery side, by the din of shattering glass – and curses! He's bothered, 'Good God, the bloody dead won't be too pleased?'

A spectre draped in a pale shroud stands up suddenly in front of us. 'Who got me this bloody shit of a DZ, hell! I fell into a greenhouse for Chrissake!'

'Not a greenhouse, in a tomb! You can ditch your winding sheet, clot!' chuckles a second ghostly arrival.

Behind them, the kingdom of the dead takes on life – between the funeral chapels surge parachutists, competing to outdo one another's bumps and bruises. I shout, 'Damn it all, who are you?'

'The SAS mission you're expecting, of course!' a lieutenant retorts. 'And I'm happy to tell you that I'm going to make a damn report on your whore of a DZ!'

'However, I'm not expecting anybody, old chap!'

'Well, okay, I'm with Commandant Robert's *Bergamotte*.'

'There's no *Bergamotte* nor Robert here!'

The lieutenant's mouth drops open, 'How's that? I am on the *Pension* DZ, aren't I, near Guéret?'

'No way! You're on *Citron*, and south of Limoges. Your navigator was only off by 50km!'

I have an idea. I guide the detachment to the village inn where Charles and Jean-Claude are ensconced. At the door, I shout out, 'Charles, people to see you!'

My major appears, then rubs his eyes in astonishment: still as statues, twenty paras in uniform present arms.

The next day, I charter two lorries and, along the narrow lanes, I drive them to Creuse, to Commandant Robert, of the BCRA, who has been waiting for them as if for the Messiah.

All is calm on the Limousin front. The Germans no longer leave their barracks. Only the Casserole dares to venture on the 40km or so that I kept intact so the buses can continue their local service. One evening, we learn that the Casserole is getting ready to spend the night at Masseret station – an affront that Charles wishes to avenge: 'Everyone on the bridge!.'

At daybreak, as the blackbirds sing their morning chorus, I take up my position behind a large oak tree. Under the ballast, in the well-hollowed-out space that was mined during the night, sleeps around 100kg of ammonal, enough to overturn a locomotive and several carriages. The site has been chosen carefully. Fifty metres further away there is a rail section with a bridge at each end spanning a cutting. Charles, the OGs and the SAS set up an ambush there. Classic scenario – the train crosses the booby-trapped section, its engine blows up over my mine, then the Bazookas, Bren guns and Gammon grenades bombs enter the fray!

Erratic hissing – the Casserole approaches. Suddenly, the splutters are silent; the train stops! Beyond the bridge a strand of smoke stretches out. Minutes pass. Suddenly a burst of cannon fire, machine guns and submachine guns mix in the pandemonium. I crawl as far as the bridge and risk a glance over the parapet. Far below, the locomotive is smoking and lower still, a dozen or so *Feldgrau*, Schmeissers at their hip, search the bank. They catch sight of my head. Get a fix on me. The bullets brush over the parapet. I roll down the ramp, gather my men. We race to reach the rallying point 2km away.

One of the SAS calls on me as a witness, 'It doesn't make sense, captain! The train stopped, I don't know why, well before our position. Two Krauts got out, reconnoitered the railway, under our very eyes, had a chat, a cigarette butt in their face, as if nothing were happening. Five minutes later a gun gets us in its sights!'

Charles arrives last, out of breath but, as is his habit, impassive, 'One of ours must have been camouflaged badly. The two Krauts, pros, spotted him but didn't react. Useless going on about it. Who's missing?'

'Three SAS and Captain Larson.'

Hours pass. No survivor comes forth. Charles is champing at the bit, 'Go get some news! I want to know what has become of Larson and these three SAS, and by what mysterious thing this goddamned train stopped. Take Dufour with you, he knows the country. I'm convinced the Casserole is no longer there; it won't run the risk of spending the night in the middle of the countryside. Be careful anyhow!'

We approach the railway using extreme stealth. it is deathly silent. Just as Charles predicted, the Casserole has gone. The cutting is full of empty cartridges. Hordes of bluebottles swarm over puddles of dried blood.

About 100m further along, we discover the key to the mystery: before the war, the Paris–Toulouse was electrified; under Pétain, lacking kilowatts, they went back to steam. The suspended overhead power cable was neglected and fell into disrepair. A braided conductor wire of about 100m in length of the electric cable blighted with verdigris fell on to the railway line. The mechanic braked to a screeching stop. Our setback – it's just bad luck.

In the morning, in a village, I locate the captain. He has been laid out on a big country bed with a starred flag of yesteryear and a jug of meadow flowers. His blood has dripped through the base and spread over the linoleum. Behind the priest, women in headscarves, men in black suits pray. The mayor whispers to me, 'We cut him from the barbed wire, gutted by one of those bloody grenades that our boys carry on their belt. The pin simply got caught in the brambles. Well, he wanted to be like them! He'll be buried beside the monument to the dead, don't worry.'

As for the three SAS, the Germans took them, untouched, wounded or dead, we don't know.

On 12 August, the Resistance in London sends a message via us, which Staunton undertakes to deliver to Guingouin in person: General Koenig is putting the colonel at the head of all the forces of the Resistance, all the Maquis of the Haute Vienne, whoever they are, FTP, AS, ORA. Georges is over the moon. In a stroke, he puts the gendarmes on notice to rally around, if not … and 'summons' Colonel Besson – who is head of the GMR and, secretly it appears, a member of the ORA – to a 'conference in Linarde on 17 August which will bring together under his presidency, Major Paquette, regional head of ORA and Major Staunton representing General Eisenhower'. On the night of the 20th, the GMRs will have become part of the Maquis.

On 15 August, the landings in Provence: Besson has grown wings. He rushes up and promises to join up with Guingouin with weapons and equipment.

The rats are fleeing the sinking ship, particularly in Brive. Its *Kommandant*, Colonel Boehmer, would ne more than ready to throw in the towel if he were to be threatened by forces backed by the allies. Staunton's counterpart in Corrèze, Nestor, is ready to pick up the pieces. An idea – yet another one – comes to Charles, 'Perhaps Nestor hasn't got available regulars, like we do, SAS, OGs? So take four SAS to Brive and play the famous "allies". If they are needed, telephone me and I'll turn up with the major part of our forces.'

On the beat-up tinpot's windscreen, I set up a Bren gun and a Bazooka in firing position. We cross the *département* of Uzerche, still sleeping, at dawn. The air is pure, and the route is wide until we reach Donzenac. Suddenly, in the south, there is an uproar of explosions accompanied by black smoke.

'They're bombing Brive,' exclaims an SAS. 'And worse, there's a plane flying in this direction!'

It is at this moment that the tinpot, which has never gone wrong before, decides to have a fit of the vapours, hiccups and shuts down! Try as I might to encourage the choke and blower control into life, she merely digs her heels in and remains glued to the asphalt. The marauding Messerschmitt dives – a white limpet with a black chimney clinging to a French highway is hardly an everyday sight. We manage to push the car into a sunken roadway just before the fighter gets us in its sights. Its first burst skims past our backside; it will pass once, twice, six times, tracing dotted lines over the earth left and right but never in the centre, leaving the tinpot and us undamaged. Does fear really give you wings? Silence falls again. At the first press on the choke, the tinpot snorts and takes us off as fast as you like to Brive! The town is jubilant. In one square, the FFI automatically kick an unfortunate Fritz. I hail one of them, 'Is there an English officer around here?'

'Yes, Major Peters, you'll find him in the town hall.'

At the *mairie*, it turns out I have just missed the major. 'He's just left for a tour of inspection.' Well then, back to Limoges.

On 16 August, when a general strike shakes Limoges, Baker Street advises us that the last forces of the Wehrmacht barracked in Entre-Deux-Mers, particularly the 159th Infantry Division, could well bring assistance to the town's garrison! It's up to me to cut off their route.

In Saint-Germain-les-Belles, north of Masseret, the départementale 5 passes over the railway on a good old masonry bridge. A hundred kilos of nitrate reduces it to 100 tons of rubble, which completely fills in the cutting. Round about we lay anti-tank mines and '*Achtung Minen!*'

signs. Not far away, in Fombelaux, on each side of the crossroads of the départementale and the N20, use plastic to uproot the 100m of plane trees, and their tangled branches form an inextricable mangrove, which I stuff with booby traps, detonated by super sensitive igniters and tied by wire so fine that it is practically invisible. The slightest vibration and everything blows! As busy as bees the SAS, OGs and Brown dig an anti-tank pit and finish it off by laying mines along with placing the usual signs. Charles is in seventh heaven.

'Our rear is secure and we move forward, my good man! Boehmer has had an impact on General Gleiniger, who's in command in Limoges and who's listening to the song of the sirens ... the Swiss consul, d'Albis, who is already in discussions with Guingouin. However, after George's ultimatum, which only comprised of one article as curt as a cudgel: "Capitulate unconditionally!" he hit back. "No question of surrending to these terrorists. I will only lay down our arms into the hands of the forces of the legitimate government of France!"'

'In other words, to Pétain! He has a sense of humour!'

'I knocked together a new ultimatum with ten articles, more subtle, leaving him a margin for negotiation with an "Allied" delegation, which will be presided over by Major Staunton of the British Army, mandated by Eisenhower, from whom I received an official delegation, by wireless. Gleiniger bit. Tomorrow at 4 p.m., d'Albis will allow us to enter Limoges.'

'What? You have confidence in a Nazi?'

'Gleiniger isn't a Nazi, he's one of the old guard! And then, I wouldn't miss this face-to-face for all the gold in the world. Actually, I adore a good game of poker! To bluff Limoges into defeat is a dream! It'll be you who'll drive me as far as the gates of the town. There, d'Albis will take me in charge!'

The next day, fresh, ironed and boots polished, at the wheel of his gleaming Citroën 15/6 I drive the 'delegation' composed of Charles, Viguier, Guéry, who is a Free French Forces captain, and Brown 'of the US Cavalry', lest we forget! 'He'll look fine in the picture,' explains my boss to me. 'And if he opens his big mouth too much, I shall shut it for him.'

In the suburb of Sablard, on the Vienne river, Consul d'Albis' car, flying a Swiss pennant, takes up the relay. Charles confides to me, 'We will have finished by 7 p.m. You know what you have to do, don't you?'

'Of course, boss!'

My seventeen Vikings, my seven SAS, Guiet, Dufour and me take our position in front of the post office in Soudanas, a suburb from where you can look down over the town in the valley. My mission is simple. At 7 p.m., a telephone call from my major to the telephonist on duty will confirm that Gleiniger has surrendered. I will catch him up at the Hôtel de la Paix. There, in the presence of my 'detachment of allied forces', the general and his headquarters will hand over their weapons to Major Staunton 'representing General Eisenhower', and in particular to the 'liberators! Colonel Guingouin in majesty!'

A torrid day comes to an end. At the moment when, for the fifth time, I question the young telephonist, the town blazes up, explosions and a resonating fusillade. And Charles is in the middle of all that? The dice and girls fly. My blokes jump into lorries. I drive at full throttle; Dufour guides me along the deserted streets. I reach a square, brake in front of a long tasteful façade: the Hotel de la Paix.

Surrounded by my troop, I push the glass door, I cross a hall under the nose of the porter, who stares at me open-mouthed; I go into a large chandeliered hall, plastered ceiling and columns. A dozen or so officers and *Unteroffizieren* stand up. There is a look of relief in their eyes; they were expecting to be treated badly by the terrorists, but here are regulars in uniform. Helmets under the elbow, an officer clicks his heels, '*Ich bin Herr Hauptmann Knoll, Adjudant des General Mayor Gleiniger*!'

In my primary school German, I respond, '*Hauptmann Mortier von das Kanadishes Wehrmacht*!' Then at the end of my vocabulary. 'Vous parlez français, anglais?'

'French, *Herr Hauptmann.*'

'So, tell me, who started shooting? Do you know where the Allied delegation is?'

'No! Our general left to read the act of capitulation to the units in the town. He ordered us to wait for him here. You are the first enemy – I mean the first ally that I have seen. I have the order to hand our weapons over to you. If you would ...'

At that moment, the door is slammed open. A group of Maquisards, machine guns pointed, barges in shouting, 'There're those bastard Boches! Give us your shooters or we gun you down where you stand!'

Pale, Knoll recoils, brings his hand to his pistol. I interpose, 'The act of capitulation specifies that the officers have the right to keep their weapons!'

'Your act, you can shove it! And who are you anyway?'

I contain myself, point to my men, who have lifted their Tommy guns automatically, 'The commander of these Allied parachutists. And you, where do you come from?'

'From Excideuil, in Charentes. We're from the Bataillon Bernard.'

The Charentais Maquis got here before Guingouin's boys? How did that happen? Obtuse, they remain planted on the spot, their machine guns pointed at me, the screen in front of Knoll, hand on belt. My men have them in their line of fire. A vaudeville act, as if I didn't know what a sensitive trigger these detestable Stens have! And they're in the hands of these hysterical bastards! To die from a burst of friendly fire under the nose of the Germans, on the evening of victory, that's just a bit much! We are in a tense stand-off when the door opens again. Charles is in front, escorted by a commandant of 'our' Maquis! I could've hugged him! My major, who's not in the mood to discuss, says, 'Who the devil put this mess together? I'm the one who's signed the act of surrender. The conditions will be respected – to the letter!'

The Maquis leader backs him up so well that the 'Charentais fellows' withdraw grumbling. Capt. Knoll extends his hand to us: 'Zank you, *Herr Mayor*, zank you *Herr Hauptmnn*!'

I am quick to follow him: 'Thank you Charles. Without you … tell me, this gunfire in the town, who do we owe that lot to?'

Charles explains, 'To the SS, old chap. When the general signalled to them that they would have to capitulate, they liquidated his escort, kidnapped him and left the town in force. Be reassured, the rest of the garrison consented to surrender! Ah, those negotiations will go down in history. This old fox, Gleiniger, nitpicked over every article after having devised his responses with his chief of headquarters. As for me, I refuted his arguments before he had a chance to finish formulating them. You know he didn't know that I spoke German from the cradle! I floored him in Prussian: "The RAF is ready to launch a Mosquito raid on your garrison. I took it upon myself to adjourn it. Lacking a consensus, I'll be obliged to revise my position! An American division approaches the Loire. On one word from me, they will push on into Limoges! The flow of blood will be such that 20,000 Maquisards who are circling you will not give a quarter."

'I found myself with d'Albis' when the firing started. Fearing betrayal by Gleiniger, I advised Guingouin to keep his troops back until the situation was clarified. Apparently, your "Charentais fellows" were not in the loop! As for you, you stepped up, bravo!'

'Which allowed me the honour of getting into Limoges first, and to receive the rendition of the garrison before Guingouin! Not foreseen in the programme.

'Sleep well! Your exploit will be erased quick as you like, but still, well done! We won't appear in the annals, be sure of that! Hold on, here's Georges!'

Behind his thick glasses, the grey eyes of the Préfet Rouge sparkle. He embraces us tightly in his big arms,

'Ah my friends, after four years, what joy! Come on, Staunton, they're waiting for us at the Town Hall!'

The peace is attributed to my troop. Guiet and I share a room. We pull a cable for the antenna from one wall to another and send the victory message before lying flat out on our beds, exhausted. Alas, no question of some shut eye: every quarter of an hour a wave of so-called 'advance' Maquisards bursts through our door and, noticing our wireless, believe they are flushing out Nazi spies sending a final SOS to Berlin so they stick the barrels of their machine guns in our stomachs! However, in spite of the heat, Jean-Claude and I are wearing our blousons, his with the US flag, mine with a 'Canada' flash.

At daybreak, only, do I come up with a solution. I stick a page of our notebook of messages struck with the arms of His Majesty on the door. I write in large letters: Bureau of the Intelligence Service. Entry Prohibited!

The Intelligence Service will have gained such respect even on the banks of the Vienne that at this moment, the thugs who consider themselves soldiers no longer approach our room except on the tips of their boots, and whispering!

16

The Day of the Grand Evening

The imposing entrance to 'the Gestapo's hotel', rue Louvrier de Lajolais, moulded oak and bronze handles, opens on to a stone staircase. Vertiginous ceiling, Corinthian columns, clad in modern ceramic tiles in dominant blue.

'*Obersturmführer* Meier had delusions of grandeur,' spat Charles.

'Just to traumatise his victims before submitting them to interrogation. You're thinking about Violette, aren't you?'

'Yes, I can just see her. She comes in, lifts her eyes to the hall, gathers her courage – she spat in the face of the SS who captured her, didn't she? Meier certainly didn't get anything out of her.'

Guingouin gifted this cave to Major Staunton, saying, 'You have earned it, particularly putting that poor Gleiniger in your pocket – whom Meier shot on the Saint-Léonard route.'

The sight of the master bedroom stops us short: they are fully spread with black silver-edged drapes, walls, curtains, canopies, bedspreads and even rugs thrown over stretches of dark oak; the colours, for want of a better words, of the SS!

'You've been sleeping with the maggots, my friend,' chuckles Charles. 'This evening you'll sleep in a coffin. Heck, you're not the first! Sarah Bernhardt …'

Peace had come, the Jedburgh Inter-Allied and SOE teams who operated in the region are rallying to our funeral parlour, which has been promoted to a centre of repatriation: de Guelis, Bissett, Simon, Thomas, Viguier, their adjutants, their wireless ops, two doctors, Forster and Mackenzie, a super efficient Irish woman, Paddy O'Sullivan, Jack Shannon and a *bon vivant*

American major. The maids' bedrooms are registered as full. Ted Fraser and his adjutant, a solid Quebecois called Collette, only come back late in the evening. From dawn to twilight, they slave away to get Limoges airfield back into shape with the means available.

'You're in charge,' Charles tells me. 'You proved yourself at La Vialle.'

I don't lack for house staff, among which is a first-rate cordon bleu. Our table, well known, attracts pretty middle-class ladies. Irresistible, wouldn't you say, a hero in silver-edged black sheets!

The first C-47 lands at last on the patched up runway. Others follow. 'The Gestapo' is instructed to leave. A warrior's rest is fleeting.

At the end of August, at the head of our SAS and OG *Harka*, Charles, Brown, Guiet, Dufour and I head for a section of the National 10 between Angoulême and Poitiers that is are scattered with the debris of the German units fleeing the Gironde. 'You have freedom of action,' stated Buckmaster.

Along the way, a pilgrimage is imperative ...

Of Oradour, only stones, ashes, wisps of trees and twisted branches that still smell of burning like matches burnt to a cinder, skeletal woodwork, bits of blackened wall through windows opened to the blue of the sky. A flag has been unfurled on the still standing bell tower. The cracked and broken altar, at the foot of which some 350 women and children were massacred, stands intact against the wind.

Silence endures. Charles groans, 'Can't wait until we've finished with this mob. Let's go!'

We cross the Vienne river, then Rochechouart and La Rochefoucauld Bivouac at the Braconne camp, abandoned a short while ago by the enemy. About 15km to the north of Angoulême, near the village of Tourriers, the National continues in a wide but vague curve and turns into a thin furrow. Elsewhere it runs straight on and flat out. A wood borders the embankment. In the evening, we take our positions; Lieutenant Rieder – I only know his first name – who has replaced Larson, spreads out his OGs evenly on my left. An ambush just like the others, except for the fact that Staunton has decided to try his luck elsewhere: 'You're going to be tight with thirty on this narrow bank! I'm leaving you to it.' And off he went with the SAS and Brown.

Ritual: a humming announces a convoy. Backfiring from the lead motorbikes. The greater part of the troops arrives unexpectedly. Well lodged on my knee, the phosphorescent sight of my Marlin pierces the mass of the third lorry; I let off some short bursts of fire which, I know, inexorably hit the jackpot. At my sides, Dufour's carbine M1 fires calmly. The wood is ablaze: Bren guns, gammons and Bazookas create an infernal racket. The howls of the wounded mix in as do the yells of the *Unteroffizieren*. No delay in the riposte, at first, badly aimed: grenades bouncing too short, machine guns firing too high, mortars, too far. Afterwards, it starts to spoil. We decamp under a hail of branches lopped by a volley of bullets.

At the entrance of the Braconne camp, Rieder looks pale. 'The attack on the armoured train turned out so badly; it was a baptism of fire for my boys. Larson's death traumatised them dreadfully, you know! I thought I had got them back on track, but tonight, they panicked, fled leaving two Brens on the ground. there are already rumours among the SAS that it was one of mine, badly camouflaged, who was spotted by the two Casserole scouts. Add in abandoning weapons in the face of the enemy, and ... well, if Brown learns of it ... they're good for a court martial, those boys are! Perhaps you could get them out of it?'

'Given a miracle – that the Krauts haven't sneaked off with your Brens!'

As day is breaking, Dufour and I approach the point of ambush on all fours. No one in sight! On the asphalt, rivers of well-worn blood, masses of empty cartridges and shell casings shine like nuggets in the sun. In the shelter of the bank two silent Brens are bathing in the dew!

'I know someone who's going to be pleased!' says Jacques. 'As for the Krauts, we must've treated ourselves to a good dozen. That's at least something in return for Oradour! In my opinion it's their rearguard that we wiped out. Look, the way ahead is free! Why don't we do a little reconnaissance? With these two Bren guns lodged under the windscreen, where's the risk?'

As far as the eye can see, the route is deserted. It is so tempting. It isn't the tinpot that carries us any more but, the C-47 having delivered us loads of petrol, an extremely powerful Citroën 15/6. Let's go. En route and at 150kph an hour I only slow down at the sight of the Angoulême ramparts. Everywhere, flags, garlands, just like in Brive! The town hall is invaded by bustling FFI bods; in the mayor's majestic armchair *Aristide* is seated, or rather Major Landes of SOE, boss of the *Actor* circuit. From Bordeaux he covers the major part of Aquitaine. I came across him at Orchard Court. He's philosophical: 'I came to check things out with the local chiefs. They have things in hand. There's nothing else for me than to do except back home. You can get on with the rest, right?'

I drive carefully through narrow and steep streets. Suddenly, two silhouettes at a window wave their arms, shouting: 'Sir! Sir! Stop! We are English!'

They are rear-gunners of a downed Lancaster that some good people picked up and kept cooped up at the rear of their apartment; they haven't seen the sun for three months! Heart-rending farewells. The two young and pretty girls of the house sob their hearts out. During this long cohabitation, the Entente Cordiale was, it would seem, respected to the letter, strictly!

I come back covered in glory; I give the Brens discreetly back to Rieder, then, back in Limoges, I hand over my two survivors to Ted to be repatriated on the first aircraft.

Two days later, we're on the road again, going north. Our objective – these same fleeing Germans we've just taken down a peg or two. According to London, they're attempting to make their way towards the *Vaterland* by the Sologne, Bourbonnais, the Belfort opening. Some GMRs offer to make up our advance guard. They have so much to make up for and gain pardon. We also tow the two Vickers machine guns, heavy, water cooling, that no one has learned to use.

An American colonel surprises us in a village in Sologne. Blonde, steely looking, curved back and loaded with Colts! It's Colonel, and 'Cossack', Obolensky in pursuit of the sections of his troop let loose in Finistère, Vendée, in Cantel and at Vassivière. Good prince, he consents to let *Percy Red* – code name of the Rieder group – be temporarily at Staunton's disposition. Then he takes up the quest for his lost children once more.

A Maquis chief informs us that in the Claveau, a country seat 4km from Mézières-en-Brenne, a PC of the Wehrmacht is lodged. Lower down, by the départmentale roadway that links Châtellerault to Châteauroux, the Germans are beating a retreat.

In the shelter of an embankment, I see a modest manor, Le Claveau, flanked by two stocky corner towers. A door on the same level opens on to a moon-shaped lawn; a motorbike, two cars and a bus are dozing; the roof is loaded with a machine gun. A washing line hangs on a cord extended from the bus to a balcony. Beyond the lawn there is a dovecote; and a very hoarse rooster. Behind me are deployed the OGs, SAS and GMRs, who are busy around the heavy Vickers that Charles has foisted on them, 'Sort it!'

Only the rooster dares to trouble the peace of dawn; the rooster, and Charles who, at my sides, adjusts his megaphone, '*Achtung Deutsche*

Soldaten! You are surrounded by an Allied unit. You have no chance of escaping! Surrender!'

Half-naked silhouettes show themselves at the windows, the door, and rush for vehicles. A big devil, athletic, tanned, climbs in two bounds up the bus ladder, reaches the machine gun.

'What bloody idiots, these Krauts are!' yells Charles . '*Halt, Dummkopf!*'

Through the eyepiece of my carbine I keep the *Dummkopf*, the idiot, in the line of sight. When I think about my saintly woman of a mother who has always held me, religiously, at a distance from engines of death: 'Never kill.' Today I kill, in the name of Gaston, Fernand Bonnier, Violette and the children of Oradour disintegrated in the phosphorous.

The hand of the acrobat grabs the machine gun; it pivots …

'Fire!' yells Charles.

Forty weapons spit. The Vickers can be heard with their distinctive heavy pom pom. The acrobat comes a cropper on his carriage; the jumping jacks are weakening. At openings, white rags wave. Hands crossed on their head, about a dozen dazed *Feldgrau* fidget facing the rows of SAS and Vikings.

The matter is dealt with promptly. Charles shouts out, 'Bury the dead, evacuate these vehicles to the woods near ours, recover weapons, search, bring me any documents you find. I'm dealing with the interrogationof prisoners. Bob and Dufour, go and mount the guard near the roadway.'

A darkened lane leads to the départmentale road. After having made our way from tree to tree, we wedge ourselves between the roots of a plane tree, about 50m from the roadway. Not a living soul; I doze off.

Dufour, a bulimic, stretches and says: 'I'm going to get a little snack.' Just imagine, he hasn't had a bite since dawn!

The quarter hours pass slowly. Down below suddenly two cyclists, clearly German, pass by whistling. Two others arrive unexpectedly, put their feet on the ground, drink a mouthful, set off again. An agitator goes off to have a dump in the gutter! The occasion is too good to miss, nicking one of these unaware chaps; we'll know more about these fugitives, their number, their destination. I slide behind a hedge bordering the route.

A tinkling of a bell alerts me – I jump out. My supernatural apparition produces a reversing effect on four cyclists, all dressed in green, pedalling side by side. They brake, skid, fall and get in a tangle. The first four, then the ranks who follow, as there are so many cyclists, as far as the horizon.

I stay stock still, carbine pointed on a pile of bikes and paralysed men, wide-eyed. Imitating Charles's Prussian accent, I yell, '*Deutsche Soldaten*! *Ich bin ein Englisch offizier*! You are encircled, surrender!'

Is it really reasonable to convince 1,000 Germans that they are surrounded by a single man?

A burst of rifle fire. Struck by a blow from a great big mitt, my arm describes a circle. My carbine flies off. Before it touches the ground, a rugby pack fells me to the ground. An order snaps out: the fray disbands. A young lieutenant wearing the edelweiss ensign of the mountain troops shakes my hand smiling, saying in English, 'Sorry, but there is a war on, you know!'

An *Unteroffizier* wearing a Red Cross arm band runs up and seizes my arm trickling blood, 'Internazional Red Cross, *mein Herr. Ach*, you had arm against chest? Two centimetres closer, bullet middle heart! Now, bone not even broken! You, big luck, ha!'

Here I am, arm in a scarf, and prisoner. Crouched in the ditches, my victors aim their weapons to the four cardinal points. The lieutenant leans forward, 'So, Captain – for that is your rank, is it not? – tell me a little what brings you here.'

I tell him my name, my number, which, as per the terms of the Geneva Convention, he has the right to demand. After that, I embroider on the effectiveness of the 3rd SAS, to which I claim to belong: 400 commandos parachuted in the surrounding area. He is astonished that I got separated. I reply, 'I wanted to save lives. You won't be getting much further, you know!'

He gives me a friendly, almost complicit look, 'That's for the bosses to decide ...'

A weary-looking bus stops in front of us. The young officer invites me to get in. I give a last look around. Why hasn't Charles intervened?

Because – as I'll learn later on – he didn't hear anything. Pulled back a good kilometre from there, he was interrogating prisoners. One of Brown's many reports will say more:

> After the Le Claveau attack, our troop fell back 400m metres into a wood. I posted myself on a hillock dominating the départementale road. Two hours later, I heard a burst of gunfire coming from the route then I saw thirty to forty Germans who were deploying towards us apparently to encircle us. I immediately gave the order to fall back, since we were only thirty-five in total and I was convinced that there were many more enemy

combatants than we could see. I was right. Later, we learnt that 100 to 200 cyclists were sent on reconnaissance.

Evening falls. God it's dark in this bus! The stink of sweat and suppurating sores catch in my throat. Wounded are sprawled on the benches and even on the ground. For sure, victims of ambushes who aren't too pleased with me! I settle down as best I can in a corner. Soon I'm shaking with fever. Imperceptibly, as if pushed by the jolts of the bus, a cover slides over my knees; a hand brushes against me. On the defensive, I seize it. It hands me a cigarette. The flame from the lighter briefly lights up a smiling face under a bloody turban, '*Nehmen Sie, bitte … Krieg ist schrecklich*!' ['Take it, please … war is horrible!']

And that isn't the last of the surprises for me …

The bus stops; the door opens on to a major, who shines a torch on me: 'You killed the whole garrison at Le Claveau!'

'No, *Herr Major*. Only those who ignored the orders. The others will be treated as prisoners of war.'

'You deserve to be shot!'

'No, I don't! Shoot me and my people will find you. *Krieg ist schrecklich – und fertig* for you. You've lost it!'

He slams the door. My neighbour offers me a second cigarette, '*Major*, bad – us not!'

We set off again. I fall asleep. Gunfire, yappings, '*Terroristen*!'

We stop abruptly. Bullets whine past. This night, we just roll along in stops and starts, from one ambush to another,

At dawn on 5 September, the driver finally shuts off the engine. My guardian angel from the Red Cross comes over, 'This is Lazaret – hospital.'

A courtyard of miracles, more like it, peopled by the lame, amputees, mummies spread out on a lawn bordered by blocks. I ask him, 'Where are we, then? In Nevers?'

'*Gar nicht*, Châteauroux!'

So, in one night we covered less than 50km? At this rate, Dijon is a good week on the road and we'll see the *Vaterland* at the end of time!

Inside the grounds, a big devil covered in dressings tells me that he is just waiting for me to break out. If I agree that my people will hide him, we will escape through a breech he discovered in the fencing. Alas, an aggressive *Feldwebel* – who will attach himself to me from now on and whom I nickname the Pug – sets upon us. My large scoundrel takes off and never comes back. At nightfall I'm pushed on to the flatbed of a lorry between a pyramid of shell crates and six drums of fuel, under the eye of a guard whose Mauser doesn't move its line of sight from me even when we thrice come under fire – which, fortunately, merely reaches for the stars.

At the crack of dawn, the vehicles take refuge in the barns in the woods; it's not a good idea tobe driving around during the daytime: the day before yesterday, a dozen Mustangs caused carnage among the lorries near Argenton-sur-Creuse.

After having saluted me, clicking his heels, my driver, an old corporal with a weather-beaten face, takes me to a farm and advises the farmer treats me like a lord. Behind his little iron-rimmed glasses he is all smiles, 'Me, Fritz, Rhénan, cousin of the Alsatians, 52 years old, farmer, not soldier, auxiliary only. Never shot, never killed! I'm protecting you, *Herr Hauptmann*!'

Now his acolytes, among whom is the ferocious sentry who kept me in his sights the night before, also fall into line: Knut, the mechanic, is Austrian, not Nazi! The other, Hermann is only 18; Sudetenland, so hardly German, he was forced to join up. I will never have better valets. From then on, if Hermann is on guard duty, it is to warn of the approach of Little Squirt. Of course, there're some awkward customers like this Nazi who, just like Major de Mézières-en-Brenne, yells, 'You, terrorist, I shoot you!'

I waved my official identity plaque under his nose, 'I'm an officer of the regular forces. You, you will never reach Germany! So ...'

He paled, lifted his hand, hesitated, slapped his thigh with all his force then turned on his heels.

'*Schön, ganz schön, Herr Hauptmann*! – good, very good,' murmured Fritz!

At the next day's stop, my host whispers to me, 'Someone wants to see you in the kitchen ...'

It's the 'delegate' of the Résistance network of which, of course, my farmer is a member. He lets me know that I'm a prisoner of a bunch of fugitives and runaways commanded, for want of a better word, by a General Elster who was occupying Mont-de-Marsan. Yesterday 200 lorries loaded with Luftwaffe units from the base at Châteauroux attempted to rejoin Sancoins; attacked without let up by the Maquisards, they didn't even cover 100km in thirty-six hours.

'I'll give your news to London by radio,' he assures me.

When I get back to the room, Fritz, who's watching the Pug, grimaces, '*Herr Hauptmann*, *Feldwebel* said that if you *weg* Knut, Hermann, me, shot ... You keep repeating, "Belfort gap closed!" So if you soon free, you not leave before, *bitte*?'

He is so pathetic, the old corporal. In spite of hooch compresses that the farmers' wives who're sheltering me apply to me, my wound becomes septic; I'm no longer up to getting over the wall: 'No, Fritz, don't worry.'

On the afternoon of 8 September, after a night sacrificed to the usual ambushes, the edelweiss lieutenant, pilots and sailors visit me. I repeat to them, embellishing, what the BBC has just informed me, Allied fighters have strafed units which, behind us, were leaving Châteauroux: 400 dead. More to the east, de Lattre occupies Dijon and Autun. The route to the *Vaterland* is well and truly cut off! I go on about the three-star comforts of the prisoner camps in Scotland and Canada. Shortly after, the Résistance member on duty passes me a message from London: a person named Salesman wishes me '*Bon courage*!'

On the 10th before dawn, the Krauts set out across an interminable bridge; it spans a large bed of gravel with a drizzle of water running through, all that remains of a great river at the end of this summer. A medieval fortress stands on a cliff dominating the opposite bank. Caught up in a tide of carts, cyclists and pedestrians, our coach rolls along at walking speed. Suddenly, the cliff is in flames, the thunderbolt strikes – bullets, shells rain down, mowing down men and horses. Vehicles crumple. The panic is indescribable. Hanging on to his steering wheel, Fritz executes a fantastic U-turn and then criss-crosses, horns blaring, between the wrecks, the corpses of beasts and people. The cabin is riddled with bullets, the windscreen shattered. He sets off, accelerator to the floor, and doesn't let up until we reach the first town, Marcenat-sur-Allier, 2km from the bridge.

I don't have time to catch my breath, the Pug – who, alas, has survived – pushes me into the village school and locks me in a store shed. I sit right on the beaten mud floor, back to the wall.

A little later, four *Feldgrau* come in, and without glancing at me, put a fresh pine coffin dripping blood beside me. Ten minutes later they come back with another coffin. Soon I have six caskets to keep me company. Under the sheet metal roof – turned red by the midday sun – I am stifling. Squadrons of green flies buzz in the seas of blood. I exterminate those flies that attempt to feast on my wounded arm.

A medical colonel enters: 'Sir, I have no more dressings nor medicines and many wounded. From the village mayor I have learned that opposite, in Billy, there are almost regular units called ORA, commanded by real officers, who have attacked us. Officer to officer, I thought you could possibly convince them to have our wounded hospitalised.'

'But, Colonel, why not put down your arms, quite simply? You're caught in a rat's trap. What's the use of having men killed, like this morning?'

'Our general refuses to surrender to "irregulars"!'

'But I'm a "regular"!'

'Doubtless that's the case but you don't have the power to ...'

'You think? During the day, by radio, I can receive a delegation from General Eisenhower!'

He looks me up and down, perplexed, 'I'm going to refer that to my general. Don't move!'

I burst out laughing, 'Move? You're joking!' Then showing him the coffins: 'If I could only get a little fresh air!'

He goes off leaving the door open. Straight away, Fritz brings me a lard tart and ersatz coffee that I eat stretched out in the sunshine. My breakfast hardly digested, the doctor reappears. 'I haven't succeeded in contacting my general, and my wounded cannot wait ... Do you accept my proposition?'

Six ambulances bearing a white flag line up before the school; they are stuffed with wounded accompanied by nurses, the *Souris Grises* – the 'grey mice' – soiled and shabby from weeks of effort and struggle. Violette already thought them frumpy when they were at the peak of their glory. In front, a line of honour: frozen standing to attention, my Alpine, some sailors, pilots, Hermann, Knut and Fritz, who whispers to me: 'This time, *Herr Hauptmann*, *Krieg* well *fertig*!'

I pass them in review; I shake their hand. Fritz has a tear in his eye. It just lacks *God save the King* ...

The colonel invites me to take my place in the cabin of the head ambulance, 'So, in the event of betrayal, the first bullet will be for you.' Half a smile steals across his face.

At the wheel, a *Gretchen* with a sombre look and white-blonde hair! When we reach the opposite bank of the Allier she represses a *Mein Gott* at the sight of a Scottish major wearing a beret with a pompom of his clan, as favoured by Edward VII, and a great russet moustache, who shouts to me, 'Welcome home, Bob! Buck knows how you captured around thirty enemy personnel, even worn out. Staunton will come and get you,' while giving my

Amazonian a Hollywood smile. The mouse is terrified. In the Wehrmacht, as straight as a die, she has never set eyes on a *Herr Major* disguised as a clown and, in addition, turning on the charm to a female soldier!

ColonelMortier is camped in a maisonette at the foot of the fortress. He commands the reconstituted units of *tirailleurs* who tore us to pieces.

'In November '42, demobilised, these brave sharpshooters got lost in the wild. We got them back and made them fit again,' he points out. 'Damned warriors, don't you agree?'

'Absolutely. Thank you!'

'As for "Colonel Elster", he is not, properly speaking, a colonel, rather three or four groups of 4 to 5,000 men. One was stopped short at Decize by the FFL. Yours was trying to proceed between Moulins and Vichy. You saw, I was there! The 4th SAS of Colonel Bourgouin bolted from Brittany, the 83rd American Division from Orléans. We're told that Elster only wants to surrender to his boss, General Macon. Imagine, if your doctor had been able to get to him, perhaps you would have had 5,000 prisoners? Go on, I'll lend you two motorcyclists to clear your route.'

After having pretended to search for our common ancestors, Mortier, while we clearly know that our patronymic is false, we leave one another as good friends.

The Moulins hospital is venerable. A nun wearing a cornette is at the foot of each bed; my wounded are at the party. As for me, I'm bandaged, bathed and pampered like little Jesus and tucked in the white bed in a cell by the prioress in person. I fill in the admittance register religiously.

The next day I have lunch at the Hotel de Paris, the establishment with the most stars in the town. The staff watches this first Allied officer curiously. I am puffed up: here I am – a hero! Naive more like. The bill, excessively steep, puts me in my place! Between Occupiers and Liberators they show no favouritism; both get the same fatal gunshot. The mark is dead, so now they fire on the dollar! Hopefully Vera won't know anything about it ...

Charles picks me up after a coffee, which costs its weight in gold.

In Limoges, the Gestapo still holds open house. I happily reacquaint myself with my hospital sheets. Alas, very early in the morning, a telephone call pulls me from these delights.

'Captain Mortier! This is Colonel Rivier, commander of the region. Was it you who mined a crossroads on the National 20? Ah well, gotta un-mine it for me!'

'I stuffed it with booby traps ...'

'With what?'

'Hidden traps ...'

'Come again? You made a map of your minefield, didn't you?'

'Er, no. That day, I didn't have much time, you know.'

'But what do they teach you then in your Saint-Cyr of Canada, Captain?'

'I've never been to Saint-Cyr, Colonel!'

'Evidently!' grumbles Rivier, a technician. 'Whatever is needed, do it!'

The crossroad is just as I left it. A jumble of plane branches broken one against the other. At the side of the group of signs reading '*Achtung Minen*' lies a dismembered light cart still harnessed to a disembowelled horse, stiff legs. A pair of trousers hang from a branch of a tree. A farmhand says to me. 'It's Pierre, a farmer, stubborn as a mule and well away on a half-a-bottle. The other evening he shouted, "These signs, it's a gimmick! I'm off on the shortest route!" He was buried in bits.'

I put my feet in the rut hollowed out by a cart's wheel; I unroll long slabs of explosives from one end to the other. Their explosion detonated the mines. From slab to slab, I manage to clear the trees. I spot one of these invisible deadly wires, I follow it without touching it until the first booby trap; I defuse it. I go after another at the speed of a tortoise; one false move and I leave in smoke. By the time night is falling, I have neutralised six traps, I'm shattered, my wounded arm refuses to work. Up to then, my luck has held out.Yet there remain a good dozen more booby traps.

I deal with Colonel Rivier late in the evening and only at some distance, by telephone: 'Defusing mines by hand in that mess is suicide. Need a tractor to clear these trees – at a good distance. That way the booby traps will blow one after the other without doing any damage. As for the mines, only an engineering unit armed with frying pans will be able to neutralise them.'

I don't wait for the colonel to explode. I hang up. Afterwards, I feign death. Fortunately, he has other worries – organising Liberation parties ... On the fairground, fanfares and Croix de Guerre are handed out like sweets to the glorious allies, however much time spent in France, the actions led, the dangers run.

Charles is mocking: 'When he invented the Légion d'Honneur, Napoleon said that medals were only baubles, yet he decorated his Old Guard by order of merit anyway. You only had to be a major! Even if you've only been dropped in after the liberation, you're rewarded.'

The Maquisards are being inspected. At the head of one section, two of them, blonde, tall, bronzed, stand taller by a head at least than their companions at arms, hired soldiers whose parade style leaves much to be desired. These two parade stomach in, chin high, leg bent. Real military men, without a doubt. When they notice Charles, their face lights up with a large smile and they cry out, '*Wie geht's, Herr Major*?'

My boss responds to them with a high salute, saying to me; 'But, my word, that's my two from the Das Reich! They look fit as a fiddles.'

Their sergeant does not hold back on the praise, 'At the beginning, when they were volunteers, I didn't want either of them. I said to myself – they're going to shoot us in the back! They are crack sharpshooters, I can tell you. You've should have seen how many of their friends they brought down!'

The town hall offers a vin d'honneur to the 'authorities': the new mayor, Georges Guingouin, the préfet Chaintron, regional 'delegates', a commissaire of the Republic. The *Centre Libre* doesn't skimp on the flattery: 'Major Staunton has replied to the discourse of the government's commissaire in impeccable French.' After the last flute of champagne, Georges Guingouin embraces me in his long arms, 'Bob, adieu. Safe return to the country.'

'Adieu, Colonel. You have well and truly won your peace!'

He stares at me as if inspired: '"My" peace? No, yours! Mine will only come with the Great Day!'

His faith transfigures him, an apostle, that is what he is. In his soul and conscience, the paradise of the Soviets is that of the just. On the Great Day, Saint Stalin, father and redeemer of the people, will impose on them his universal fraternity with blows of the hammer and sickle.

17

V-2s to the Samurai

'I'll stay in Limoges for the time it takes to settle our affairs; I want to leave everything tidy,' Charles tells me. 'We'll meet up again in Paris.'

Jean-Claude and I leave 'the Gestapo' in my Citroën filled with jerry cans full of petrol; from today we won't find any more anywhere. Blow me, how empty the road home is; I remember it blocked by the pitiful throng of the Exodus! This time we pass just a few rare civilian vehicles and at times a military convoy. On the other hand, in Orly there is a forest of wreckage as far as the eye can see; bombers, fighters, liaison craft, all crammed together like sardines in a tin.

The streets of Paris are as quiet as the routes of France. On the pavements policemen with white batons who, yesterday under the Occupier's boot, brought to heel pedestrians crossing the roads outside of the pedestrian crossings, stare fixedly at the sky when the same parishioners make it a point of honour to cross anywhere except within the pedestrian crossings. It isn't the time to make waves; they have these peccadilloes on their conscience. Now, Allied flags have taken the place of swastika banners on the façades of buildings.

I am thinking of my family – no news for a year now. What kind of a shock am I going to cause them? I opt for the soft approach. Madeleine Ducroquet, my friend's mother, answers on the first knock at the door.

'My God, it's you? Yesterday, your father was getting desperate: "Paris has been liberated more than a month and 'the little one' still hasn't shown up!" I'm going to announce your return to them with kid gloves. My sons aren't here; they've resumed their studies again after having got in on the action at the Préfecture de Police. How happy they would have been to welcome you back! But what am I thinking! I've one last bottle of Duval-Leroy, uncork it while I clear a corner of the table. Excuse this mess – I'm ashamed of it!'

Madeleine is one of those manic hosts to whom a mote of dust, a knick-knack or a mat out of place is a cause for flurry and worry. 'It's just not me, this mess and jumble, but my housekeeper left me suddenly a week ago. Her husband was killed!'

'In the war?'

'No, he was a farmer.'

'An accident?'

'One could say so – he was blown up by a mine!'

'Near the front?'

'Not at all – in deepest France. An out-of-the-way village, in Limousin.'

'In Limousin? Do you remember its name by any chance?'

'Yes, Fombelaux.'

I give Jean-Claude a well-aimed kick under the table to nail his beak shut.

My return to the fold, will be pathetic, full of tears, like the previous ones. We go to bed at dawn; we have so much to share. The next day before midday, I present myself at the Automobile Club of France.

'Monsieur Benoist still hasn't given us his news,' I'm told.

Le Cecil, Parisian PC of the French Section, is a four-star hotel that stands like the bow of ship at the crossroads of rue Saint Didier and rue Lauriston. On the latter, No. 93 notoriously, until very recently, accommodated the French Gestapo, the Carlingue, founded by Pierre Bonny and Henri Lafont, one a crook and the other, a corrupt cop who had been involved in the Stavisky affair and other filth. Decorated with taste, this building was brightened up with orchids, the owner's favourite flower. His 'countesses' were a battalion of whores who excelled at pillow talk. Their conversations with their naive lovers were sometimes continued in the form of muscled interrogations in the basement torture rooms. Host of a private luxury hotel in Neuilly, Lafon rode thoroughbreds in the woods, and his titled Amazons on his giant bed strewn with orchid petals. All of Paris was to be found at his bustiling receptions. Maurice Chevalier crooned his *Ma Pomme*. Lafont mingled and bowed and scraped when his friend and boss, Karl Boemelburg, honoured one of his shindigs with his presence.

Buckmaster welcomes us. God, has he got some wrinkles! His red hair streaked with grey is sparse, heavy pockets surround his eyes. Affable, warm, he is quite different! He grasps my hands in his, 'You've been wounded, Bob?'

'It's nothing but a bad memory, but Violette, Peter Newman and Claude Malraux are still alive, aren't they?'

'Yes. The Swiss Red Cross informed me they were deported. Be assured that we will see them again. As they are on their last legs the Nazis will be only too pleased to have currency to exchange!'

'I hope so. Anyway, Eliane, Diana and Eric are there, of course?'

Buck's face darkens, 'Well – no ...'

'Don't tell me that they were taken as well. In June not so long ago you confirmed to me ...'

'I lied to you. We had orders never to reveal to those operational the disappearance of their friends. I'm sure you understand – morale ... Eliane went back to the *Monk* circuit in Marseille. She sabotaged thirty locomotives near Cassis, and then the circuit was penetrated. Diana was part of the *Acrobat* circuit in Lons-le-Saunier, infiltrated by a double agent. She was later seen in the Natzweiler concentration camp. As for Eric, parachuted near Belfort, he killed a traitor. Unfortunately, he was betrayed in his turn – and killed, in Montbéliard.'

I clenched my fists and jaws before lashing out, 'That's all, I hope?'

'Yes – well, no ... there remains Bisset.'

'What, Bisset? He came back, surely!'

'No, he came back by car with Ted Fraser. They stopped in Vichy. Unloading his jeep, the groom at the hotel dropped his Marlin – safety not properly engaged – a bullet right in the heart.'

Toto, I almost curse him: senselessly, like these kids of the Maquis, like Larson! Dead for nothing.

'I hope the list is closed, Colonel. Do you know where Benoist is?'

At that instant Vera Atkins appears, impeccably coiffed and made up, smiling like a Victorian lady. She offers me her cheek, 'Bob, bad penny that you are, I was sure you'd come back!'

'Benoist,' the Colonel asks: 'Where is he?'

'Ah yes, Robert,' she murmurs. 'Betrayed by his heart. He mounted an exemplary network in Nantes. He learnt one day that his mother, whom he venerated, was at death's door. You know him; nothing could have prevented him going to her bedside. Kieffer was waiting for him. They hanged him.'

With a forced smile, Buck confides to me that, from the class of March 1943 in Wanborough, only two survivors remain: Raynaud and me. Pierre got back a short while ago, unscathed, after eighteen months of his mission in the Midi!

I salute Buck, hug Vera. I leave Le Cecil almost running. It smells of death too much!

I am surprised to find myself wondering whether maybe Maguy, too … But no, she answers at the first ring, fully alive, mad with joy.

'You? I'll give you ten minutes, no more, to find me at Ciro's.'

I present myself at Le Ciro's in uniform, amaranth beret on my head, stick under my arm, imagining, 'What a shock I'm going to give her!'

Without a flicker, without a word, she throws herself in my arms. A long minute later, after having caught her breath, she exclaims, 'The uniform suits you well, my darling!'

I remain stupefied, 'That's all you …'

'Ah yes. You could have spared yourself the trouble, René! But you're probably not called René, are you? Before you left for – Turkey, your absences without leaving an address, your open secrets, all had the alarm bells ringing. You may as well have confided in me.'

'And what about your uncle?'

'Uncle the *Oberst?* A pacifist who adored me so much he would have protected you! I told him nothing, of course. Yesterday, luck didn't smile on you: Maman saw you coming out of the Cecil, which is just two steps from us, you know. On her return, she was all a-tremble: "Your René is an English spy! He saw my brother in uniform; he's going to denounce us!" I reassured her. I got ready to contact the Cecil. You called me…'

For days it was victory parties for us – sleepless nights in a Paris that could easily be mistaken for those of yesteryear. No break for the black market. Free Paris traffics Luckies, nylons, GI rations and military petrol, however pink it might be to protect and ensure its provenance. Pros and society women go from *Feldgrau* to *Fieldgreen* without a pause. Blasé, Gabriel Chartrand, the man from Quebec who went to Rouen before I did in 1943! Big boss of public relations of the Canadian Forces, he is paid court to by all these petty collaborationist crooks looking to whitewash themselves. They besiege his suite at the Hotel Napoleon, the palace on avenue Friedland.

'Just imagine,' he tells me, 'Jules Berry – a must-see star of the cinema and the boulevard – has begged me to intercede in favour of his wife, herself a star who let herself be screwed by the Germans.'

Gaby objects, telling him: 'It's just too gross!'

'Come on, my dear, be kind!' insists the actor, in his voice eroded by cigars and Scotch. 'Like every woman, Josette obeys her fanny, the universal law! Unfortunately, a fanny – and she's got a damned great one, believe me – is blind; it doesn't see the difference between a German prick and a French prick!'

Gaby gets indignant! The majority of leading lights in the art, letters and movie world signed on at the Continental, licked the boots of Otto Abetz, the Reich ambassador in Paris or, in Berlin, those of Goebbels and Goering. Tino Rossi is hiding. Chevalier is paying big money to the good works of the PCF so that they will pardon him. Guitry vegetates in Drancy. Is he ruminating on his past glory when, in the first rank of a collaborationist *Harka* and big shots of the Wehrmacht, he welcomed Hitler's offering, Aiglon's ashes? And when it come to the art of collaboration, the world of 'business' beats that of the intelligentsia by far!

'You can't be good at everything,' mocks Charles, who had arrived in Paris. 'France may well be beaten in war but she is unbeatable in scheming and dirty tricks. You're young and ingenuous but you'll get there. Come on come to dinner at the house.'

'You've got a house in Paris?'

The 'house' is just an apartment, but in a smart building in the Faubourg of Saint-Germain. On the landing a young elegant woman, hair cut like a tomboy, welcomes me, 'I'm Maryse, Philippe's wife.'

'Philippe? But it's Charles who ...'

'Come in, he'll explain to you.'

Charles appears, 'No, Bob, Major Charles Mark Geoffrey Staunton is finished! In front of you is Philippe Liewer, French 100 per cent ... and Jewish.'

All becomes clear: the tears in his eyes, I remember, when he had opened the doors to the Jews at the internment camp, for example.

Charles-Philippe smiles crookedly at me. 'Let me explain to you, old man – the Liewers, established in Strasbourg since forever, withdrew to Paris in 1871 so as not to become Prussians. At home, by tradition, we learn German and English from the cradle. As per my right under the law, I joined Havas News Agency, I covered the farce that was Munich until the SD discovered I was a Jew and expelled me. In 1940, I was an interpreter with British headquarters. I was one of those evacuees from Dunkirk ready to sign on again. But Maryse was in Nice! I left to look for her. The debacle – I remained blocked. End of 1940, I was contacted. You know the rest.'

The Liewers belong to tout-Paris. Born at the home of the Weill-Harlé, which brings scientists and professors into the world, Maryse launched herself into the French adaptation of the *Hauts de Hurlevent* (*Wuthering Heights*). My friends drag me in a worldly whirlwind. Maryse and Maguy, wearing haute couture dresses, eclipse the starlets, the bluestockings and the transient poets, and the Le Tabou club's existentialists.

While waiting for the elections, which are to take place God knew when, de Gaulle keeps everyone happy. The CP, 'party of 75,000 shot!', who we know are well armed, marches to the tune of the Kremlin. Thorez will be minister.

Herriot, the old flag, though threadbare, is still flying. Unlike his comrades of the Third République, he wasn't condemned to the Vichy Riom Trials in 1942 and interned. He was depressed for a very long time. In August 1944 he was the impeccable host of a rest home in Lorraine. 'Before the Germans packed their bags, Laval figured that he could launder him,' Philippe recounts to me. 'He invited Herriot to a lavish lunch at the Préfecture of Paris and said to him: "You can have the throne; you, the last president of the Assembly, legitimate successor to the head of state. If the marshal retires – and I will watch out for that – Roosevelt, who cannot bear de Gaulle, will crown you. That done, you will return me the favour." Stuffed with foie gras and grands crus, head in the clouds, *le Gros* replies: "Since I believe in de Gaulle about as much as I do in Pétain, I'm in!"'

'He signed his death warrant, then!'

'Not a chance! Hitler saved him. He refused to back the scheme; he had him sent to Germany! So, *le Gros*, "captured by the enemy" made a martyr, who will one day have more streets in his name than de Gaulle, you'll see! The French have such a short memory. They assemble in Paris by the 300,000 to see the Grand Charles (de Gaulle); no fewer turned out in April last when Guitry – yes, him again! – gave the sugar grand-daddy, in great pomp, an autographed letter of Napoleon's.

Mitterrand's another who'll find his way through, too. In Vichy, he was in the Légion's Documentation Service. He buttered up the marshal so he would award him the Vichy Order of the Gallic Francisque, number 2202 – such a truly rare gong that it needed to be requested in writing, don't forget. He mounted a phony network of prisoners and deportees – as if they were capable of resisting! He went to sweet-talk Giraud in Algiers, while still carefully remaining out of the general's reach. When the liberation happened, he boasted having taken, almost at the point of a bayonet, the Minister of Anciens Combattants – but the Germans had fled three days previously. At present, he is general secretary to the Ministry of Prisoners, among whom one day 1 to 2 million will be voters. Be in no doubt – the "flag" will lend him a hand!'

One person who has never drifted is Maman. In 1915 she founded the Paquet du Soldat in New York, which sent dozens of thousands of parcels to our squaddies. In June 1940 she threw the grateful letter that Pétain had written in his own hand to the bottom of a drawer. Thirty years later, she conceived the French Welcome Committee, a reception centre for Allied soldiers exposed to the temptations of the city of light, its little ladies, its sleazy bars and low dives. She trawled the high society world for sponsors, recruiting Lady Astor, Mrs Eden, Lady Decima Moor, a respectable aristocrat whom I knew in London, and General Carthew-Yorstoun, who commands the British garrison. In a large apartment in place de la Madeleine, she commands an irreproachable battalion of hostesses from good families!

When I visit her, an English sergeant pushes a large Wehrmacht motorbike, a Zündapp, under the entry porch. Dressed in a strange uniform, jodhpurs, laced boots over white socks, with black wavy hair, his moustache of a young premier, velvet eyes, he has the face of a handsome man. I whistle, 'What a beautiful machine!'

'War booty, Captain! Its owner was an *Unteroffizier of the Panzer SS Hitler Jungend*. I laid him out on the Orne in July. I know motorbikes. In '40 I was a machine gunner on a bike in the Czech army. I was wounded in Orléans.'

'Get out of here! In '40 you were too young, for sure! And then, you speak English without an accent!'

'I have a gift for languages! I speak Russian, Rumanian, Hungarian and German. I was born in a hole in the Carpathian Mountains that changed nationality like a shirt. I'm going to tell you a secret: as of now, legally, I'm a Soviet!'

He offers me a Du Maurier, a luxury cigarette. 'I smoke the same.'

'Ah well, you've got good taste, Sir, as I'm Leslie du Maurier, a *nom de guerre* of course.'

He tells me the twists and turns of his life: flight from the Ukraine in 1939 before the Germans, through Bulgaria, Turkey, Lebanon, the Foreign Legion and then the Czech army, England and even a lady who taught him English in pillow talk. Then he asks me, 'In fact, to whom do I have the honour, Sir?'

'Captain Mortier, actually Bob Maloubier.'

'So, you're the son of Madame President? Élisabeth has spoken to me of you ... Good God, but she's waiting for me! Sorry Sir!' he yells as he runs on up the staircase.

In the full to bursting living room, I see him bending low over a pretty girl with a fine face, framed in long chestnut hair.

'Ah, here you are at last!' my mother launches at me.

'I was delayed by a strange sergeant who says he's Russian ...'

'Ah, then you've met Leslie? What a cheek he has! He seduced my protégée, Élisabeth Meynard, from a good Lyonnais family. Her mother is worried – her girl – infatuated with a little Central European Jew! Nevertheless, Carthew praises him to the skies. He has assured me that he would be decorated, promoted to officer, even naturalised, and that he was worthy of Élisabeth. He's looking for a command for him in a prestigious unit. But I am in an embarrassing position nonetheless, as his father, officer of the Cadre Noir,[1] a hero of the Great War and Protestant' – virtue par excellence in the eyes of Maman, inveterate Huguenot – 'is cross with me!'

'France is liberated, the French Section of SOE, no longer needing agents, is going to turn you over to the BCRA,' Vera announces to me; she sounds disillusioned. 'But I fear it won't have much to offer you!'

Philippe is also concerned about my future, 'You were dreaming of flying, weren't you?' One of my good friends, Corniglion-Molinier, who was Malraux's pilot, could perhaps pull some strings for you. Unconditionally Gaullist, he is one of these rare fighter pilots who brought back victories from both wars. Additionally, he is a doctor in law, has produced films and is, I believe, owner of Victorine studios. Fresh from being made a general, he is Vallin's second today, the head of French aviation.'

Fine figure, young with two stars, slim, tanned, eagle profile, silver hair and affable, 'Philippe told me a lot about you,' says Corniglion-Molinier. 'But only Vallin ... I'll telephone him. Go and see him!'

From his office in Boulevard Victor, the big boss dominates the aerodrome of Issy-les-Moulineaux, as congested as that of Gibraltar. He is debonair. 'I can get you into a training school – which, at the end of hostilities will

1 Corps of *ecuyers*, or instructors, at the French military riding academy École Nationale d'Équitation at Saumur

close. And if you haven't qualified by then, which I fear you won't, you will be left on the streets and frustrated. Think about it.'

I didn't reflect for long. I had started this war, it deserved that I finish it. Adieu to my childhood dream.

Indian summer on the congested Champs Elysées, and in the shambling military crowd is a turbaned pilot, one leg and one arm in plaster, leaning on the side on a crutch, on the other on a little plump woman with red coppery hair wrapped up in a mink coat. Déricourt and his Jeannot! He hugs me to his bandaged chest: 'The Jerries got me two months ago. Some Maquisards pulled me out of my crushed aircraft for burial. Two legs, eight ribs and one arm broken, fractured skull, perforated lungs, burst spleen and I forget what else! It wasn't my best time. Let's go have a drink to that!'

For the brigade of La Lorraine, a top-class brasserie in Place des Ternes; from the maître d'hôtel to Madame Pipi, each and every one calls him Monsieur Henri. Champagne! He recounts his many setbacks to me.

'Since we parted ways, I've had a hard time. Neither the Free French Air Force nor the RAF wanted me: too old to be a war pilot, but young enough to jump out of a plane with a parachute! One day, Corniglion-Molinier got me out of the mess. In France he recuperated some old cuckoos to carry out liaison flights, performed by old pilots. One day, at the commands of an Auster from the time of the Crusades, I was flying by sight, very low. I cut the route of a German column ...'

Born raconteur, Henri describes the shells striking his engine as a direct hit, the crash in a field, his death – as true as mine a year earlier – as one recounts a trump in bridge. All ears, Maguy, breathless, devours Henri the enchanter with her eyes.

Philippe takes me to Rouen. He's keen to do an autopsy – the term is his – of the mortal remains of *Salesman*, our circuit, to piece together its fall, aid the victims and their heirs, comfort the widows and the orphans.

What a shock coming into the lower part of town! The quays disappear under a pile up of wrecked tanks and lorries, scraps of German columns that, in retreat, had bottlenecked up on the banks and been shredded by a hurricane of bombs. The bridges have collapsed. Of 12 rue Jeanne d'Arc, not one stone remains on top of another. Saint-Maclou and rue Molière are spared. Madeleine crumples against me sobbing, while Maurice claps his hand on my back. In July, Denise Desvaux had put the key under the door just in time; she hugs us to her generous chest. Broni Piontek was deported,

Paccaud and the Francheterres scraped through, but their son Raymond was arrested, and they're unaware why. Together, we establish a list of the disappeared.

In Le Havre, the damage has been severe. Juliette Mayer reports how Roger was taken, betrayed by the principal of the college who, terrorised, hid from him the fact that the Gestapo were waiting for him. Philippe confronts the 'commissar' Alie at the Bonne-Nouvelle prison where he is detained. An insignificant little man except for his very mobile black eyes. He plays the gallant knight who backed a bad horse.

Philippe cuts him off. 'Saint Paul ordered useless chatterers to keep quiet! Only the thirst for power incited you to send your people to the abattoir. You're nothing but a filthy traitor! I shall be asking the court to have you shot. And if by miracle, you escape the firing squad, I will personally have your guts for garters and ensure that you burn over a slow heat. And I will not be alone, will I, Bob?'

The satisfied smirk disappears; the little man keeps his own counsel.

Once again Philippe sees correctly: 'We won't have to pursue Alie; he will be shot.'

Farewell dinner at the Francheterres, who live on Rouen's left bank in places des Emmurées. The name intrigues me. Francheterre gives me the key to it: 'We find ourselves on the site of a cloistered convent, 1,000 years old; back then you'd only have left it in a coffin, hence the workers who were digging the foundations of this building exhumed a tomb stone bearing this epitaph:

> I was abbess of these premises only six years.
> The sky took me to itself in the April of my age,
> But since we only come here to gain Heaven,
> I never had any need to stay longer.

'Makes a shiver run down the spine, doesn't it?'

'Six months ago Violette said the same thing to me!'

If Paris is having a party, London is still at war. Hardly had I put my foot on the ground than a block of flats disintegrated before my eyes in a hurricane of dust – without a plane in the sky, without the howling of an engine, without even being preceded by the shriek that always announces the arrival of an honest bomb! No, this shrieking comes afterwards. As I remain with my eyes raised to the sky, an RAF cadet accosts me, 'Never heard of the V-2s, Sir? They arrive just like that, faster than sound, through the stratosphere. the warning comes afterwards! Pretty mess, hey? A ton of high explosives crashes down at more than 2,000ft a second. It makes a fine hole, doesn't it? Next to that the V-1 looks like a load of crap. Do you remember them?'

'I haven't "heard" either one of them, I was abroad.'

'Ah. Well, 10,000 V-1s fell – a quarter of them on London. Five thousand dead and 15,000 wounded! As for the V-2s, you'll get all you want and more, ten come down a day – I know all that because I'm in the section that counts flying bombs!'

In point of fact, in the day, V-2s thunder all over London. A block of flats here, a section of a street there, all fall into dust. The King, the Queen, their daughters Elizabeth and Margaret – in uniform, one in the ATS, the other a girl guide – and Churchill spend hours climbing over ruins and bombsites, comforting those who have been disaster victims.

In Baker Street I am honourably discharged. In Duke Street, headquarters of the BCRA, I fill in a pile of documents and I swap my captain's pips for captain's braids. Stuck with her submarines, Ann cannot get away from Weymouth. On the telephone she swears in a tearful voice that she'll remember me 'forever'!

One evening I get to know Nancy, a female auxiliary pilot of the US Army Air Force which convoys in light bombers coming out of American factories to England. I don't believe my ears; she is fragile, with harpist's hands.

'Yes,' she assures me. 'I even do several rotations a month.'

She invites me to the Rainbow Corner post exchange – a multifaceted hostel, post office, drugstore, bar, restaurant and dance hall for American troops – at the corner of Piccadilly Circus and Shaftsbury Avenue. That evening, Glenn Miller and his orchestra get the GIs dancing. A table is reserved permanently for the female pilots and their boss, Jacqueline Cochran, a famous, record-holding female aviator. I'm welcomed American fashion, open armed; I even have the chance of exchanging a few words with Glenn, who, learning that I'm going back to France, says to me, 'Ah, I am surely going to visit there! So, see you in Paris, Bob!'

In a pissy dawn, through masses of showers, I disembark in Arromanches, an immense floating port protected from undertow by a semi-circular water break constructed with a chain of wrecks and Mulberries, those caissons invented by Churchill. A bunch of ships discharge, loaded to the brim. The roadstead and the inner harbour are crawling with small craft, hulks and pontoons as well as lorries. I end up on the shore, a cesspool where walking means sinking up to the calves. Against a background of Norman cottages holed like colanders and burnt bunkers, beach teams congregated around multicolour signs are waving their arms around, regulating the traffic of 'ducks' and tanks.

'Heading to Paris?' grumbles an officer. 'Jump in this GMC trying to get itself out of this shit-house.'

Battling with the steering wheel, three gears, as many pedals and an engine howling to death, a beanpole, black as ink, pulls his truck out of the bog. Four hours later, he drops me at my place, loaded with four jerry cans of petrol.

The *Direction générale des etudes et recherché* (DGER), which succeeded the *Direction générale des services spéciaux* (DGSS), which is taking over from the BCRA in London, is nicknamed *La Muette* [The Mute], because it squats in a luxury block of flats dominating the roundabout of the Muette, originally a Bloch-Rothschild building confiscated by the Kriegsmarine which, daubing them green and black, made them, in the heart of the Bois de Boulogne, a small fort of the Atlantic Wall. Around, hundreds of cars plastered with stars, the Croix de Lorraine, hammer and sickle. Inside, an ants' nest of civilians and military come from God knows where, doing God knows what. It's a secret service dump for London and Algiers – and Vichy. It's like entering a windmill. It will be known that Doctor Petiot outdid Landu in burning Jews in his boiler after having plucked them of their assets. He claimed he was trying to get them to Spain, after they visited him as an FFI captain. After Colonel Passy, the ethnologist Jacques Soustelle takes over. He might have been able to juggle the Zapotecs, Toltecs, Chichimecs, Tepanecs and Aztecs, but at La Muette the wheels came off!

As for me, I interrupted the typing pool of innumerable secretaries and disturbed the siesta of a number of deputy chief clerks simply for them to suggest missions each one more suicidal than the last, but 'right up my street', concocted doubtless by non-repentant Vichyists worried about losing their positions to a 'Gaullist'.

Buck got me out of it: 'A Colonel Carlton-Smith who commands Force 136, a sort of SOE of the Far East, is looking for volunteers to jump on the back of the Japs ...'

For some days, I lay siege to the bedlam to deliver the indispensable order of secondment signed by Koenig, of which copy after copy goes astray.

The newsreels broadcast a scene of 'a whole division surrendering to four valiant American combatants' – that is, four flabbergasted GIs, assailed by a horde of enthusiastic *Feldgrau*. In the first row, Fritz, Hermann and Knut, beaming.

Philippe lowers his arms, 'I will not be following you, old thing. My stomach isn't doing too well. I'm taking a holiday.'

'You really do deserve it, Major.'

'No, not major, marshal of a dwelling, i.e. a sergeant, which I was in 1940. As I'm not signing on again, grateful France refuses to ratify my British rank and Major Charles Mark Geoffrey Staunton becomes Sergeant Liewer again. Doesn't make me feel optimistic. The demagogues are starting to promise the people milk and honey galore – whereas in fact the war has ruined France and everything will have to be rebuilt with blood, sweat and tears. I don't think Churchill and de Gaulle will last long.'

'Come on, they're not going to budge!'

'Keep dreaming, dear innocent!'

When I announce my coming departure to her, Maman doesn't hold back the tears!

'Your father, your brother, you, I have seen you leave too often. To wait is the fate of women, of course. Just imagine, Élisabeth Meynard, my protégée, is going to wait for this Don Juan of a Leslie. He has promised to marry her when he gets back from war, an officer. General Carthew confirmed to me that if they adopt a Scottish name, he would also get his naturalisation. So Leslie chose "Bob Maxwell". One more point in common between you. Your journeys look alike, you're about the same age and now the same initials!'

Maguy is still so beautiful as to knock your socks off, but a realist, 'There you are away again, far, very far from me. You will leave me with no news, for months, years, maybe. This time, I will not have the strength to wait for you, you know that, don't you? I only promise you one thing, I shall never, ever forget you.'

I have never forgotten her, either.

December comes to an end. Since the thick fog, poisoning the Channel for a very long month, is dispersing, I shall fly to London, the base from which I will depart for South East Asia so we can dislodge the Japs.

This pea soup of a fog has claimed for its own one illustrious victim; the radios of the free world announced it: 'On the night of 16 December, the plane carrying the celebrated band leader Glenn Miller from London to Belgium crashed in the Channel.'

'*See you in Paris, Bob*'? Alas no!

On christmas Eve, the fog fades away and I fly away ...

À moi les Samouraïs!

Postmortem

In August 1946, I disembark from the *Orient*, disorientated, in the Le Bourget arrival hall. The flight captain, small but athletic, throws himself into my arms. Jean Kisling! Another survivor.

'Picture it. On 8 November 1942, all the staff at the Tunis base of El Aouina were evacuated except three staff in the officers' mess – one of which – me! The very same evening, a German colonel called me: "*Ach*, here's Moïse Kisling's son, this *schwein* of a Jewish 'painter' who fled to America!" And he had me banged up in a mess cave used as a potato store!

'In the dawn, a guard opened up. A delivery man deposited on the ground a sack of potatoes, made a half-turn; the guard then did the same.

'Without reflecting, I lifted up the sack, 25 kilos, like it was a feather, and I knocked out the Jerry with it. Then I drew his bayonet and I ran him through! Already out in the corridor, delivery man. I climbed the staircase on tiptoe. At the top a sentry had turned his back. I stuck him like a pig before he had the time to say "ouf"! I jumped into the delivery van, burst through the entry barrier of the base, and sped to the Tunis brothel where the madame had a soft spot for me. Once the Germans had abandoned their search, I drove to Morocco. There an old friend of the family, Saint-Exupéry, helped me along a bit, which opened up a place at a pilot's school for me in Alabama. He arrived from New York where he was having a slanging match with my father, Gaullist and severely wounded of 14–18. Antoine, a Pétanist, refused to serve de Gaulle! A broken and old pilot, the modern machines were no long a part of his era, but what a symbol! So, Valin forced the Americans' hand. Saint-Ex died because of it. I finished the war as a fighter pilot. But I've got a timetable to keep and a ton of crayfish to load in Corsica. Let's meet up again in a week. Papa will be delighted to see you again!'

In Croydon, one fine day, a customs official reports that the attaché case of Commander Déricourt appears very heavy.[1] In truth, it 'weighs' a fortune in gold and silver ingots, and wads of pounds sterling. Henri presents himself at the hearing of the modest provincial court flanked by a top barrister from London, a KC (King's Counsel), assisted by two juniors who overwhelm the chief justice to such a point that he inflicts no more than a fine of £500; a trifle considering such an infraction could be punished by several months locked up.

So who mobilised and paid this star of the assizes? Not Colonel Sir Claude Edward Marjoribanks Dansey! He has just lost his SIS! His death, discreet, in his manor in Bath, will be mourned by his faithful friends, who flatter him outrageously as the 'greatest servant of His Majesty'. Lady Frances, his very young wife, will reduce his ultra-secret archives to ashes. Thus of his collusion with Admiral Canaris, the boss of the *Abwehr*, with Bodington or Déricourt, whom he drove behind Buckmaster's back, there will remain nothing. In the autumn of 1945, the archives of the dissolved SOE are given to MI6. A providential fire devoured the larger part of them! From then on, ask for information from a file that smells like trouble and they will reply, 'Sorry, it was burnt!'

If it was not Dansey in person who inspired this KC, who other than the IS, faithful executor of his last wishes, could have taken it on?

But a misfortune never comes alone …

One morning in November 1946, two civilians lock up the fine Déricourt in Fresnes. The DST[2] had picked through the Paris Gestapo archives – in which is found the file of an agent 'BOE 48', dealt with personally by Boemelburg and who devilishly resembles Déricourt! While Boemelburg disappeared and Kieffer had hanged, the artisans of Nazi counter-terrorism detained by the Allies, among them Bleicher, the quick-change artist of the *Abwehr* and Götz, and master of the *Funkspiel*, whispered to the examining magistrate how his head would roll.

1 Jean Lartéguy and Bob Maloubier, *Triple Jeu* (Paris, Robert Laffont, 1992).

2 *Direction de la surveillance du territoire*; French domestic intelligence agency.

At the hearing on 8 June 1948, a dramatic turn of events, those ferocious accusers become deaf, dumb, sheep overcome by the early onset of Alzheimer's disease! On this, the defence, Advocate Moro de Giaferri, a Gaullist big shot of the Bar, produces forty witnesses of good faith, among them Philippe, me ... and François Mitterrand: 'They passed through Déricourt's hands – air movement officer – they're still alive, aren't they? So ...'

A dramatic turn of events just before the curtain falls. At the eleventh hour, coming from nowhere, the guest: 'I am Colonel Bodington, deputy to Colonel Buckmaster – "We" were in the frame with regard to Déricourt's collusions. He acted under orders!'

Henri is acquitted on the spot!

Three investigators, sick at heart, confide to me, 'Multiple demands for information that we passed to the Foreign Office Home Office, War Office SOE and to Colonel Buckmaster in person have remained unanswered and receipt was not acknowledged. So, where does that leave things? And the about-turn of witnesses, who fixed that?'

An enigmatic 'Monsieur Robert' may well have preached the good word to the witnesses right up to their cell ...

Nick Bodington had been separated from the French Section at the end of 1943 and demobilised a long time now, had no status any longer as a colonel, still less as Buck's deputy. However, '*once a spy, forever a spy*'. The intelligence services hold on to you until death!

So, who other than MI6 could have manipulated the Nazi witnesses and 'driver' Bodington?

Henri toasts his release with a night of champagne galore in rue Pergolèse. Disheartened by so much injustice he confides to me, 'They've given me back my honour, but are they going to compensate me for my eighteen months of prison? No more flying. I'm retiring to the countryside, chicken breeder for ever more. My door will always be open to you.'

Déricourt, *grand cru*!

In 1957, an Armagnac four-engine craft of a branch of Air France turns turtle on Orly airport, downed in the fog. 'No piloting fault is attributable to the captain on board, Henri Déricourt,' concludes Inspector General Maurice Bellonte. From then on, Henri discovers a taste for more exotic climes: Air Liban, Air Laos – and a young, romantic English journalist, Jean Overton Fuller. The 'thing judged' now guarantees him cast-iron immunity, so he lets drop a hotchpotch of various tall variations of the truth – which she publishes. 'Bodington and Henri were in cahoots. They worked for "a different" service of His Majesty. They brainwashed their friend "Boe", from time to time handing over to him one of the agents given into to their care – Colonel Bonotaux, among others.'

'The life of a Bonotaux – what's that in wartime?' says Henri to his confidant, Jean.

The 'cousin' Emile Bonotaux really did enter the Resistance at the end of 1942 under the orders of General Frère, away from de Gaulle, of course. He took himself off to Algiers. On his return he was unable to obtain a place on the submarine shuttling between Algiers and Ramatuelle. He had to fall back on a Lysander of Déricourt's 'Line'. His fate was sealed. Déricourt sold him to Boemelburg. He died of typhus in Dachau, less than two months before the German capitulation.

At the end of November 1962, top personalities, ambassadors and the movers and shakers of Vientiane, capital of Laos, saluted Déricourt's remains, pioneer of the air, hero of the RA and Gaullist aviation, decorated with the most prestigious Allied gongs. His Lockheed crashed in Sayaboury, near the Burmese border. The press omits to mention that Sayaboury is a discreet airfield of the Golden Triangle and that Déricourt was the only pilot of a modest confidential airline. Commercial Air Laos, nicknamed Jam Air, or, Opium Air. He delivered the 'treacle' to the henchmen of the president of Vietnam, Ngô Dinh Diêm, on the makeshift landing sites around Saigon. But peace on his soul, if he ever had a soul, and if it had really left him! It is claimed that he has been seen recently in Barcelona on the arm of a ravishing young woman whom he had seduced in Hong Kong!

Incidentally, on 9 September 1944, Henri was not brought down by German flak but, flying at hedge height, through a high-tension line. To the south of Issoudun, it seems. Not far from Col. Elster's column. He, really too anxious to escape the bomber fighters, was not going to show his position by firing his cannon on anybody at all, I guarantee it!

In the 1930s, hadn't they already nicknamed him the death-cheater?[3]

I knew other death-cheaters …

3 Cf *Triple Jeu*; Jean Lartéguy and Bob Maloubier; ed. Robert Laffond*;* Bob Maloubier, ed. Calmann-Lévy, *Les Coups Tordus de Churchill* (Paris).

On 17 April 1956, *The Times* sings detente. Co-dictators of the USSR, Khrushchev and Bulganin, have just disembarked in Portsmouth from the cruiser, *Ordzhonikidze*, jewel of their navy.

26 April 1956: 'The Commander of the Reserve, Crabb, who was testing a diving suit of a new type in Stokes Bay, 5 miles from Portsmouth, a week ago, did not reappear!' the Admiralty announces.

The commander of the *Ordzhnikidze*, proclaims, 'I saw a frogman prowling about my boat!'

The press takes the bull by the horns. 'A Mr Smith came down to the Sally Port, a cliffotp hotel. In the evening he went out; no one saw him again. The next day, two gentlemen collected his luggage and papers, and removed four pages from the register of guests.'

Called before the Commons, the Prime Minister, Anthony Eden, gives a slight cough, 'Things produced at our initiation … to reveal them, contrary to the interests of the Crown, etc …' *Pravda*, Radio Moscow, followed by the worldwide media orchestrated by Khrushchev from his command post at the UN, went on the rampage.

Commander Crabb-Smith, a sales rep and barfly – he had all the necessary qualities – was engaged in some little tasks for the intelligence services: to reconnoitre the hull of a cruiser that does 15 knots more than the fastest Navy runner, for example. Another little job that they talked about at the base in Portsmouth where I had completed two frogmen courses: to test, in a caisson, the resistance of the human body to underwater explosions. In several occasions, I had met up with the gentleman at the Anchor, a pub beside the sea whose barmaid was so beautiful she took both our breath away – his and mine. We had chatted about far distant memories of Gibraltar, no more.

A detail that bothered me: when English frogmen were teaching me to splash about in the bay, an old fisherman had said to me: 'I dunno what these tides are playing at but those drowned in the bay are always bought back to the shore by the sea in less than forty-eight hours!'

Tabloid headlines: 'Déricourt has been kidnapped!'

Fourteen months later, in Chichester bay, 10 miles from there, a fisherman hooks in a corpse half-eaten by crabs. No more face, nor hands but strips of a frogman's wetsuit.

'It's Déricourt!' concludes the country coroner in spite of the fact that neither his ex-wife nor his mistress formally identified him.

The pros don't give an opinion either. Is it him? Drowned? Killed by the Russians? Is it a phony corpse much like that of 'the man who never was' served up by the English for Hitler's consumption in 1942?[4] If so, did they really grab the gentleman; he has so much to tell the KGB!

Whatever it was, the Crabb affair made the Crown tremble. A good lesson for all the secret services of the world. Nevertheless, it was badly taken on board by Charles Hernu and François Mitterrand, who thirty years later were to produce a remake under the title of '*Rainbow Warrior*'.

Me too, one day, I come within a hair's breadth of the kingdom of Hades – without even having been informed!

'Can I take you to Bruneval?' Morlane, head of Service Action de la DGER, who had taken me into his team on my return from the Orient, proposes to me in March 1947. 'The general is going to commemorate the first commando raid in occupied France and launch his "Gathering of the French People" [RPF]. En route we'll have lunch at my cousin's who runs a metallurgy factory in Rouen, the *Française de Métaux.*'

What a surprise! I'll have some things to tell him!

Behind the majestic doorway of the enterprise there are no *Feldgrau* searching the workers. A young couple welcome us on the threshold of the directors' wing. Morlane announces to them, 'Well now, here's a boy who boasts of having blown up your factory!'

The young woman rushes up the steps, throws herself into my arms, crying, 'My God, you're Bob, in flesh and blood? It's a miracle!'

Flabbergasted, I stammer, 'But how do you know my name, and what miracle?'

'It was my husband, then a factory engineer, who gave Delbos the plans of our factory. He was part of a small group of resisters called *La Française*, but you weren't to have known that. As for me, I was unaware of all of you, before your burial.'

'My burial, is that a joke?'

'What? No one has told you anything? Isn't that just too funny! You'd been wounded, seriously wounded, hadn't you?'

'Seriously is saying a lot. Delbos wasn't overly worried! He went on and on about it to me, "You'll be on your feet in eight days."'

4 Bob Maloubier, ed. Calmann-Lévy, *Les Coups Tordus de Churchill* (Paris)

'It was 21 December 1943, wasn't it? Ah well, in the evening he turned up at our place in a panic saying: "I'm supporting a chap by the arm who, lung, liver and intestines perforated, won't get through the night! Besides, he weighs no more than 80 kilos with a height of 1.80m, and worse, he's going to die on the fifth floor of a tower block! No question of waiting for rigor mortis, the staircase is narrow and we can only get him down if we bend him! I'm waiting for his last breath before I wrap him up!" I sewed three potato sacks end to end as your shroud. My husband found some pig-irons and chains. We chose a bucolic corner of the Seine to immerse you at Croisset in front of Flaubert's house. My men parked my husband's van lower down from you. A member of staff from the factory working for the Germans had petrol, SP and *Ausweis*. Delbos went up ... and came back down in time to get back before curfew: "He's still breathing, I'll be damned, but he won't last the night! So for that reason, I'll need to keep his body warm tomorrow. I'm going to concoct some camphor and eucalyptus fumigations – for the smell, you see!' Coming back the next night, stammering, he muttered: "He's stronger than I thought, the bugger, but it's just a question of hours!" The third night: "He's tough but the damage is irreversible – everything has an end!" The fourth: "He just defies all the scientific data, but science always has the last word." The fifth: "I've known some cases of remission, temporary of course!" The sixth: "I refuse to believe in miracles!"

'I pointed out to him,' the young woman went on, 'that, Lisieux wasn't so far, perhaps Sainte Thérèse ... Didn't make him laugh. Anyhow, at the end of the week we put back the pigs, chain and shroud and we drank to your reincarnation.'

That day at *La Française*, we lifted our glasses for my resurrection after having observed a minute's silence in memory of the good Doctor Delbos, who had died shortly after his return from deportation.

In Bruneval, proclaiming the advent of his RPF, the General, too, alluded to a new tenacity.

In 1954, very few would have bet on the survival of Georges Guingouin. 'The doctors of the Marchand Hospital in Toulouse decline to pronounce upon the chances of recovery to health of the "person detained",' announces the press. Detained, Georges? I am stupefied. Ten years ago, when I left him, his star was rising to the stratosphere. Liberator, soon mayor of Limoges, cherished child of the Party, the days before him would hum! I had forgotten Philippe's words: 'When Chaintron and his people will announce his ruin!'

In 1947, he lost 'his' town hall. Afterwards, Chaintron ousted him from the election lists of the fiefdom, and then reduced him from the rank of Secretary of the Central Committee to that of a simple member, an underling – but not without a voice! Last of the just, Georges condemns the Germano–Soviet Pacts and the bloodbath in Tulle. However, a diktat from Moscow had announced, 'All matters pertaining to undercover activities have been settled once and for all and cannot be re-examined!' The apparatchiks have given out the Marxist–Leninist glossaries, 'Titoist, lecherous viper, Trotso-Hitlerist'. And so forth. He doesn't give a fig. Pronounced deviationists, Tillon and Marty are purged. In defending them, Georges becomes the target of Thorez and company and ... signs his death warrant.'

'The money that Tillon and Guingouin have is party money. I permit no deviation!' spits Duclos during one meeting.

Money might matter to Duclos, the 'little cake-maker' plump and become gentrified who, under Pétain, prostrated himself before Abetz, claiming in *L'Humanité*, 'We are the party of brotherhood. We are without hate with regard to the German soldiers.' But what is money for an apostle such as Georges? I see his patched-up glasses again, his down-at-heel boots, the greenish beret that he would have given to someone poorer than he was. Furthermore, he took his place again at the blackboard, the modest pawn in the eyes of many, put in the corner with a dunce's cap. The Party wanted this 'pawn's' skin; it mobilised the cops who, under Vichy, had already hunted the Préfet Rouge, and magistrates who hadn't exactly excelled for deeds in the Resistance during the Occupation! One of them was content to pursue Guingouin, another more of a collaborator than the others had even been condemned, a third had scraped through.

On 24 December 1953, summoned as a witness to a nebulous affair going back to the good old times of the Occupation, Georges went to the Palais de Justice in Tulle, hands in his pockets – to almost disappear. By good fortune since the war secrets can be filtered in Morse through walls, 'SOS! Georges Guingouin has been bludgeoned almost to death in a dirty ditch of Brive prison. But he survived!' The League of the Rights of Man get involved, a committee of defence sees the light of day, Roland Dumas, son of a resister, leads the charge. The media bangs the drums. A siege is mounted in front of the Toulouse prison, where he has been locked up with no form of process, in the greatest secrecy. A new version of the Iron Mask.

On 6 June 1954, tenth anniversary of the 'longest day', the 'accused' Georges is let out – having been detained for what reason if not by 'royal decree'? During rearguard battles the collaborating judges will deliver sentences of five years before they finally dismiss the case.

Five years ... more than *Herr General* Lammerding, butcher of Oradour, who set up a flourishing business and died in his bed, and more than *Sturmbannführer* Boemelburg, peaceful librarian of a Bavarian squire, who ended up sliding on a patch of black ice, succumbing to a fracture of the skull and being buried in a country tomb at the foot of an oak.

If there is one person who has never had a set-to with justice, it really is Sergeant Leslie du Maurier. Promoted to officer, he marries Élizabeth. In the name of the Intelligence Service and by virtue of his gift for languages, he interrogates war criminals detained in Berlin. He confirms that the SOE parachuted agents into the arms of the Nazis deliberately to dupe them with regard to where the D-Day landings would take place and that Déricourt really was a 'double'.

Liaison officer with the Red Army in Berlin, then at the head of a supply commission in 1946, Bob Maxwell plays the game so well that the Socialists and the Christian Democrats owe him the triumph of the first 'free' elections, although manipulated by the Soviets one doesn't doubt. Elected, the Communists would be able to demand that the Red Army occupy the entire town. The Berliners had a narrow escape! Eternal gratitude. The crown of major is promised to Maxwell; in the long term why not the stars of a general? He declines; he has his idea: for five years, reserved exclusively to only the scientists of the Reich, the German scientific publications are kept under lock and key, a mine of data, on nuclear physics for example. Maxwell buys. He interests Sir Charles Hambro, president of Hambros Bank, prince of finance and ex-boss of SOE, as well as the count of Saint-Empire van den Heuvel, former section head of MI6 in Berne. At the head of 139 magazines, Pergamon Press will spread over five continents. In England his Mirror Group publications flirt with sales figures of 24 million and his fortune can be counted in billions of pounds. Oracle in geopolitics, he is the host of the greats in this world. At 68, he has it all ...

On 5 November 1991, a bomb makes the planet tremble: 'Bob Maxwell, the titan of the media, has disappeared from his yacht *Lady Ghislaine*, cruising the ocean around the Canaries.' After days of intolerable suspense for the family and – the stock exchanges – a Spanish helicopter spots his body floating at sea. 'Natural death,' conclude the Spanish pathologists.

The press doesn't give up: how was he able to tumble over the chest-high handrail while the captain, officers, sailors and his maître d' were on watch on the bridge and the decks? Afterwards, stupor: the state of Israel confers on him an almost national funeral and a tomb on the Mount of Olives, a sacred place dedicated to legendary heroes called to enjoy priority access to immortality: 'The Jews entombed at the Mount of Olives will be the first resurrected when the Messiah comes.'

The *Jewish Chronicle* is not deceived: 'He could only be a super Jew, not in the religious sense, but in the natural sense.' In the natural sense, fighting against the Nazis, then the James Bond of the Mossad, for sure. In fact, he laid in state at the Palais of the Nation then is taken to the tomb of emblematic figures of Israel: Elie Wiesel, Yitzak Shamir, Ariel Sharon, Shimon Peres, Moshe Arens and the rabbis, generals as well as the upper crust of the Mossad.

Between times, Israeli pathologists have put into doubt the verdict of their Iberian colleagues, 'We have noticed contusions, due to shocks or to blows.'

The *Chronicle* jumps feet first into the detective story: who has killed this guaranteed hero without a stain ... until the closure of Pergamon accounts. Horror – the pension funds of the employees are empty, relieved of 400 million pounds dedicated to refloating a group running out of steam. Enquiry. The assets of companies are frozen, the quotations suspended, and Bob's sons indicted. From white knight to black night, obese, drunk, a drug addict, swindler, megalomaniac, womaniser!

Of course, he is far from the lanky Sergeant du Maurier that he was who conquered his Zündapp at the point of a Bazooka and seduced his Élisabeth – and Maman – with his legend, his fine face, his gift of the gab in five languages. Cigars, scotch, banquets and a too-pretty secretary from time to time have rounded out his belly and damaged his heart, for sure.

But his script surely wasn't loaded with all the sins of the world; otherwise the God of Israel wouldn't have elected him!

Speaking of heroes, of Israel and elsewhere, on my return from the Far East, Philippe looked after my malaria attacks, pampered me. Then he eschewed journalism, left for Morocco. We exchanged a few words. The last: 'I'm waiting for you in Casa. I offer you sunshine, sea, tennis, golf and possibly the company of one or two nymphets, if you haven't radically changed. Do I need to come and get you?'

I promised to come but the Cold War in which I was mixed up, modestly, was urgent.

One morning, there I stand between the monuments of the Montparnasse cemetery, a red rose in my hand in front of an open tomb. I throw it; it falls among so many others, on a beautiful oak coffin, at the level of the copper plaque engraved, 'Philippe Liewer 1911–1950'. One night a telephone call had pulled me from my bed: Marie-Louise, his sister, was sobbing: 'He's dead. His stomach, you know, it was his heart. Sudden and lethal coronary.'

At the cemetery, the last of the 'Rouennais bunch' was following on my heels in their Sunday best: Hugues Paccaud, the Pionteks and Georges Philippon – returned from Buchenwald in a zombie envelope weighing just 30 kg; since then the butter of Normandy has done its work; he has recovered his rosy tint.

I push through the imposing crowd and kiss Maryse, Marie-Louise and her children.

The evening before the cemetery closes, I come back. The lanes are deserted, the earth freshly moved covered with a heap of bouquets, sprays of flowers and wreaths. We are alone.

For more than a half a century, once a year, I visit him. We chat, 'What's new, big man?'

One year I tell him, 'Limoges has dedicated one of its streets to you.'

'Super! What's it called?'

'Rue Major Staunton, alias Philippe Liewer.'

'So, back to front! Is it well situated anyway, I hope?'

What d'you think? In the old brothels quarter!'

I think I heard him burst out laughing, 'Ah, perfect!'

Summer 2000. In the majestic park of Lord Montagu of Beaulieu, seat of Group B, before the Security School, a handful of survivors from SOE celebrate the sixtieth anniversary of the birth of Churchill's baby. On an English green lawn enshrined between the ruined columns of the cloister, some Scottish bagpipes, white shoulder belt on panther skin, a complicated drill is taking place. That is the moment that Vera Atkins chooses discreetly to leave us.

She has not been offered $2m^2$ on the Mount of Olives, but she was just as Jewish as the little Ludvik Koch-Maxwell. We gather together in St Paul's Church in Knightsbridge then knock back great quantities of champagne to her memory in our old spies' club, situated behind Harrods. The full-length portrait of the Queen Mother overlooks the bar; the staircase is covered with portraits of agents, disappeared, who, like Violette photographed in the fullness of their youth, seem to mock their old accomplices who have difficulty in climbing the steps.

Born in Bucharest, the *Petit Paris* of the Balkans, Vera Rosenberg went to the best colleges in Europe. The war surprised her in London and she became engaged to an RAF pilot. 'SOE found me by chance,' she had told me. Let's see. In Bucharest she belonged to the British diplomatic circle which, we all know, is closely linked with MI6. Among them was Leslie Humphreys, future head of the French section ... Vera will one day be its general secretary whom 'Buck consulted on everything', if one should listen to the wagging tongues.

When I teased her on the 'affairs' of the Section and the damage that Götz's diabolic Funkspiel had caused, her porcelain blue eyes stared into mine: 'Just a single one of our circuits was penetrated, Bob, and we had only parachuted matériel to it, nothing more! No money, no arms, no men – do you understand me!'

Bloody liar, our Vera! In the white marble of the memorial of the French Section, at Valençay, in the Indre, 104 names are engraved in letters of gold. Among them fourteen victims of the *Funkspiel* and according to the plaque 'arrested on arrival', or 'shortly after their arrival' – that is to say, into the arms of the Gestapo. Not forgetting those sold by Déricourt ...

Buckmaster, BP, Jacques de Guelis, Gerry Morel, Nick Bodington, Dédé Simon preceded Dear Vera in the tomb, and it isn't her, silent as a tomb, who would have betrayed their secrets! With the exception of Bodington's secrets, perhaps, 'The morning of Déricourt's trial, I came across Nick in front of my hotel, the Scribe,' she told me. 'I dotted the 'i's: "If you are a witness don't forget to tell the truth, nothing but the truth!" I never said another word to this double-crosser!'

Occasionally I pushed her to the wall, 'Why didn't you appear as a witness, yourself? Why didn't Buck show himself?'

Then she closed up tighter than a clam, 'There's the statute of limitations!'

At the end of 1945 SOE was dissolved. Buckmaster and his people were back in three-piece suits. Churchill was relegated to the sidelines, For the dead, the deported, widows and orphans, all that remained for them was to do battle with windmills to assert their rights. After having rung all the bells of the establishment in vain, Vera, outraged, threatened the ex-great chief of SOE, Colin Gubbins, general of the headquarters still on duty, with the use of the press and an intervention in the Commons. He nabbed her a post at the Commission on War Crimes.

Squadron Officer, 'Commander' of the RAF, she sets off to be reckoned with, her auburn hair rolled close to her head, her cigarette-holder pointed like a pistol between her rings, weighed down with the list of fifty-two missing persons from the French Section.

Kieffer was in the hands of an SAS battalion in the British occupied zone in Germany, which was preparing to hang him. In July '44, his SS had captured five SAS parachutists in France. The Führer's orders? Shoot them ... discreetly! Kieffer disguised them in civil clothing then killed them. However, two succeeded in escaping! The SAS launched a merciless search.

Vera confronts the little *Hauptsturmführer* in his cell.

'In his eyes, I was only a woman, less than nothing,' she reported to me. 'On the other hand a major, superior in rank, who spoke better German than he did! He decided to get it off his chest, revealed to me that BOE 48 really was Déricourt ... whom he hated. But Boemelburg was ever protective of him, was "dealing" with him at his home with no witnesses.

"His confidences and the courier of the networks that he was setting up made the most indomitable of your agents fall by persuading them that they were betrayed by a mole infiltrated into Baker Street," he revealed to me. As a consequence, I sent report after report to my own Commission and to the War Office. They were buried, as you know, but thanks to Kieffer's confidences I reconstructed the calvary that "my girls" faced.'

Andrée Borrel, Sonia Olschanesky, Vera Leigh and Diana Rowden – 'my Diana' – arrived in Struthof Alsace's concentration camp on a lovely summer's day in 1944. Their morale was high as the SS led them to their barracks: with Germany ready to give in, their status as British officers guaranteed them that their lives would be saved, they were sure. Suddenly their guards threw themselves on them, stuck syringes anywhere in their flesh, undressed them, then, dead or alive, dragged them to the crematorium. A flaming red mouth opened, and they tipped them, one after the other, into the furnace. When the hair of the first girl caught fire an SS who was too sensitive vomited and fled. Later, he confessed to the judges.

In Dachau, not far from Munich, shortly after the liberation of Paris, Noor Inayat Khan, Madeleine Damerment, Yolande Beckman and Eliane Plewman – 'my sister' – fearfully skinny, but all feeling protected by their English status, chatted in light-hearted fashion while the guards were leading them the length of a sandy yard. Suddenly rusty coloured splattering staining the base of a wall made them jump. The men then grabbed them, pressed them down by the shoulders. The emaciated legs of the women failed them; they fell to their knees. Using whatever strength they had left they grasped, grasped the hand of their companion. Calmly an SS applied the barrel of his Luger against the neck of each one of them, pulled the trigger, four times. Four heads burst ...

Of eight women who had been young, beautiful and brave, there remains nothing, not even an ounce of ash – as much as what remains of the Reich of a Thousand Years, in fact!

From 8 May 1945, victory day, the Bushells moved heaven and earth to find Violette. As the War Office and the Red Cross passed the buck with no results, the Bushells alerted the press. Some survivors from the camps came forward – they had come across three English women, one of whom was Violette, during the winter of 1944.

In August 1944, in a third-class compartment stripped of its seats, in one of the last trains with deportees reaching Germany, nineteen captives are crowded in, among them Robert Benoist, Yeo Thomas – the 'White Rabbit' – and Harry Peulevé, head of the Dordogne network, whose deputy was Roland Malraux.

RAF fighter-bombers have targeted the train, machine-gunned and bombed it. It comes to a screeching halt. The guards bolt the doors and throw themselves into the bushes. In a deafening fracas, bullets lacerate the metal, bombs make the convoy reel. Soon, the burning sun turns the wagon roof red, turns the overcrowded compartment into a furnace. Seeing themselves condemned to being torn apart or burnt alive, terrorised prisoners howl to their death. Then, in the corridor, appear two women chained together, each carrying a can! The SS didn't lock the female prisoners' compartment, at the end of the wagon: they had chained their ankles together in twos so they felt there was no fear of seeing them escape! Without caring about the heat, the machine guns and bombs, the two prisoners, jug in hand scuttle between the toilets and the compartment, giving water to the men.

One of them leads, getting her companion to help. Benoist and Peulevé both recognize her. It's Violette, Violette Szabó! At first glance Violette identifies Peulevé. It's Harry, Jack Peters' friend, who, in London, had confirmed without laughing that he was a military pen-pusher! They took her for a ride, those two! She winks at him conspiratorially.

When, calm having returned, the SS come back on to the train, the galvanised deportees straighten up. 'She was acting so very cheerfully, giving us her best beautiful smile,' is how would be remembered by Peulevé until his death. 'Even in tatters, without make-up, God she was pretty!!'

More prosaic Yeo Thomas: 'What balls Violette had!'

That's the opinion, the picture, that two of her sisters in misery shared, Huguette Deshors, her cell companion in Limoges prison; and Marie Lecomte, who did not leave her from Fresnes to Ravensbrück.

A bomb having destroyed its locomotive, the train remained anchored to the rails. Trucks took up the relay and arrive in Reims at the end of the day. The SS park the deportees in a stable; they chain them to the feeding troughs, women on one side men on the other. The chains are released. Keeping close as possible to the central ally and watched over by the guards posted at each end, Violette and Harry manage to exchange news in whispers, 'I was the one who gave your profile to Jepson, the SOE recruiter,' admits Harry Peulevé. 'Being part of the French Section ... like you, it wasn't Italy I was heading for, it was the Dordogne and Roland Malraux. In March 1944, a Catherine arrived from Rouen, friend of his brother Claude who had just been arrested. I keyed a message putting a Clément on guard ...'

'So you were, if I recall, MacKintosh Red?'

'You know? You'll explain to me by what mysterious ... I was myself arrested shortly after. Fortunately, my assistant was away. You know him – it was Jack Peters ...'

'"Our" friend Peters ... that I bumped into in the place de la Madeleine, in April last ...'

'God be thanked, he's still alive then. He must have succeeded me as head of Nestor, our circuit that covered the Dordogne and the Corrèze.'

'Nestor, that I was supposed to contact on 10 June, it was him, then! If God and the *Das Reich* had allowed it what a surprise we would have had! What a coincidence! If a writer stuck that in a novel no one would take it seriously!'

At break of day, their whisperings are interrupted by low rumblings. Men are led away to Buchenwald, the women to Ravensbrück.

In 1946, Vera had set off again on the trail of most of her 'little ones' fallen into the hands of the Nazis. She knew that Violette had been incarcerated in Ravensbrück After that – mystery ... The *Lagerführer*, head of the camp, Schwarzhüber, had up to this point sat in arrogant silence opposite his interrogators.

'This *Totenkopf*, this death's head, I was resolved to have his skin, in reality and figuratively!' Vera told me. 'When the SS saw a female come into his cell, he smiled with such scorn that I lost my temper.' She didn't comment on how she dealt with him but he to: 'The prisoner Szabó? One who wouldn't submit either in the factory or in the camp!' An homage, of a sort ...

Conceived to hold 2,000 captives, Ravensbrück, by the end of the war, contained more than *40,000*, fed on water, peelings, rubbish. *La Binz*, the sadistic head female guard, a mastiff in heels, whipped the zombies in striped rags if they didn't get out of her way quickly enough. Roll call was at 3 a.m. in temperatures 20 degrees under zero: the sick would collapse while standing attention. In the dawn, those who had slept on the frozen ground took the wooden planks in the place of those who had died during the night.

'In January '45,' Schwarzhüber remembered, 'I received a specific order from Berlin concerning three English women. I extracted them from their cell ...'

Liliane Rolf and Denise Bloch, who had assisted Robert Benoist, are so weak that the SS carry them under their arms. Violette is still standing. At the end of a path, a square of grass between two walls. The three women, ghosts, are pushed to the ground by the SS. They just have the strength to lift their chins in a final act of defiance. On her knees, Violette looks with full hatred and scorn at those watching – doctor, the dentist and the underlings. SS Schult unholsters his Mauser ...

Vera Rosenberg pursued the torturers and murderers with implacable hatred. She had Schwarzhüber, Binz the 'Bitch' and many like them hanged.

When King George VI pins onto the chest of Tania Szabó the George Cross awarded to her mother, the highest distinction ever given to a woman, he will not quote Yeo Thomas in the original words, but he will murmur, 'I would never have had the courage to do what she did!"

Easter 1958, as each year, Marie Lecomte, the Breton woman who had shared the hellish ordeal with Violette, went to the church in Morlaix to pray for the soul of her defunct sisters. Thirteen years ago, in Ravensbrück, when they were separated, Violette emaciated and filthy, embraced her seven times: 'For each of my family, my parents, my brothers and me. If ever you get out of here, swear to me to give them these kisses! Here's my address, I've written it with my blood, she added while sliding her a torn piece of a newspaper between her fingers,

'I swear it on my head!' whispers Marie, inserting the miniscule roll in the hem of her skirt.

But, in February 1945, here she is fidgeting in an interminable queue leading to a gas chamber just put into service as the bullets and the injections were no longer sufficient for the demand for executions! Miracle – without a cry of alarm, someone pulls her out of the rows. It is a French kapo who whispers to her: 'You'll be seeing me again, won't you?'

In May, the Red Cross takes possession of the camp and of one of these living dead who has no memory of anything. Neither her vow, not the shred of newspaper scrawled in blood and rolled into a hem. She was undressed, washed and dried; her rags are burned.

For thirteen years Marie is annoyed with herself but what can she do about it? Suddenly, during that Easter mass, the Virgin appears on a washed out tapestry and speaks to her! Marie runs home, goes straight to a commode, opens a drawer; at the back a greenish wallet. In the wallet, on the yellowish cutting from an English newspaper, a search notice, a photo of Violette – and her address! The next day, Marie leaves for London to throw herself into the arms of the Bushells.

Previously, Vera had sent me an English journalist, R.J. Minney, who was passionate about Violette's epic tale. We travelled across Normandy, the Limousin. He published *Carve Her Name with Pride*, a tale that the producer Arthur Rank turned into a film distortion à la James Bond. From London Buck telephones me, 'Don't go to see this tripe, Bob.' However, this film hit the bullseye: bouquets of flowers at the steps of the Bushell house, at the entrance to the school where Violette climbed over the wall along with her brothers and on the steps of the town hall in Lambeth. Without forgetting a mural at the monument to the dead of Stockwell, and a bronze bust of Violette on the Albert Embankment.

Half a century after her death her name is inscribed and that of her companions at the corner of the crematorium at Ravensbrück, there where Schult murdered her. Finally a horticulturist named a mauve fuchsia 'Violette'.

In 1998 one evening, in a cottage in Wormelow a woman named Rigby, 'felt' the immaterial presence of a young woman who, from the beyond, commanded her to create a museum. This cottage was The Olde Kennels, whose history she was unaware of until after this revelation. It was funded by the dog keeper, Harry Lucas, Violette's uncle. She had spent her holidays there.

'Don't fall asleep there, you have a plane to catch!' Philippe had reminded her at the end of May in 1944.

On 24 June 2000, the Violette Szabó GC Memorial Museum was inaugurated in the presence of stars, deputies, bishops, generals, a FANY detachment, representatives of the Special Forces, 3,000 spectators and a crowd of journalists and cameramen coming out of a flotilla of television trucks.

In the year 2000 Guingouin's 'old men' also remembered '*la petite Anglaise*', who had enough balls to keep her head until her last bullet was fired at the Panzer grenadiers of Das Reich. They raised a monument on the corner of Le Clos, the meadow where we landed.

On 6 June each year, after the 'authorities' have pronounced their discourse and placed their sprays of flowers, the bell for the dead rolls over a valley scattered with wild meadow flowers.

A minute's silence.

On a base of poppies and buttercups, 'the silhouette of a "little brown thing full of mischief and a ravishing smile" appears to me,' said Leo Marks, the prince of codes. She hums a refrain of *I'll be Around*, the Mills Brothers tune that was all the rage in 1944 and sketches out an arabesque of the pasa doble. The savant spins around draped in a transient Scottish veil signed Molyneux. She gives me a smile.

I smile back murmuring:

> The peace of these years in the long, green grass,
> Is yours, yours and only yours.
> And your death ... will be but a pause."

Acknowledgements

With special thanks to Mark Yeats, who never gave up the idea to publish Bob's book *Agent Secret de Churchill* in England, even though French publishers were so reluctant to take the risk. This is a dream coming true for Bob to have his book published in English. He must be very happy wherever he is ...

Also, of course, tremendous thanks to Bob for all he did for us and for having bequeathed his literary works to me. Without this kind of extraordinary man we would never have been freed at that time!

Marie Hélène France
Bob Maloubier's widow
Houilles, France
January 2016

Index